THE
ESSENTIALS

To our community—for opening their homes and lives to us—without them, we wouldn't have a book.

THE ESSENTIALS

THE ART OF INTERIOR DESIGN

CAITLIN FLEMMING & JULIE GOEBEL

PHOTOGRAPHY BY STEPHANIE RUSSO

ABRAMS, NEW YORK

CONTENTS

INTRODUCTION	9
CHAPTER ONE: TRAINING YOUR EYE	13
Travel WITH GRANT GIBSON	17
Historical Homes WITH LEAH O'CONNELL	25
Museums WITH VICENTE WOLF	33
Nature WITH JILL SHARP WEEKS	39
Designer Showhouses WITH CATHERINE KWONG	43
Shops WITH LAURIE FERBER	49
Books WITH BUNNY WILLIAMS AND ELIZABETH LAWRENCE	55
CHAPTER TWO: WORKING ELEMENTS	67
Hardware WITH SUSAN BRINSON	71
Outdoor Spaces WITH MICHAEL TRAPP	77
Textiles WITH KATHARINE POLE	83
Color WITH HEIDI CAILLIER	91
Lighting WITH TAMSIN SAUNDERS	97
Furniture WITH NATE BERKUS AND LULU LYTLE	105
Art WITH JOSH YOUNG	115
Handcrafted Items WITH DEBORAH NEEDLEMAN	123
Flooring WITH AMBER LEWIS	131
Window Treatments WITH DAVINA OGILVIE	137
Accessories WITH CAITLIN FLEMMING	147
CHAPTER THREE: NINE HOMES FOR INSPIRATION	153
Calhoun Sumrall NEW ORLEANS, LOUISIANA	156
Kristin Ellen Hockman BERKELEY COUNTY, SOUTH CAROLINA	172
Rachel Allen LONDON, ENGLAND	188
Charlotte Boundy LONDON, ENGLAND	198
Glenn Ban EAST HAMPTON, NEW YORK	212
Josh Young MIDDLEBURG, VIRGINIA	226
Courtnay Daniels NEW YORK, NEW YORK	242
Lan Jaenicke SAN FRANCISCO, CALIFORNIA	254
Amy Meier RANCHO SANTA FE, CALIFORNIA	266
LITTLE BLACK BOOK	281
ACKNOWLEDGMENTS	300
ABOUT THE AUTHORS	303

SAN FRANCISCO,
CALIFORNIA

INTRODUCTION

DESIGNING A HOME can seem like a daunting task to accomplish on your own. At the same time, no one knows your taste and what you love more than you do. And luckily, we have discovered that finding the courage and developing the expertise to design your home becomes so much easier and more fun when you are open to the beauty and inspiration that surrounds you. For us, falling in love with design happened through decorating our own spaces, collecting antiques from all over the world, and, in Caitlin's case, running a thriving interior design practice. Together, we became the authors of two interior design books, *Travel Home* and *Sense of Place*, which feature both our designs and the work of other designers we admire.

After the experience of writing these books, we began to realize that we had learned so much from the designers who opened up their homes to us. In *Travel Home*, we heard a multitude of perspectives on how travel can have a large impact on the design decisions the designers make in their own homes as well as in the homes of their clients. In *Sense of Place*, our focus shifted to how the cultures and environments where we live have an impact on our homes. In the dozens of homes we visited, there was much more we learned about good design. Although what we saw was never the same from one home to the next, we began to realize there was a teachable art to creating a harmonious home. This is when we came up with the idea for *The Essentials*: a design bible that divulges the wisdom that is usually vouchsafed only to the professional designers but can be used by anyone who wants to improve the look of where they live.

PACIFIC GROVE,
CALIFORNIA

The book is broken down into three chapters:

🌿 In "Training Your Eye," we discuss the knowledge that seasoned designers have developed and how to approximate it without being a professional. Not everyone is born with design instincts, but they can be learned and refined. This chapter gives you practical steps for developing your own aesthetic as well as how to seek out inspiration. We offer concrete ways to do this—from spending time in nature to visiting historic homes and museums. We also bring a wide array of experts in to give additional perspective to these ways to train your eye.

🌿 In the middle and meatiest chapter, "Working Elements," we meticulously lay out the technical essentials of a home. This nuts-and-bolts chapter covers conventional wisdom on many elements of design: hardware, textiles, outdoor spaces, color and pattern, lighting, furniture, art, handcrafted items, flooring, window treatments, and accessories. We also include some words of wisdom from experts in each of these categories.

🌿 In the "Nine Homes for Inspiration" chapter, we visit the homes of nine talented designers, who offer inspiration by showing real-life examples of many of the ideas we have been talking about in the previous chapters. We present a cross-section of homes that represent a wide swath of design styles. Some are large homes; others are more modest. Each space can help you fine-tune your design aesthetic for your own home and other spaces.

We hope *The Essentials* serves as a reference that you can turn to time and again when you are considering the design of a space. Now, more than ever, people are invested in making their homes supportive, restorative, and reflective of their unique life experience. Knowledge can give you the confidence to design your home in a way that meets your needs—for cocooning, for hosting, for relaxing, for connecting, and for whatever you want to accomplish. Whether you hire an interior designer or take on the task of home design on your own, the goal of this book is to help you clarify how you want your home to look and feel and then be confident making the small and large choices and changes that go into executing your singular and worthy design vision.

LONDON,
ENGLAND

1

TRAINING YOUR EYE

NEW ORLEANS, LOUISIANA

W hile it can seem like some people are just born with a talent for design, we believe designing a home is a skill that needs to be cultivated, a muscle that can always be strengthened. No matter your starting point, whether you are a design pro or a complete novice, it is always possible to hone your instincts, find new sources of inspiration, refine your tastes, and better understand what you love. This practice of training your eye is ongoing, something we are always thinking about.

Some of the questions we ask to get to the heart of our home design goals include:
- How do you want to live?
- How do you spend time in your home?
- What rooms do you gravitate to?
- What are the functions that the different spaces in your home need to support?
- How does color make you feel?
- What do you want out of your home?

In this chapter, we dive into the specific ways we have been able to train our eyes, and we share them with you. Some may seem obvious, like referring to design books. But with the advice shared here, you will learn there are specific ways to see more and take away more actionable, practical tips from the books you read. We have broken this chapter into specific categories and have provided concrete suggestions on how to go about learning more and, ultimately, to be successful and confident in a home design approach that works for you.

For each of the following topics, we impart our ideas and tap experts in the field to share their knowledge. For travel, we turn to **GRANT GIBSON**, a former designer who now travels the world and takes others to discover the wonders of our planet. **VICENTE WOLF**, a world-class designer, explains how museums played a formative part of his education as a designer. In our pages on historical homes, we hear from **LEAH O'CONNELL**, a textile designer whose great-grandmother owned a country estate, Filoli, in California, which was later donated to the National Trust for Historic Preservation. She describes how all of us can learn by visiting historical homes. **JILL SHARP WEEKS**, an experienced designer, helps to steer us to look at nature both for inspiration and to find ways to bring it into our homes. **CATHERINE KWONG** encourages us to visit designer showhouses and gives specific ways to benefit from exposure to them. For shops, we turn our attention to **LAURIE FERBER**, co-owner of Elsie Green, a storefront in Concord, California, and an online shop that specializes in French antiques. She finds compelling reasons to visit shops and describes what you can learn from those visits. And finally, expert designers **BUNNY WILLIAMS** and **ELIZABETH LAWRENCE** explain how design books can inspire the design of your own home. Bunny, who has written over twenty books herself, understands deeply the importance of books in your life. With your eyes and mind open, you can begin to train your eye, one experience at a time.

TRAINING YOUR EYE

14

TRAVEL

Opposite: Even the simplest moments can provide inspiration. With its iron decoration and massive size, this door in Mallorca, Spain, is a perfect example. Even the graffiti seems to fit in.

Over the course of our careers, we have discovered that there is nothing that informs our design sense more than traveling. Sometimes we find inspiration on day trips close to home, but other times it comes from a more ambitious journey that we've taken to a faraway place. Being able to travel is a priority for us. We've gone so far as to sell a truckload of our prized possessions at a flea market to help pay for a trip to Istanbul. Travel fuels our creativity in a way nothing else does. And if we are completely honest, it was the desire to travel that brought us together to write *Travel Home*, our first book. For each of our three books, we traveled thousands of miles with our photographer to seek out special spaces. We felt it was important to present homes created by designers with a range of perspectives in a wide range of locales, and for this book, a primer on the practice of interior design and arguably our most ambitious to date, it was more important to us than ever. We deeply understand the value travel can have on our perspective in life. Seeing how others live has been a privilege that we want to share.

Travel allows you to live in the moment. If you venture to another country, you may not speak the language, but you observe how everyday life can be done differently. Simultaneously observing your surroundings—the style of the buildings, how rooms are furnished, even the way sidewalks are constructed—will teach you much about design, if you keep your senses tuned.

Here are just a few of the potential benefits of traveling:

PERSONAL GROWTH Having the opportunity to interact with strangers, seek the unfamiliar, and embrace new ways of doing things can help expand your view of the world and in turn can spark creativity and add fire to your passion for design.

APPRECIATION OF CRAFTSMANSHIP There are many materials, objects, and skills from other regions of the world that influence international home design, and we can learn about them in a direct way when traveling. For example, it's difficult

"Exploring various design traditions and techniques from around the world can inspire you to incorporate unique elements into your own home."
—GRANT GIBSON

to even consider buying the ikat-inspired textiles that have become popular in recent years when you have held and felt hand-loomed ikats in a stall in the Grand Bazaar of Istanbul. You quickly understand the value of finding the real thing.

AWARENESS OF TRENDS When you immerse yourself in a new culture, you will often notice different trends in design. When we were in the United Kingdom, we noticed that nearly every home we visited used an absinthe green or a salmon color on the walls. We realized these colors worked as great backdrops for art and textiles. As we had come from California, we were accustomed to neutral walls. Returning home, we thought about color in a whole new light.

INSPIRATION FROM WORLD ARCHITECTURAL WONDERS Why not learn from the best and intentionally seek out ideas from an iconic site? A great way to discover significant places that you'd like to visit is by examining World Heritage Sites listed by the United Nations Educational, Scientific, and Cultural Organization (UNESCO). They have compiled lists based on the cultural or physical significance of a place. You can look up these special sites by country. For example, the sites in Egypt range from the Great Pyramid of Giza to the Aswan Dam on the Nile. Wherever you travel, there are wonders to behold.

EXPOSURE TO A NEW AESTHETIC Travel can introduce you to unique architectural styles, art forms, and craftsmanship. This can open your world to different ways of doing things. The thatched-roof homes with their thick adobe walls in the Yucatan Peninsula might not be something you directly replicate at home, but they may spark ideas for textures or tones that you want to adopt.

ARTS AND CRAFTS Keep an eye out for local handicrafts that might augment your design at home. When you see them in your home, it will remind you of where you have been. One of the things we love to look for on our travels are vintage textiles. They are easy to pack in a suitcase, and when you return home, they can be repurposed in a variety of ways. A small yardage of lace can become a cafe curtain in a kitchen or bathroom. A beautiful vintage textile can be used as a throw pillow. The possibilities are endless.

Opposite: Look around to see how different materials and patterns work together. In Brussels, Belgium, the cobblestone streets provide a contrasting texture to the ornate facades of the buildings.

THE ESSENTIALS

GRANT GIBSON

We met Grant Gibson more than twenty years ago in San Francisco and became fast friends. Brought together by our love of both design and travel, we have taken many trips together. Grant is curious, inquisitive, and always finds unique and authentic places to visit. From Lisbon to Rajasthan, his passion for travel is contagious. Moving on from his thriving interior design business, he now has turned his attention to a travel company that organizes group trips as well as individually crafted voyages. We can't think of a better person to offer advice on ways that travel can be your best friend as a designer.

Opposite: Grant, an accomplished interior designer, now takes like-minded people on trips around the world. Above: Just like our homes, green space can provide a respite from our busy lives. This view is in Mumbai, from the Royal Yacht Club.

1 What are the ways in which travel can help to define your design aesthetic? Experiencing different cultures, architecture, art, and landscapes while traveling can help you discover new patterns, color palettes, textures, and design styles that you may not have been exposed to before. Exploring various design traditions and techniques from around the world can inspire you to incorporate unique elements into your own home. Whether it's the intricate patterns of Moroccan tiles, the minimalism of Scandinavian design, or the vibrant colors of a tropical paradise, each travel experience has the potential to shape your design sensibilities in exciting ways.

2 How has travel changed how you look at the world? I've always found that traveling to different places allows me to gain new perspectives. Experiencing new languages, foods, and customs has made me realize that there are so many ways of living and seeing things. It has also helped me become more open-minded and empathetic toward people from diverse backgrounds.

THE ESSENTIALS

3 What are the places you've visited that have influenced you the most? Why? Paris, with its iconic architecture, world-renowned museums, and elegant streets, has always inspired me with its timeless sense of style and artistic allure. The city's elegant boulevards, charming cafes, and beautiful gardens also contribute to its reputation as a source of inspiration. Paris and its style and sophisticated aesthetic have left a lasting impression on me, and this is why I return over and over again.

My experiences in India have also expanded my understanding of design and culture in ways that continue to inspire and influence my work. The vibrant colors, intricate patterns, and ornate designs found in Indian art, textiles, and architecture have left a profound impression on me. Visits to historical sites such as the Taj Mahal, the ancient temples, and the colorful streets of Jaipur have inspired me with their unique blend of tradition and craftsmanship. The warmth of the people and the sensory richness of daily life in India have shaped my creative perspective and design sensibilities.

Finally, Istanbul's unique blend of Eastern and Western influences, reflected in its architecture, cuisine, and traditions, is known to inspire creative thinking. The city's historical sites such as the Hagia Sophia and the Blue Mosque, as well as its bustling markets and vibrant neighborhoods, are huge sources of inspiration for colors, patterns, designs, and deep-rooted history. The combination of old-world charm and modern energy in Istanbul has made it a compelling source of influence for those interested in art, design, and cultural exploration.

4 For someone who hasn't traveled much, what do you recommend as a way to get started? I would recommend beginning with a local or domestic trip. Exploring nearby cities can be a great way to ease into traveling and get a taste of what it's like to be in a new environment. You can also consider joining guided tours or group travel experiences to help make the process less intimidating. I lead small groups to India, Istanbul, Morocco, Egypt, and Mexico City. Each of these destinations has its own unique cultural and historical significance. Additionally, reading travel blogs, watching travel documentaries, and talking to friends or family members who have traveled can provide inspiration and practical tips for planning your own trips. Remember, the most important thing is to take the first step and start exploring the world around you.

HISTORICAL HOMES

Opposite: While you might not want to emulate their exact style in your own home, historical homes can inform your use of color, layering, and scale. This room in Beauport, the Sleeper-McCann House in Gloucester, Massachusetts, provides lessons in many aspects.

One of our favorite things to do, both when we are traveling and when we are at home, is to visit historical homes. They come in a variety of sizes and architectural styles, from Georgian to postmodern. It's a chance for you to see the many design elements in a home up close, including experiencing simply how a room feels. This can lead you to a greater understanding of architectural design.

You will be surprised by the number of homes open to the public. Some are run in a way similar to a museum, while others are only open a few days a year. In the United States, a great place to begin is the National Register of Historic Places. In the United Kingdom, you can research National Trust buildings to discover homes to visit. We always keep an eye out for dates of home tours we want to see.

There are countless ways to learn from visiting these places, including:

EXPLORING DESIGN DECISIONS While you may loathe Victorian design (or any other style from the past), you can still get ideas from designs of other eras. For example, looking at the use of colors, textiles, and furniture styles can help you articulate what you love (or hate).

PRESERVATION If you own a home that is older and you are thinking about renovating, seeing a historical home can help you understand what might need to go into a renovation or learn about conservation techniques.

CRAFTSMANSHIP Very often, historical homes can provide examples of quality woodworking that has stood the test of time. We also love to look at their kitchens to get ideas for cabinetry, layout, and other details, such as the hardware. Old kitchens in historical homes are often places where multiple people would be working at once. Notice the layout of these spaces—they can be great examples of how you can design to accommodate efficient traffic flow. For example, baking tools may be gathered in one area, while serving dishes and cutlery can be in an entirely different part of the kitchen.

THE ESSENTIALS

Opposite: This dramatic, sparsely decorated window accentuates the beauty of the water outside. Above: A bedroom in Beauport, the historic Sleeper-McCann house in Gloucester, Massachusetts, has many layers of patterns—from the textiles on the bed to the dishes in the cabinet. Don't be afraid of mixing patterns.

THE ESSENTIALS

LEAH O'CONNELL

Interior designer and textile designer Leah O'Connell understands historical homes in a special way. Her great grandmother owned Filoli, a beautiful country estate with 16 acres (6.5 hectares) of formal gardens located in Woodside, California, until she donated it to the National Trust for Historic Preservation. Here is Leah's sage advice and her list of historical homes to visit. We can't wait to visit her recommendations and hope you get a chance to check some of them out as well.

1 What can you learn by visiting historical homes? Visiting historical homes is a bit like getting into a good novel—it's escapism at its best. We get to be voyeurs of lifestyles and traditions of the past. Visiting these homes allows us to experience history in a tangible way; they all have stories to tell. And, of course, there is the aesthetic importance. Inspiration and imagination are personal, but stepping into a well-preserved home is a feast for those of us who love design. They give a glimpse of architectural achievements and details such as superior craftsmanship, rare materials, different scales and proportions, unusual colors, historical textiles . . . I often visit my favorite houses more than once as I take away something new every time.

2 Is there any advice you'd give someone who wants to visit a historical home? I think discovery is one of the greatest joys, and this fuels inspiration. Some would probably say to do your research about a home prior to visiting, but my mind works in the opposite way—I prefer visiting a house open-minded to what I might see and then going deep down rabbit holes afterward.

Also, don't rule out the unsung. Although some historic houses like Monticello or Fallingwater are revered, deservedly so, the popularity of most is far more modest. When traveling, look at the National Register of Historic Places as you can find incredible homes, cottages, retreats, and gardens tucked away in unassuming places, lovingly protected by local people who care about the stories within. These under-the-radar homes are often the most personal (and then, of course, there's the added benefit of delight as you discover something new).

THE ESSENTIALS

Opposite, from left: A corner in the kitchen at Charleston House in Firle, England.
Leah has a special connection to Filoli, in Woodside, California, as her family owned the property.
Above: At Filoli, you can explore the formal gardens as well as the interior of the home.

3 What are the historical homes you recommend visiting? How to choose? Here's a list of five of my favorite lesser-known houses:

❦ FILOLI (Woodside, California) I'm partial to this one as it was my great grandmother's house before she gave it to the National Trust for Historic Preservation. While it's best known for its formal gardens, this was first and foremost a family house. My grandmother and I spent countless hours walking the gardens, and she knew every plant and its origin—there was a lot of love that went into creating it all. It's gorgeous year-round but particularly in the spring when the bulbs are blooming. Insider tip: Don't pass by the kitchen—it's one of the best rooms! In the butler's pantry, you'll see the house bell panel with my family's names (my grandmother is one of "the twins") and the dumbwaiter that my mother and her cousins used to ride up to the second floor when they were little.

❦ BEAUPORT, THE SLEEPER-McCANN HOUSE (Gloucester, Massachusetts) This was the summer home of America's first professional interior designer, Henry Davis Sleeper. It's one of the best houses to visit if you love design—I didn't want to leave! I was completely enamored with his collections of colored bottles, brilliantly backlit for the most magical effect. There are treasures to be appreciated in every nook.

> *"Inspiration and imagination are personal, but stepping into a well-preserved home is a feast for those of us who love design."*
> —LEAH O'CONNELL

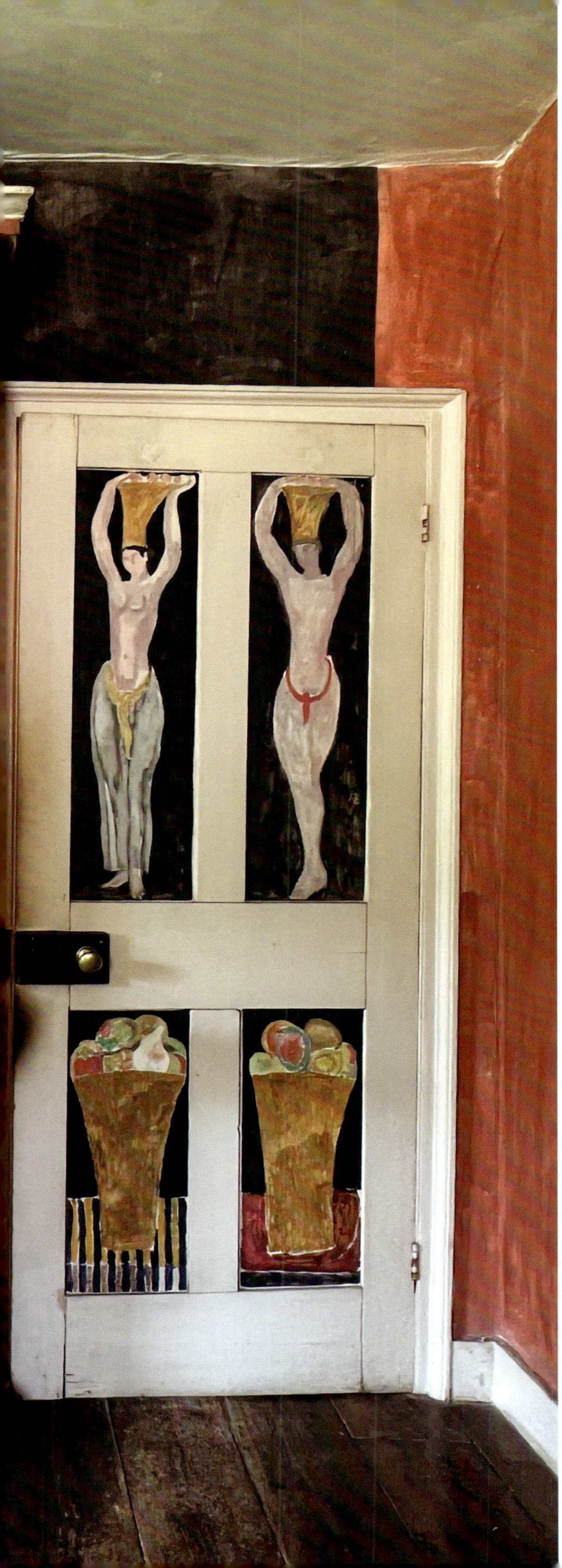

🌿 **THE MOUNT (Lenox, Massachusetts)** Edith Wharton and her architect, Ogden Codman Jr., literally wrote the book on interior design, *The Decoration of Houses* (or at least it was the go-to guide in 1897), and they introduced a new pared-down approach to designing American houses; she deemed the large mansions popular during that time ostentatious and in bad taste. For those who appreciate symmetry and proportion, this house does not disappoint. It's one of the few National Historic Landmarks dedicated to a woman, so that's reason enough to visit!

🌿 **GAMBLE HOUSE (Pasadena, California)** This is perhaps the best example of American Arts and Crafts architecture in the United States. Handcrafted details, beautiful use of natural materials (wood, stone, glass), and the interplay between indoor and outdoor spaces exemplify how good architecture is indeed like fine art. Even if you're not an Arts and Crafts enthusiast, a visit to the Gamble House will have you in awe of skill and craftsmanship that is hard to find nowadays.

🌿 **HUDSON RIVER VALLEY** There are numerous glorious estates in the Hudson River Valley that vary in architectural styles but are dramatic and historically significant, most with idyllic landscaping to boot. Visit as many as you can, but don't miss Kykuit, Lyndhurst, the Armour-Stiner Octagon House, Staatsburgh, Vanderbilt Mansion, Olana, and Boscobel.

THE ESSENTIALS

TRAINING YOUR EYE

32

MUSEUMS

Opposite: In the Victoria and Albert Museum in London, England, it's just as important to look at the details of the rooms you visit as the pieces in the collection. Here, the inlaid floors and soaring ceiling provide an ideal setting for historical relics.

There is no better way to improve your eye than to regularly visit museums. Consider purchasing a yearly pass for the museums you enjoy the most near you. Often, these can pay off in just a few visits. You can also look for the days when museums are open free to the public. For example, in San Francisco, there is residents' day every Saturday at the Legion of Honor. Each time you visit a museum, you will be honing your skills at noticing the play of color, pattern, and texture used by artists. With time, you will also begin to see the influence it has on your design decisions.

Here are several ways that museums can help you as you design your home:

ENGAGEMENT Museums often host events by experts in a variety of fields, whether they are lectures on a particular period or workshops on flower arranging, which offer unique opportunities to learn. Not only can you listen to scholars, artists, or curators, but you can join discussions and ask questions to further your knowledge of a subject.

APPRECIATION Museums often display objects that are made using a wide swath of materials, styles, and techniques. Studying these details helps to further your understanding of what goes into making beautiful, meaningful things.

ARCHITECTURE In addition to the items displayed at a museum, the building itself can be informative. Look at the spatial relationship between the items exhibited and the rooms where they are displayed. Seeing an exhibit at the Guggenheim in New York, where you can walk from the top of the building to the bottom on a circular ramp, adds more to the experience. Every time we visit the Metropolitan Museum of Art, also in New York, we sit a spell in front of the windows by the Temple of Dendur. The design of these spaces affects how you feel.

THE ESSENTIALS

CULTURAL CONTEXT There is a museum for everything, displaying items from various cultures, periods, and subjects. Any kind of museum can hold lessons for you in design. For example, in a museum of natural history, the botanical specimens can inform how texture plays a role in a design choice. You might even want to consider collecting your own specimens from your favorite places to display in your home.

MASTERS Many exhibitions display the work of design icons. This can include fashion designers and architects, along with artists. Study their techniques. What colors do they use together? We are also drawn to photography exhibits by masters such as Ansel Adams and Dorothea Lange. How do they make you feel? When you expose yourself to some of the most celebrated people in their field, you can learn from them and also understand yourself more completely. By looking at original art created by masters, you can begin to see the details of what makes their work great and stand out from other art. This can be the same when going to a museum with period furniture. The more time you spend looking at authentic, celebrated creations, the better you'll also be able to understand quality when you see it. And, quite frankly, you'll be more apt to see the flaws in a fake or "dupe."

Above, from left: Light streams into the Victoria and Albert Museum from the domes above. These remains of a church bombed in World War II are, in some ways, as beautiful as one intact. Opposite: An ornately carved staircase, originally from Brittany, France, now in the Victoria and Albert Museum, offers architectural inspiration.

THE ESSENTIALS
34

TRAINING YOUR EYE

VICENTE WOLF

Vicente Wolf has always found museums to be a part of his design classroom. When he first arrived in New York, he was sweeping the floors of the Decoration & Design Building, a mecca for design lovers, with more than one hundred showrooms. Vicente scraped together enough money to buy a pass for the Metropolitan Museum of Art. Most days, he would head there after work and let the museum teach him about color, balance, and scale, and offer a multitude of other lessons. He credits this experience with being key to how quickly he was able to succeed in the interior design world, becoming one of the most sought-after designers in the world. The following explores his ideas on why visiting museums is vital for designers.

1 How can museums help to develop your eye? I'm a visual person, and going to museums has always opened doors for me as it pertains to cultures, color, and understanding different styles, from eighteenth-century French masters, to African masks, to hip-hop. Understanding the progress of cultures, ours and others, gives one a frame of reference in creative pursuits. When you're walking through a museum, you're seeing the development of styles and how their humanity was interpreted, how people lived and created.

2 What are some things to notice? How light comes through leaves in the forestscapes, how street puddles reflect a city skyline, how objects brought into a space can help tell the story of a wonderful environment—all of this help informs my creativity. This is why I have come to love museums. Photography, sculpture, and paintings are different mediums, but they all offer the same thing: a representation of the artist's vision. After you see an object in a museum and you introduce that quality into a home design project, then you're bringing in a level of awareness that builds a richer environment, not just filling a room with furniture. I will say that when I'm looking at art, like the [Edward] Hopper exhibit at the Whitney, I step into that world. The color, the emotion, and the environment influence my perception of the artwork. Museums allow you to step into a world that may not be of your period or comfort level, and that education really can't come from books. You have to experience it.

3 Tell us about how museums have had an influence on your design work. One is not only impressed by the exhibited works, but also by the design of the spaces and the way artwork is displayed. Whether it's the coloration of the surrounding elements like the flooring and wall color, the quality and positioning of the handrails, or the juxtaposing of the works and lighting, the better museums create total environments for viewing—like at the National Gallery of Art's new East Wing designed by I. M. Pei, where he deftly created spaces within the irregular shape of the building. The Egyptian Museum in Cairo, built in the late nineteenth century, was designed to represent the antiquities exhibited within—on the inside and outside.

4 What museums would you put on the list of "must see"? The Gibbes Museum of Art in Charleston [South Carolina] is a must visit. Aside from being the only art museum in historic Charleston, they did a remarkable job in showcasing their existing collections, from the eighteenth century to the contemporary. **The Museum of Modern Art in New York** is a must for lovers of contemporary art. With its reimagined structure that was completed in 2019, it is a mecca where all the great masters of the late nineteenth century through the twenty-first are presented. **Rijksmuseum in Amsterdam**. From van Gogh to Rembrandt, it explodes with scale and width of Flemish and Dutch art. **The Nubian Museum in Aswan, Egypt**. It's an archeological museum built to preserve Nubian culture and civilization. The artifacts and art are remarkable, and the building itself is an architectural masterpiece. **The Istanbul Museum of Modern Art** has a wonderful collection of contemporary Turkish art. **The Peggy Guggenheim Museum in Venice** has excellent Surrealist works. Last but not least, the **Vatican Museum in Rome** is a treasure trove of papal art as well as sculptures and important masterpieces of Renaissance art.

THE ESSENTIALS

Above: Vicente sits on the steps of his Montauk, New York, home, where mirrored risers add light to the stairway.

TRAINING YOUR EYE

NATURE

Opposite: When you see something beautiful outside, consider bringing it into your home. Here, Jill Sharp Weeks brings simple branches into her home in Charleston, South Carolina, lining the staircase.

One of our greatest teachers is nature. For example, noticing the subtle changing colors within each season can be important in developing your understanding of the use of color. In the San Francisco Bay Area, the rolling hills of the Marin Headlands look as if they fall into the Pacific Ocean. Paying attention to how they evolve from green in the winter and spring to golden in the summer and fall, contrasting to the blue, green, and gray of the ocean, is a constant lesson in mixing colors. Here are some of the many lessons nature has to offer:

COLOR Nature can provide a wide and varied palette of color. The calm and subdued colors of the ocean or a lake can be in stark contrast to the colors of a vivid sunset. Noticing how color can change with light and shadow can help you to realize the impact of light on a room and how it can vary depending on the time of day.

MATERIALS Whenever possible, we always gravitate to natural fibers for our homes. Not only are they often healthier, but they add texture. Sisal carpet instead of synthetic rugs, woven baskets instead of plastic bins, and textiles with natural fibers bring warmth to a home. And, quite frankly, it's a win-win situation because, usually, it is also gentler for the planet.

PATTERNS AND PROPORTIONS We will never forget when we arrived at the home of designer Erica Tanov to photograph her home for *Travel Home*. On her front porch, there were beautiful ferns; they were casting a perfect shadow on the wall behind the pots. The design they cast made us stop and notice; the beautiful symmetry of this natural pattern took our breath away. When you study the intricate patterns of leaves, flower petals, pine cones, ferns, or even the bark of a tree, you can see how design exists in everything in nature. The spiraling shape of a seashell can teach you about symmetry, which can help you begin to more deeply understand how to create balance in your own design work.

When you see something beautiful outside, consider bringing it into your home. A bowl with beautiful seed pods from a tree or branches from your backyard displayed in a vase can bring life to a space.

THE ESSENTIALS

JILL SHARP WEEKS

Jill Sharp Weeks is known for designing homes that are deeply connected and influenced by both her community and the natural world. Jill and her husband, Ray Weeks, divide their time among homes in Santa Fe, New Mexico; Charleston, South Carolina; and Bray's Island, South Carolina, all of which cleverly incorporate elements from the natural world. Jill, whose former Santa Fe home was featured in *Sense of Place*, this time focuses on sharing brilliant ways to incorporate nature into our homes, explaining how it adds an unexpected value.

THE ESSENTIALS

40

1 How can looking to nature for inspiration enhance your home? I believe that gathering bits and pieces from nature and bringing those elements into a home can evoke a feeling of vitality that breathes energy into other aspects of the space.

2 How can spending time in nature help to develop your eye for design? When I was growing up, I can remember my mother saying that you need only look as far as the sky, woods, and water to understand what colors pair well with one another. Today, in her nineties, she still refers to this feeling when we talk about creativity, paintings, and homes. It has always had a great impact on me—even after schooling and training on color theory and design. There's just pure and constant inspiration in observing how interconnected nature and our interiors can be.

3 What are some elements from nature you can use in your home? I enjoy collecting large river rocks or beach stones and putting them in rows on our shower floors. Placing a petrified wood stool next to the tub adds a great touch for bath soap and a drink. Weaving twigs into the arms of chandeliers always feels unexpected. Huge cut palmetto palm fronds add great scale to a tabletop in sturdy urns. Large trays filled with curious squash or gourds bring beautiful pops of color and nubbiness. Terra-cotta pots of hellebore or geraniums are beautiful year-round in a sunny room. Silver vessels filled with porcupine quills are dramatic because of the opposing textures. Transferware platters piled high with oyster shells are a beautiful addition to any table. I adore large skeins of wool purchased from our Santa Fe farmers' market, hung on hooks in the mudroom. Tamarind pods and dried black-eyed peas in a hurricane vase with natural beeswax candles are a signature styling element for me.

4 How does nature influence your approach to design? I couldn't dream up an engaging interior space that doesn't rely on using elements that have come from our natural world. Many of my interiors are based on natural textures and an earthy color scheme. I'm drawn to reclaimed wood beams and weathered wood flooring, the patina of old stone floors, hand-applied plaster walls, and an abundance of shells and rocks displayed on windowsills, treated as importantly as an art installation.

TRAINING YOUR EYE

42

Opposite: In the living room of the decorator showcase Catherine Kwong designed in San Francisco, she could let her creativity flow. Large sweeps of white paint on traditional wood floors added an unexpected modern detail. Don't be afraid to think outside the box.

DESIGNER SHOWHOUSES

Visiting showhouses is a great way to see innovative home designs that have been completed by design professionals. These showhouses often occupy luxury properties or notable buildings that have been temporarily transformed by interior designers and are open for public viewing. Even if there aren't any happening your area, designer showhouses are often worth a trip. You usually get to see multiple interior designers' work at the same time, so you will quickly realize some work is inspirational to you while others are not. By going into it with a plan to carefully notice which rooms you gravitate to, you will begin to recognize what you prefer in the diverse world of design. Designer showcase homes can often spark creative ideas for an upcoming project. Keep in mind that this doesn't have to mean a major overhaul: They may help you tweak something in your home without necessarily changing everything.

Consider some of the following to make your trip to a showhouse worthwhile:

MEET DESIGN PROFESSIONALS The designers who have created each room are often there to answer questions. This is the perfect opportunity to inquire about how design decisions were made. With most showcase homes, a published program is included in the entrance fee and can be chock-full of valuable information on sources and vendors.

TAKE NOTE OF THE DESIGN DETAILS Designer showcase homes often present the work designers are most proud of at that time. Be sure to look at all of the details within a room:

- What colors are being used? Did they paint the woodwork the same color as the walls?
- Are there any accessories that stand out?
- Do you notice any furniture styles that seem to resonate with you? Is there a mix of styles?
- What kind of finishes are trending?

THE ESSENTIALS

TRAINING YOUR EYE

44

Opposite and above: Viewing designer showhouses, where designers can let loose and experiment, can provide you with new and creative ways to approach design.

🌿 **Study the Layout** The layout choices made in each room are another important aspect. Taking careful note of furniture placement and the flow of a room can help you to optimize how a space functions. For example, look at where there is negative space. Every well-designed room should have negative space to make statement pieces feel more special.

🌿 **See Innovative Design** Frequently, designer showcase houses are the places designers will take risks with cutting-edge ideas they have not yet used in an actual home, since they are not bound by a client's preferences or budget. Caitlin remembers that when she first started out working at a design firm, the owner created an infinity mirror with butterflies that appeared to be flying to the inner depths for the annual design festival Legends in Los Angeles. Seeing innovative design is a great way to help you think outside the box.

THE ESSENTIALS

CATHERINE KWONG

Catherine Kwong began her career in New York, where she designed flagship stores for Ralph Lauren. After moving back home to San Francisco, she launched Catherine Kwong Design in 2011. Catherine has worked on interior design projects around the world and has participated in several design showhouses. She gave us her insights into why they are the perfect place to inspire the design of your home.

1 Why are designer showhomes worth visiting? Designer showhouses are a great place to train your eye, aesthetically speaking. In a showhouse, designers are presenting a very distilled view of something they find beautiful. The time frame for showhouses can be quite short, so the rooms are capturing a moment in time; a snapshot of what feels fresh and current; what is in the conversation right now.

Because of the ephemeral nature of a showhouse, I find that designers tend to be more game to try something new, experiment with new ideas and materials, and generally push the envelope in terms of creativity. It's a great place to see unique points of view from different designers, and sometimes you notice trends or new styles emerge.

THE ESSENTIALS

2 What are the key things you should look for in designer homes? There are both budget and time constraints on producing a room for a showhouse . . . and that can actually be a great thing! It allows you to see how designers tackle architectural challenges with more practical and budget-friendly solutions. That often leads to more creative answers, which are always fun to see. You might notice stenciled walls instead of wallpaper, Ikea curtains trimmed and tailored to look very luxe, or found items used as artwork. In my 2013 Decorator Showcase room, I didn't have room in the electrical budget to add in sconces, so I used vintage fringe lights, and we just hung them up high and ran the cord down the wall to an existing outlet. And I certainly didn't know how I was going to find an existing and affordable rug for that living room . . . so we went back to our original concept boards, which included Cy Twombly paintings—and ended up asking my friend James Stancil to paint the floors instead. I fell so in love with how the painted floors turned out, and it really helped me set the tone for the rest of the room.

3 What are important lessons you can learn from visiting designer showhouses? My main piece of advice would be to walk through as many rooms as you can and really pay attention to your emotions. What do these rooms elicit in you, and is there a through line? Maybe there are rooms that make you feel calm and serene and others that excite you and make you want to gather with friends around a table. Take a step back and see if there are commonalities: maybe you are attracted to more minimalist rooms, or rooms with vivid colors and pattern-mixing. Many times, a unique layout or furniture placement really changes how people circulate and interact with the space. Interiors are a very visceral thing, and you can learn a lot by noticing what attract and repels you.

> *"Walk through as many rooms as you can and really pay attention to your emotions. What do these rooms elicit in you, and is there a through line?"*
>
> —CATHERINE KWONG

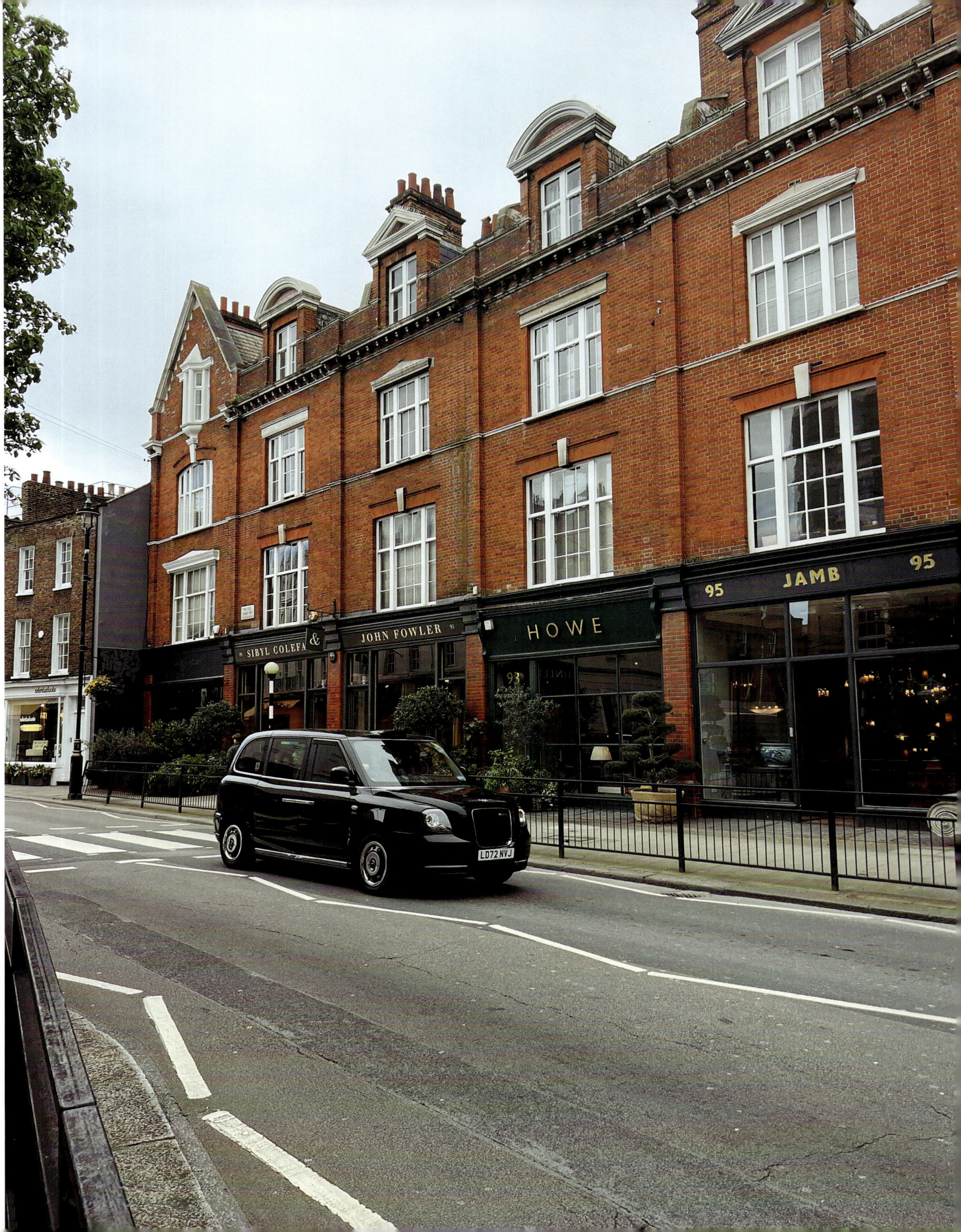
JOHN FOWLER
HOWE
95
JAMB
95

SHOPS

Opposite: When you are visiting a city, try to find the area of town known for home decor shops. In London, Pimlico Road is a treasure trove of shops where you will find inspiration in every corner.

Some of our greatest inspiration has come from the design shops we have visited both where we live and during our travels. On a recent trip to London, we kept going back day after day to the design shops found on Pimlico Road. It was an opportunity to experience design we might not be exposed to in the United States.

Keep your eyes open for shops that are featured both online and in shelter magazines. Another great place to find shops is in the back of design books. Many authors (including us!) give a comprehensive list of their favorite shops (see pages 281–299). You can widen your horizons with these retailers, browsing through a diversity of styles and design influences. Additionally, the staff at many shops can be a great resource, happy to answer the design questions you may have.

We also want to stress the importance of sitting on furniture and observing the scale of a piece in person. Sometimes it may look like it's perfect online, but when you see it in real life, it may be a slightly different color than you expected or feel a little too big. Visiting the shops and seeing and touching furnishings will help you to determine what you like and dislike.

Here are some of the things you can gain when visiting a shop, even if you don't buy anything:

INSPIRATION for ways to style the things you already own by seeing how shops arrange, group, and display different objects and furnishings.

IDEAS for how you can mix and match different colors, patterns, and materials.

EXPOSURE TO THE TRENDS AND BRANDS that seem to be making an impact. (You don't want to follow every trend or your home will feel impersonal and become dated quickly, but it can be fun to see what is new.)

THE ESSENTIALS

LAURIE FERBER

After years as a corporate executive, Laurie Ferber decided to start a shop because she loves working on displays, editing photos, and shopping the French countryside for the antiques and collectibles she has become known for. Her shop, Elsie Green, began in 2010 and specializes in French antiques, custom furniture, and unique curiosities. She shares her insights into how shops can provide inspiration when you are creating your home.

1 Your shop has a focus on vintage furniture and pillows made from vintage textiles. How can vintage elements improve a room? There will always be newly made furniture in a design because sometimes vintage just won't work, but to add one or two vintage pieces can add a soulfulness to a room that a new piece just can't pull off. And I think it reflects well on a designer to be able to have some sources for one-of-a-kind pieces in his/her arsenal. It's a fun trick to be able to present a gorgeous set of vintage dining chairs to surprise and delight your client.

Vintage textiles have the same effect—they add a touch of soul to a room, and often they are one-of-a-kind pieces so your client (and his/her friends) will be seeing them for the first and only time in your design.

Bonus points for understanding the story behind a vintage piece when you present it to the client. Ninety-nine percent of the time, the shopkeeper or dealer will have a great story about a vintage convent table (usually they have drawers all along the apron on both sides so the nuns could store their own plate and spoon at their place) or whatever piece you've selected. Just ask. Your client will love it and will no doubt share it with friends.

2 What kind of shops are good for developing your eye in design? I think smaller boutique shops are better than the big stores for finding ideas and inspiration. The displays tend to be more curated, less sales-y, and more creative. I also think the shops that are not as well curated are a great

THE ESSENTIALS

Opposite, from left: A corner of Elise Green, Laurie Ferber's shop in Concord, California. Laurie in Morocco. Above: Beautiful textiles in Robert Kime on Pimlico Road in London.

> *"If you can walk into a charity shop and find the one Baccarat glass in there, that's a skill that will serve you as a designer every day."*
> —LAURIE FERBER

place to hone your editor's eye. If you can walk into a charity shop and find the one Baccarat glass in there, that's a skill that will serve you as a designer every day.

Also, don't just look to fill your well of inspiration from shops or other designers; restaurants are great sources of inspiration for lighting, placement of art, and floral design, and hotels are great for bathroom design. And look to museums or galleries for inspiration on how to hang, light, and feature art in a space. The wall colors at the Met are a master class.

3 Which shops do you find particularly inspiring? When I'm looking for inspiration, I try to seek out shops that other people in my field are not going to visit regularly. So I love Merci Paris, for example, but I'm not necessarily going to find an idea there that will feel unique.

I'm lucky that my job takes me to Europe at least twice a year, so some of the best inspiration comes from [shops in] some of my favorite European cities:
- Bailey's House & Garden in the UK
- Galerie du Disordre and Maison Hand in Lyon
- Deyrolle (not a home shop, but great inspiration for color) in Paris

Some of my favorites in the US:
- Aimé Lèon Dore and Paula Rubenstein in NYC
- Galerie Half in LA
- Wyeth, The Quiet Botanist, and Finch in Upstate NY

I also always visit perfume and jewelry shops when I'm traveling. They are usually great inspiration for featuring small things in a meaningful way, they usually have good art collections, and the lighting is always pristine.

THE ESSENTIALS

4 Where should someone look to find interesting shops when visiting a new place? I always visit Paula Flynn's Shopkeeper's website, theshopkeepers.com, for small, intriguing shops to visit while I'm traveling. And our blog, *Etcetera*, has a series of city guides that feature shopping recommendations based on our own travel experiences.

5 Why is it important to see items in person before purchasing them? For furniture, I think scale is the number-one reason to view an item in person before making a purchase. Sometimes something is much bigger or much smaller than you imagine it will be. If you have your eye on something online and you're not able to see it in person, ask the shopkeeper to FaceTime with you so you can see it in human scale. Most of the small shops will be happy to oblige.

For upholstered furniture, often you want to sit on the piece before committing—most important for focal pieces like sofas and sectionals. Accent chairs can be more forgiving since not everyone who lives in or visits your house is going to use them every day.

For textiles, color [that you see online vs. actual textile color] is a function of how well your computer screen is calibrated, how well the photographer captured the true color, and how different the lighting conditions in the shop are from the lighting conditions in your client's home. Whether you're buying in person or online, make sure you're clear on the return policy before you take something out, as the color may shift once you place an item in your project.

Center: Nellie's of Amagansett
Above: Nushka in London

CREATIVE LIVING
THE FRENCH COUNTRY HOUSE
GARDENS
ONE MAN'S FOLLY
DÉCORS BARBARES
MORE IS MORE
The Lives of Others
Simon Watson
DESIGN BY NATURE
WESTERN GARDENS
HAUTE BOHEMIANS
Golden Light
Isabel Lopez-Quesada AT HOME
THE TUDORS
A WANDERING EYE

BOOKS

Opposite: Books can provide an enduring source of inspiration for designing your home. This home library, designed by Patricia Giffen, was placed in the entry of the cottage she created for Julie Forrest.

One of the most important parts of our design education has originated from books. When we first started out in design, we would spend hours at bookstores and libraries reading design books and familiarizing ourselves with good design from eras past and present. With time, we have both amassed our own extensive libraries. It's very helpful to have concrete visual references when you can't figure out a design solution. Some books are almost like old friends that we return to repeatedly, with notes and worn pages throughout. Additionally, we even pay attention to the descriptions of rooms in novels and biographies and try to envision what they look like. And now, having written three books, we also have a deeper appreciation for what goes into creating a book and feel honored to be able to pass along what we have learned in this special format that allows space for more in-depth analysis.

Here are a few of the many ways books can help you:

LEARNING Design is an area that is always in a state of evolution. The ways our homes function with technological advances have made our lives easier in some ways and more complex in others. In addition, cultural shifts and trends happen at a fast pace, with the sharing of ideas and the saturation of images on social media deeming things in or out at lightning speed. Design books can help keep all of this change in check. Books are built to be permanent and are also an antidote to information overload. They are curated and authoritative, and so they cut through the noise we are often bombarded with on social media. Books have been carefully edited by editors, and the best ideas are discussed. They are made to be collected and kept for years to come, which can, in turn, encourage us to make long-lasting, timeless design choices.

METHODS Books on interiors can often offer an understanding of a particular designer's creative process. Every designer develops their own set of principles, and this can help you develop your own perspective on how to complete a project.

THE ESSENTIALS

AESTHETICS Books explore many different kinds of design, allowing you to learn about a wide range of different ideas and styles, and they have the space to provide well-researched, comprehensive, in-depth information on a particular subject in a way that an article in a shelter magazine or an Instagram post does not. If you are drawn to the style of a particular designer, look to see if they have written any books or if their work has been featured in another author's book.

FUNDAMENTALS Books often delve into the principles of design and offer concrete examples of them in action. You can learn lessons in balance, color, proportion, and scale by studying the images. Analyzing photographs that point out these concepts can help you gain a deeper understanding of how the design of a room works and the things you need to take into consideration in your own space.

Above: Even in the smallest of homes, like in Rachel Allen's barge, there is always room for books. Opposite: In the home of Calhoun Sumrall, the dining room also serves as space for his vast book collection.

THE ESSENTIALS

TRAINING YOUR EYE

In the London studio of textile collector Katharine Pole, the smallest of bookshelves house her reference books, which provide her endless inspiration.

CHICK PEAS
PRODUCE OF U.S.A.
HISTOIRE SINGULIÈRE DE L'IMPRESSION TEXTILE
LE COTON, L'IMPRESSION
Micheline VISEUX
QUILTS of PROVENCE
Berenson
Les Belles de Mai
THE FABRIC OF INDIA
CLOTH THAT CHANGED THE WORLD
Yale
FRENCH TEXTILES
FROM 1760 TO THE PRESENT
Mary Schoeser
Kathleen Dejardin
Made in Neuchâtel
EN JUPON PIQUÉ ET ROBE D'INDIENNE
MICHEL BIEHN
JEANNE LAFFITTE
indigo
EGYPTIAN MUMMIES TO BLUE JEANS
Jenny Balfour-Paul
STYLES FRANÇAIS
matisse
HIS ART AND HIS TEXTILES
Edited by ANNA MASON
19th Century Textiles

Top shelf
- DE MONTPARNASSE
- WOODLANDS
- THE PEREGRINE
- CURTIS SITTENFELD — American Wife
- GREAT LIVES (The Times)
- LIONEL SHRIVER — So Much For That

Middle shelf
- A Wandering Eye
- 36 Hours: 125 Weekends in Europe (The New York Times) — TASCHEN
- Adventures Among Birds — W H Hudson
- Nature Near London — R. Jefferies
- Ian McEwan — Atonement
- Martin Amis — Experience
- Island Beneath the Sea — Isabel Allende
- the stylist's guide to NYC — sibella court
- Julian Barnes — Keeping an Eye Open
- Coco Chanel — Justine Picardie
- The Birth of Modern Britain — Francis Pryor
- Dan Cruickshank's Bridges
- The War Poets — Robert Giddings
- Drawings by Thomas Rowlandson in the Huntington Collection by Robert R. Wark — Huntington Library
- Matisse & the Joy of Drawing — Lloyd — Modern Art Press
- Matisse in the Studio — RA
- Picasso Portraits — Elizabeth Cowling — NPG

Bottom shelf
- Burma
- Wilfred Thesiger — A Vanished World
- Home-Made Vintage — Christina Strutt
- Robert Kime: The Personal Collection
- Christie's New York — The Collection of Arthur & Charlotte Vershbow, Part Three
- Flemming & Goebel — WA
- Sense of Place
- Making Modernism
- Strang · Cumming · Fowle
- Live Forever — S. J. Peploe — Elizabeth P...
- New Museum, 235 Bowery, New York NY

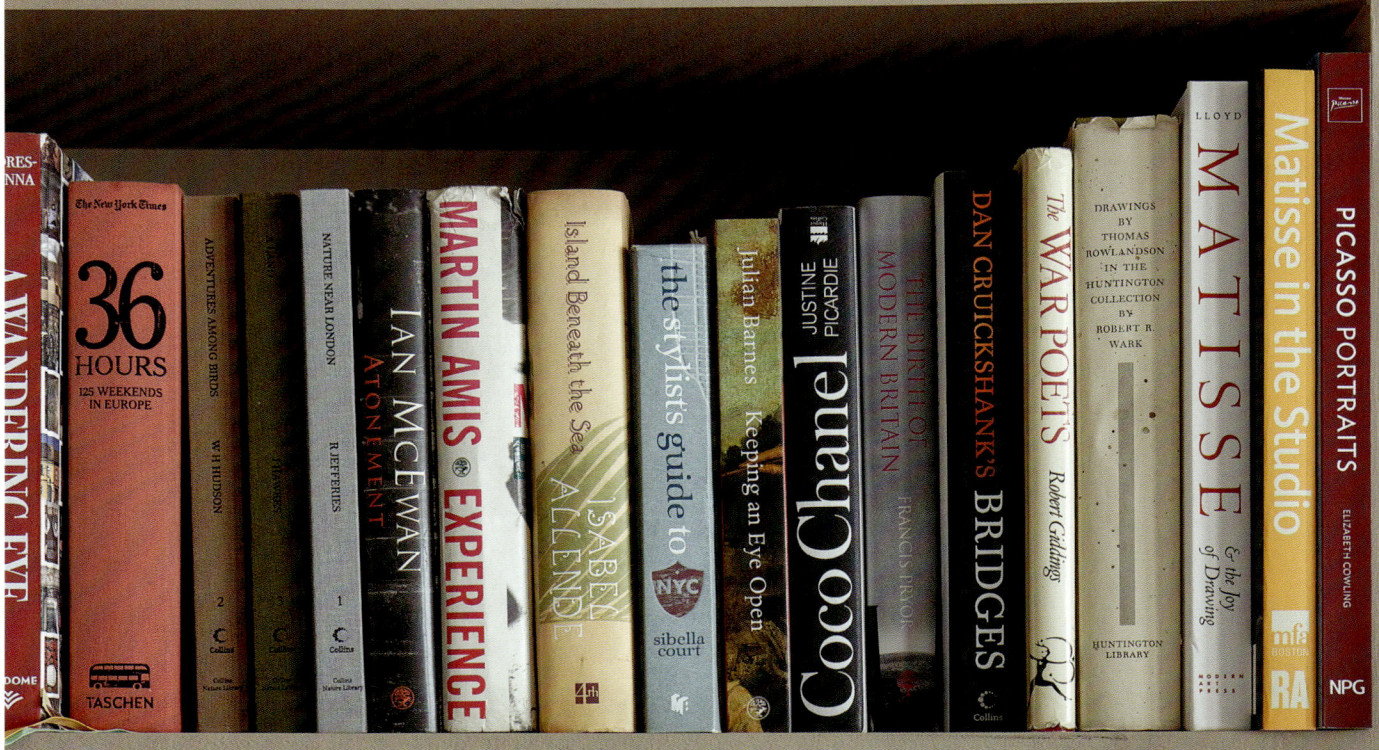

Opposite: Books can also be an important element of your decor. In this close-up, you can see Charlotte Boundy's impressive book collection. Right: The library in Courtnay Daniels's New York home accentuates her reading nook.

> *"As a designer, your education should be ongoing—you should always be learning—and books are an essential piece of that education."*
>
> —BUNNY WILLIAMS AND ELIZABETH LAWRENCE

VOCABULARY Knowing the technical terminology that professionals use will enable you to be able to communicate more effectively with colleagues, architects, and contractors. There is no better place to learn this than from books.

HISTORY Understanding how design history has evolved will give you a perspective on how the past informs design today. Additionally, while many very talented designers are no longer with us, their work lives on in books. You can often find their books, even if they are no longer in print, in secondhand shops or online. Caitlin recently became entranced by the work of Jaime Parladé, a Spanish designer. She found a copy [of his book] online, and it has been a constant source of inspiration.

THE ESSENTIALS

TRAINING YOUR EYE

62

BUNNY WILLIAMS & ELIZABETH LAWRENCE

Founded by design legend Bunny Williams in 1988, Bunny Williams Interior Design was renamed Williams Lawrence in 2023, as leadership is now shared between Bunny and her business partner, Elizabeth Lawrence. For over three decades, their design work is considered to be the best in the field. They are celebrated for their warm, welcoming, and approachable appeal, which is embedded in both tradition and history. Bunny is the author of more than twenty books on design, and both she and Elizabeth have great insights into what concrete takeaways you can glean from books about design.

1 How can books (all types!) play a role in developing your eye as a designer?
Bunny and Elizabeth: As a designer, your education should be ongoing—you should always be learning—and books are an essential piece of that education. We have an extensive library of design, architecture, and garden books in our office, and we reference them all the time. Seeing rooms from the past, and knowing what kinds of rooms resonate now, are important for training your eye. Oftentimes, when we are creating something like a painted floor for a client, we reference classical books to get inspired by historic patterns, and then we put our own twist on them. Books also offer a deeper dive into projects and a designer or artist's philosophy than other kinds of media [do], and reading the text is as important as looking at the photos.

2 What books would you recommend as essential for someone building a design library?

ELIZABETH'S PICKS

Roomscapes: The Decorative Architecture of Renzo Mongiardino by Renzo Mongiardino: This book is a treasure trove of inspiration from one of the great design maestros. From the range of effects and faux finishes that he perfected to the illuminating text that covers, in his own words, his theories of design and solutions to various design dilemmas, this book is a must have for any designer or design lover.

Life in the Garden by Bunny Williams: I've been fortunate to spend my career working alongside, and learning from, Bunny. Her country house and garden are magical, and she was able to capture the feeling you experience being there with her in her truly beautiful latest book. It is as much an experience as it is a love letter on how to live well. Every single page is a visual feast and a testament to why she's already a design legend.

Our office library is filled with older, slightly more academic books (many of which are now out of print) that we look to regularly for inspiration. A few of my favorite and most-referenced titles—and ones I think are worth searching out at used bookstores and vintage shops—are *American Painted Furniture 1660–1880* by Dean A. Fales, Jr.; *Period Rooms in the Metropolitan Museum of Art* by Amelia Peck; *Chinoiserie* by Dawn Jacobson; and *Craftsmen and Interior Decoration in England 1660–1820* by Geoffrey Beard. Happy hunting!

BUNNY'S PICKS

The Decoration of Houses by Edith Wharton and Ogden Codman Jr.: Edith Wharton was a renaissance woman. She had incredible taste, loved to garden, and could capture the world and its nuances beautifully on the page. This book is full of little gems of wisdom and an essential read for anyone who wants to have a career in design.

Education of a Gardener by Russell Page: As much as I love books filled with beautiful imagery, insights from the text are just as important. This autobiography by one of my favorite gardeners and landscape designers shows what it is to fall in love with the land, what makes for good design, and some incredibly charming insights and pointed observations about people to boot.

Sister Parish: The Life of the Legendary American Interior Designer: Working alongside Sister Parish and her partner, Albert Hadley, at their firm Parish Hadley was pivotal in my own development as a designer. So many of the top talents in the country today came out of their firm. This biography features a lovely foreword by Albert. I was honored to be asked to contribute an essay of appreciation for it, too.

Opposite: Bunny and Elizabeth, our experts on books, have experience in both curating personal libraries as well as writing publications on design.

3 How can reading books be key to professional development for designers?
Elizabeth: The summer before I went to design school, I read everything I could find about the design greats—including *Nancy Lancaster: Her Life, Her World, Her Art*; *Frances Elkins: Interior Design*; and the really wonderful biography of Sister Parish, *Sister: The Life of Legendary American Interior Decorator Mrs. Henry Parish II*. Being immersed in their worlds, learning about their influences and clients and what inspired them, really informed where I was going.

I say this often to the young designers in our office, "You need to know where design, and the industry, has been before you can know where you're going." You can't move forward if you don't understand who's come before you and what kind of work they did. There are so many design heroes, and reading about the things that went wrong and the mistakes they made, as well the projects that changed their careers, you begin to shape and understand your own style, and better understand how to navigate your own client relationships and project management.

And, as educational as these books are, they're also quite fun. You get a sense of how people used to live versus how we live now. Even how designers used to shop was different!

4 How can books provide inspiration for a design project?
Elizabeth and Bunny: We have some incredible historic and out-of-print books on topics ranging from Spanish and Venetian villas to Portuguese design, and these have been inspiring for some of our Palm Beach projects. There's a very Mediterranean influence in Palm Beach, and our clients often want their homes to feel anchored in the traditions of the area without feeling too referential. Understanding these periods of design and the architectural details that define different eras is important for every designer, and books are one of the most important resources in that education.

As much as we love Pinterest and Instagram, you don't always get the deep historical architectural information that's important when working in a specific style. You need to source from books that cover subject matter in a more comprehensive way. That's why building a library is so important. If you see a book that inspires you at a vintage shop, buy it! You never know when it will come in handy.

THE ESSENTIALS

Above: The floor-to-ceiling shelves create an enticing wall of books, beckoning you to come into the room and stay awhile in the home of Julie Forrest, designed by Patricia Giffen.

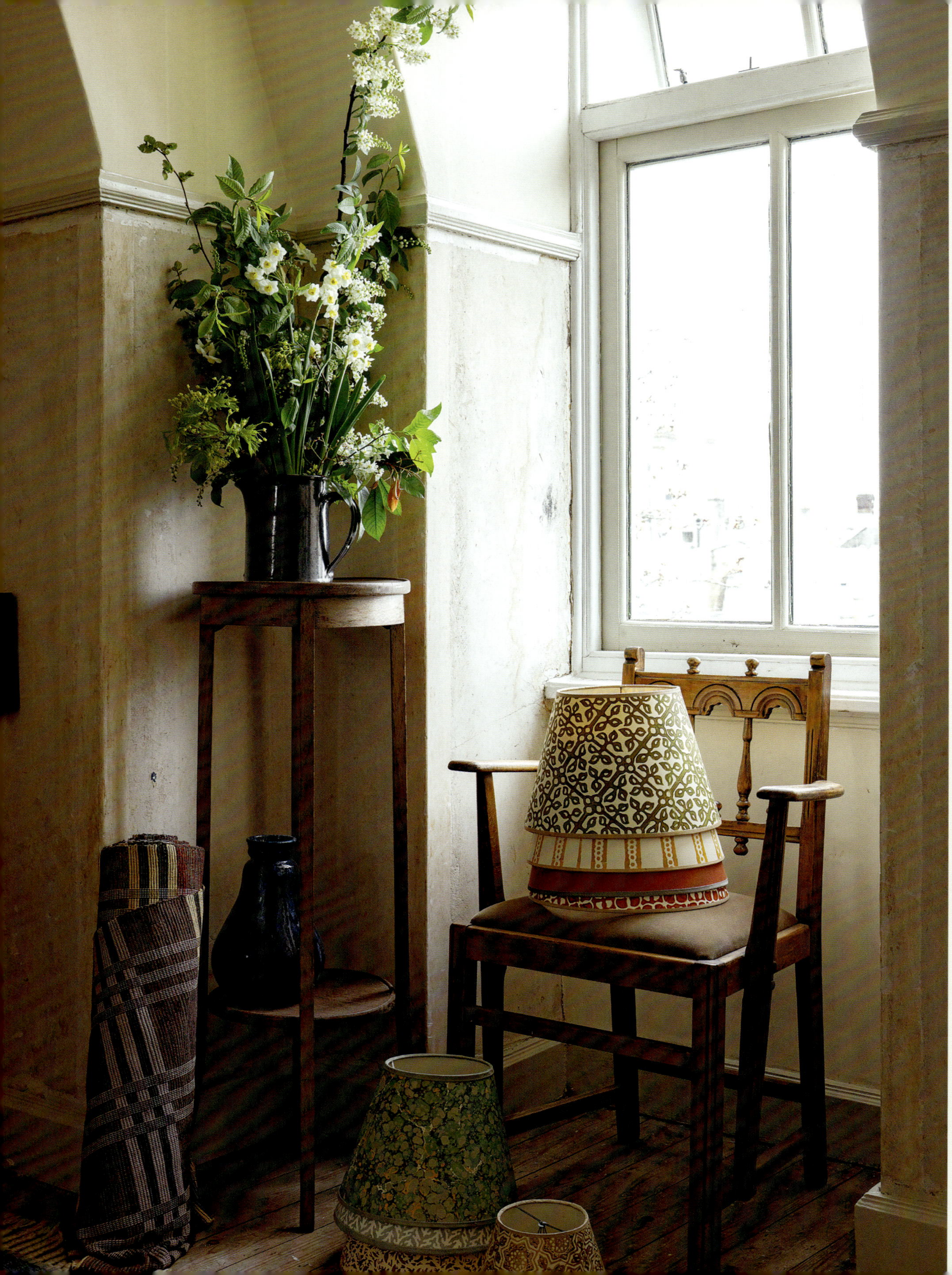

LONDON,
ENGLAND

2

WORKING ELEMENTS

In this chapter, we move on from looking at ways to train your eye and find inspiration to learning concrete methods for designing your home—the real nuts and bolts of design. We've broken this down into specific categories. Within each of these sections, we also have sage advice from the designers and creatives we admire most. For our hardware section, we have **SUSAN BRINSON**, who, with her husband, Will, has been lovingly restoring Stony Ford in Upstate New York and chronicling the improvements on *House of Brinson*. For outdoor spaces, we didn't know of anyone who has cultivated more beautiful outdoor environments than the ones **MICHAEL TRAPP** has created. For textiles, we traveled to London to see the collection of **KATHARINE POLE** and get her thoughts on how textiles can transform a space. In our section on color, we looked for advice from **HEIDI CAILLIER**, whose use of color sets her apart from her designer peers. For lighting, we had the opportunity to sit down with **TAMSIN SAUNDERS** in the garden of a pub to discuss the importance of lighting in your home. For furniture, we have the sage advice of both **LULU LYTLE** and **NATE BERKUS**, who explain why timeless pieces and how they are made, matters to both your health as well as the planet. For art, we had the pleasure of stepping into the art studio of **JOSH YOUNG** and learning how he himself collects art. For handcrafted items, **DEBORAH NEEDLEMAN** opened up about her love affair with basketry. For floors we asked **AMBER LEWIS** her thoughts on what works best. **DAVINA OGILVIE** gives her advice on window treatments and how they can make an immense difference to a home. And finally, yours truly, **CAITLIN FLEMMING**, talks about how accessories in a home can tell your story.

LONDON, ENGLAND

Lucas Hollweg Good Things to Eat
THE RIVER CAFE COOK BOOK
River Cottage
wild garlic
Sweet Things
QUOTATIONS
ELIZABETH KNOWLES
AT HOME IN THE COTSWOLDS
THE COLOURFUL PAST
THE DRAWING ROOM
GEORGIAN FURNITURE
JOHN FOWLER
COLEFAX & FOWLER
EAT DRINK NAP
Giorgio Locatelli Made In Italy
JERUSALEM YOTAM OTTOLENGHI SAMI TAMIMI
Parisian Chic City Guide
WORLD ATLAS

WORKING ELEMENTS

70

HARDWARE

Opposite: This exquisite example of hardware, found in the home of Courtnay Daniels, has become a part of the expression of the room.

Hardware—everything from door handles to cabinet knobs to drawer pulls to hinges, rails, hooks, and locks—is sometimes considered the finishing touch of design work. But, of course, hardware isn't just decoration. It plays an important functional role as well. The hardware you choose has an important influence on how your design plan works for you. The variety of materials—from wood to ceramic, glass, or even leather—on offer can be daunting. And even if you go for the standard metal, there's the finish to consider and then the style. You may prefer a warmer finish to your hardware, such as brass. But what style do you prefer? Traditional or more modern? By noticing hardware in a home, you will begin to put together an idea of what to use in your own home. When you choose wisely, hardware can be the finishing touch that makes all the elements of your design work together, so keep the following key things in mind:

STYLE Hardware should enhance the overarching style of your home, so select pieces that complement this style—traditional, modern, eclectic, or country, for example. There will be a style that can work for you. We recommend that you steer away from trendier choices, as they will look dated very quickly.

FUNCTION Just as important as the style is how you need the hardware to function. For example, the hardware on an exterior door needs to consider safety as well as design. Additionally, take a deep look into what you are most comfortable with. Are you someone who prefers a cleaner look? Unpolished brass might not be the best choice for you, and something like polished nickel might work better. But if you love the natural way brass can age over time to add patina, it's the perfect choice for you.

MATERIALS AND FINISHES Whether you love brass or chrome or both, you need to think about how the finishes you choose work together. That being said, we fully embrace the idea of mixing metals in your home. If everything in your home matches, it may feel too homogeneous or less interesting.

QUALITY When you choose higher-quality hardware, it will not only last longer but also function better. Areas of heavy use, such as kitchens and bathrooms, need the best quality materials, like brass, stainless steel, and bronze.

THE ESSENTIALS

Being able to see and feel the hardware is the easiest way to know if you really like it.

FIND INSPIRATION This is where you take a deep dive into your favorite shelter magazines, books, and social media to look with a critical eye at the finishes and hardware you like. Notice how finishes can be mixed and make an effort to absorb the details in a room that you might overlook at first glance, like doorknobs! Consider keeping files—both digital and physical—with the things you are drawn to.

ORDER SAMPLES OF FINISHES Being able to touch and feel the different finishes will help you narrow down your choices. Mix the different finishes together and see how you like the combination.

BUDGET Once you understand the range of hardware and what it can cost, you should put a budget together that is realistic. Perhaps splurge in a few places and cut back elsewhere to stay within your budget. For example, you may want to spend a little more on the faucet in a kitchen and cut back on the pulls on your cabinets. You could find affordable wood pulls and paint them the color of the kitchen cabinets.

Opposite: Finding the right hardware is primarily about personal taste: It's important for you to see and touch the different options in order to find your preference.

HARDWARE FINISHES

Once you have chosen your preferred finishes, you should play around with how they work together. Then you can choose what will go where. Mixing your finishes is now done frequently, but you want to try this out with samples to see if you like the effect before you install anything. In the kitchen, take into consideration the range and other appliances you are using and what finishes they have.

UNLACQUERED BRASS	AGED BRASS	POLISHED NICKEL	CHROME
SATIN NICKEL	BLACK	WHITE	OILED BRONZE

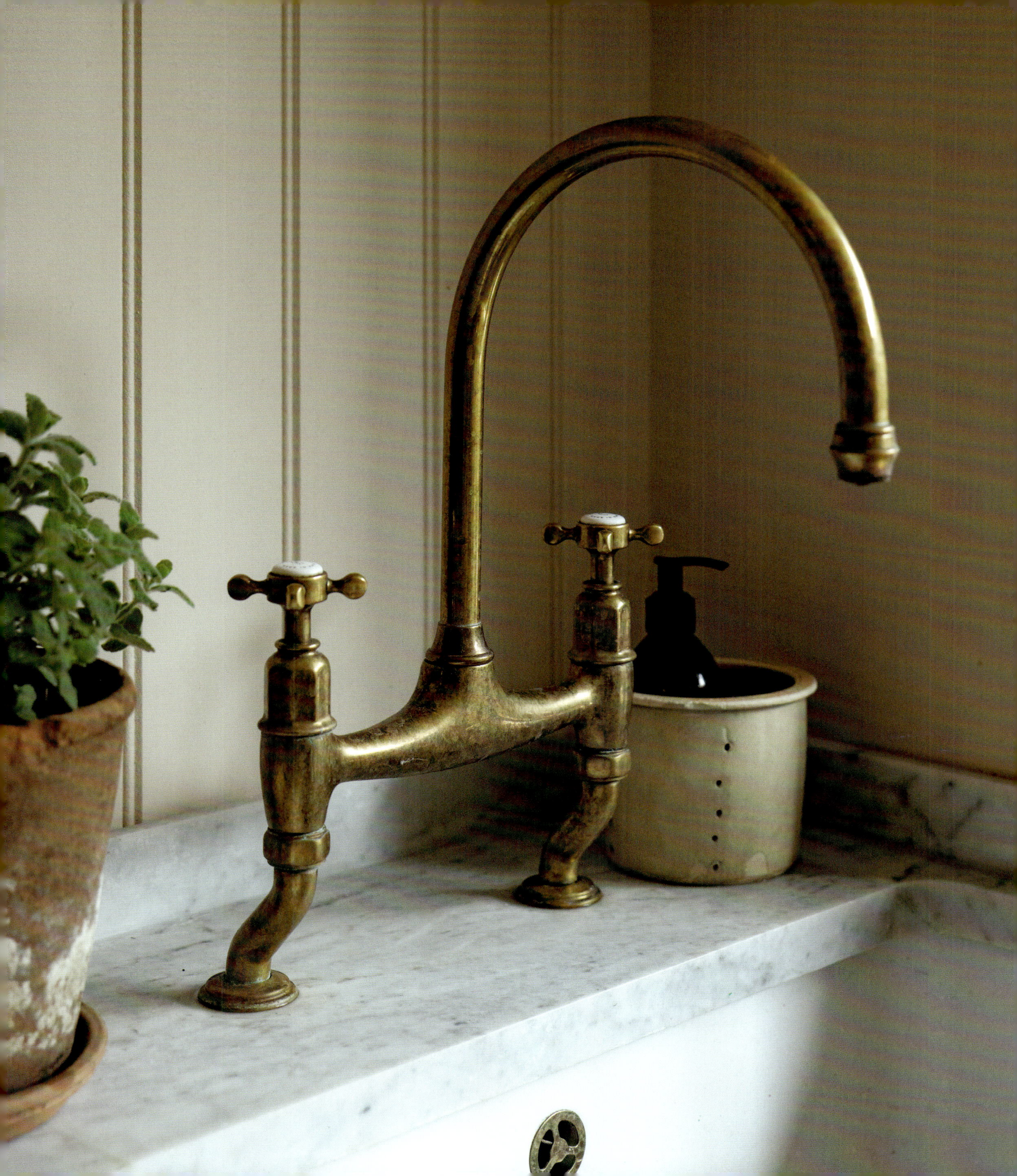

SUSAN BRINSON

Susan Brinson graduated from Savannah College of Art and Design and began her career in New York City, where she worked as a designer in advertising. In 2013, she and her husband, Will Brinson, began collaborating at Studio Brinson. They also started their blog, *House of Brinson*, in 2009 when they purchased Stony Ford, a run-down mansion in the Hudson Valley. They have been lovingly renovating it room by room. Susan gives us valuable insights into both noticing and choosing hardware for your home.

1 What should someone take into consideration when choosing the hardware for their home? One aspect of hardware I like to discuss is the level of formality. Hardware can provide visual cues to the type and style of the home. Is the home very formal with decorated, ornate, polished hardware or a simple cottage with painted wooden knobs? These details contribute to the larger story.

2 When is using vintage or antique hardware a good idea? I love using vintage hardware and always think it's a good idea! It does require a few additional details like double-checking the sizes, since standard sizes weren't always a thing in the past. You'll also need to review the finish to see if you need to remove paint or polish it up, and to confirm that items will fit with new standards, especially for plumbing pieces. The warmth and quality craftsmanship of antique hardware is difficult to re-create.

THE ESSENTIALS

"The weight of a solid brass item will feel substantial and luxe compared to something hollow. If you are making selections for the whole house, make sure to visit a showroom or order samples to feel the weight of each item."

—SUSAN BRINSON

3 Are there ways to avoid common pitfalls when selecting hardware? I avoid hardware that doesn't have a nice weight, especially if it's a piece of hardware you touch, like a knob. The weight of a solid brass item will feel substantial and luxe compared to something hollow. If you are making selections for the whole house, make sure to visit a showroom or order samples to feel the weight of each item.

4 Where would you look to gain inspiration for the hardware you use in a room? I visit historic places, especially in Europe. I love seeing custom metal work or historic solutions to common problems that have been fading from our society. Shutter hardware is my current obsession. I also love visiting historic homes with bathrooms from the 1890s to 1910s. The rooms and hardware are so classic and elegantly utilitarian.

5 Do you prefer to match all of the hardware in your home or have a mix of different finishes? We have mixed hardware in our home, and I love it; the hardware tells the story of time. Our home is from around 1840 and so many things have been changed or added since the house was built, making a collection of unmatched hardware. The hinges are cast iron in some places (which are very old), the bathrooms have nickel or brass, and most of the doorknobs are porcelain. The visual story is wonderful because each area of the house is unique. One thing to note is we like to limit the materials and style for certain areas so the house doesn't look too scattered. For instance, on the second floor, all the doorknobs are either nickel and porcelain, whereas on other floors the doorknobs shift to brass and porcelain. There is a consistency in the porcelain finish; however, nothing is exactly matching.

WORKING ELEMENTS

76

OUTDOOR SPACES

Opposite: Your outdoor space is an integral part of your home and should be designed as carefully as the inside. This garden at the home and shop of Michael Trapp provides space to wander and seek inspiration from nature.

By making the outdoor areas surrounding your home comfortable and beautiful places to spend time, you are creating alternative places where you can dine and entertain or simply sit and enjoy the fresh air with a cup of coffee. Today, the lines are blurred between indoor and outdoor design. You may want to have an indoor/outdoor rug outside to add more warmth. Also consider patterns in the cushions you might use on a bench or swing. You can completely transform an outdoor space with design into an intimate and inviting room—just like you do indoors.

Here are a few of the reasons we believe that you should design your home in way that encourages spending time outdoors:

ENHANCING YOUR MOOD Connecting with nature is shown to reduce stress. Taking a few minutes out of your day to be in the garden can give you a tremendous boost. Spending time outdoors can be the perfect antidote for a busy life.

APPRECIATING COLOR AND BEAUTY Noticing the changing seasons can provide a lesson in color and tone. There is nothing more beautiful than Upstate New York in the fall when the leaves are turning. You see the subtle changes of color, and this can inspire you to see color in a whole new way, with simple differences in tone. The same is true for your own garden. By paying attention, you will notice which colors you gravitate toward. This can help you understand the colors you might wish to surround yourself with in your home.

THE ESSENTIALS

EXTENDING YOUR LIVING SPACE It's always good to have a few extra places to spend time, but it's not simply about going outside. By creating "rooms" in your outdoor space, you will be more apt to use the areas around your home. This can be outfitting a patio, deck, or porch with a few key items. It can also be a strategically placed bench on the lawn, where you can enjoy a moment's reprieve. On my wraparound porch, I have several areas to enjoy. We find ourselves outside all the time, now that I have added a few chairs, tables, soft cushions, and some lights. Depending on the time of day, I can move to a different side of the house to enjoy the shade on a warm day, the sunshine when it's colder out, or turn on a lantern when the sun is setting.

DINING AND ENTERTAINING There is nothing more beautiful than a candlelight dinner outside. If you have a garden, consider adding a few tables and chairs there, as outdoor gatherings feel relaxed, less formal than ones in the dining room, but still special. Lighting can be a challenge at night, but there are many battery-run lamps that are fun to use outdoors in combination with candles, which create a great mood.

THE ESSENTIALS

Opposite: A dining table in the garden can provide additional space for entertaining. Above: In the garden of this home in Healdsburg, California, the landscaping blends in with the natural environment.

MICHAEL TRAPP

Michael Trapp, whose gardens are an extension of his beautiful homes, has lived in West Cornwall, Connecticut, since 1987. He is a landscape architect as well as an interior designer. What has made a tremendous impact on his design work has been his strong pull to travel around the world. His father was in the Air Force, so the family moved around; they lived outside of Paris and in Zaragoza, Spain, when Michael was a child. This exposure, along with his continued devotion to trips, has influenced his eye for design—both indoors and in his gardens. He has created outdoor rooms throughout his properties. His shop and home are settled on a hillside above the Housatonic River, where the gardens are a mix of Mediterranean and old-world influence. Although they had no initial plan, they have grown and matured over the years. We saw his interior spaces in our last book, *Sense of Place*; here he explains how to approach the design of your exterior spaces.

1 How do you make the outdoor space of a home an extension of the indoor living space? One creates rooms off the house that become an extension of the house. Gardens are all about creating external rooms.

2 How can your gardens help you have a deeper connection with nature? The simple act of growing something connects you to a much larger picture.

3 What are some decorative items you could add to a garden? I use things that help me create structures, walls, and rooms: urns, pots, pedestals, columns, all sorts of things.

4 What is the key to creating spaces that really feel like rooms outdoors? You can imply corners or make walls with stonework or hedges, lay a carpet of stone, erect a balustrade. There are thousands of ways to make rooms.

WORKING ELEMENTS

82

TEXTILES

Opposite: Using textiles in your home, such as these antique fabrics and trim from the studio of Katharine Pole, can add both depth and dimension.

How you use textiles can make a huge impact on how your home looks and feels. And textiles are one of the easiest ways to introduce color and pattern into a space. However, color and pattern don't just come from the fabrics you choose for the obvious things like sofas, throw pillows, or bedding; consider your rugs, wallpaper, lampshades, and so much more. Over the years, we have found ourselves using more vintage textiles, as well as embracing pattern-on-pattern in our rooms. Figuring out how you like to use pattern is not only one of the most rewarding parts of the design plan, it's the part that can reveal your tastes the most clearly.

Here are some things to consider when adding textiles and pattern to your home:

LAYERING Combining a variety of textiles and patterns in one space adds dimension. This is the fun part! Play around with fabric swatches to find a good balance. We try to always add in some form of vintage textiles as well. A small vintage piece can be turned into a pillow that gives more nuance and meaning to your design, for example.

PERSONAL TOUCH Textiles and patterns are a great way to put more of your own personal preferences into your home. If you love bold and bright colors, embrace them fully. But if you want to create a calm environment, consider choosing softer tones and patterns. It is worth it to spend the time looking through magazines, books, and social media to figure out what you are drawn to, which will make it easier for you to decide among the many options out there.

BALANCE It's key to find balance in your choices of textiles and patterns. In many ways, it's almost like a dance among the different things you are drawn to until you find a harmonious grouping. Continuity between rooms should also be considered, but this doesn't mean that everything needs to match. Instead, work with the different patterns until they seem to have compatibility. For example, in my living room (Caitlin), I have placed a French antique quilt over the back of my sofa. It not only adds pattern, but also softens the room. At the same time, it is in the same tones as the pillows in the room, so it adds balance. As you move into my entry area, the patterns are different, but they share a similar look with my living room. Finally, my kitchen has more patterns on the cushions of the chairs, the tablecloth, and the towels. They definitely don't match the patterns in other rooms, but they do coordinate to make a cohesive whole.

TEXTURE Pattern not only comes from printed textiles; woven, knitted, and handsewn fabrics can offer both pattern and a pleasing tactile quality. Plaid wools, homespun cotton, and bouclé (the nubby-textured fabric made from looped yarn) can give a room a rich and warm dimension. We often include an antique quilt as a way of adding texture and preventing the room from looking too generic.

TACTILITY Velvets, faux fur, and other choices can be a perfect way to both soften a room and provide added comfort. How a rug feels under your feet and the softness of a towel are all textures you want to consider.

ACCENTS There is nothing more beautiful than adding a vibrant pattern as a special moment or eye-catching detail in a space. This adds visual interest and variety. Even when most of a home has a minimal aesthetic, a small powder room that has been wallpapered in a vibrant pattern can be such a nice surprise. It almost feels like a jewelry box.

Above and opposite: Details in the design studio of textile collector Katharine Pole reflect her passion for the whimsical and colorful.

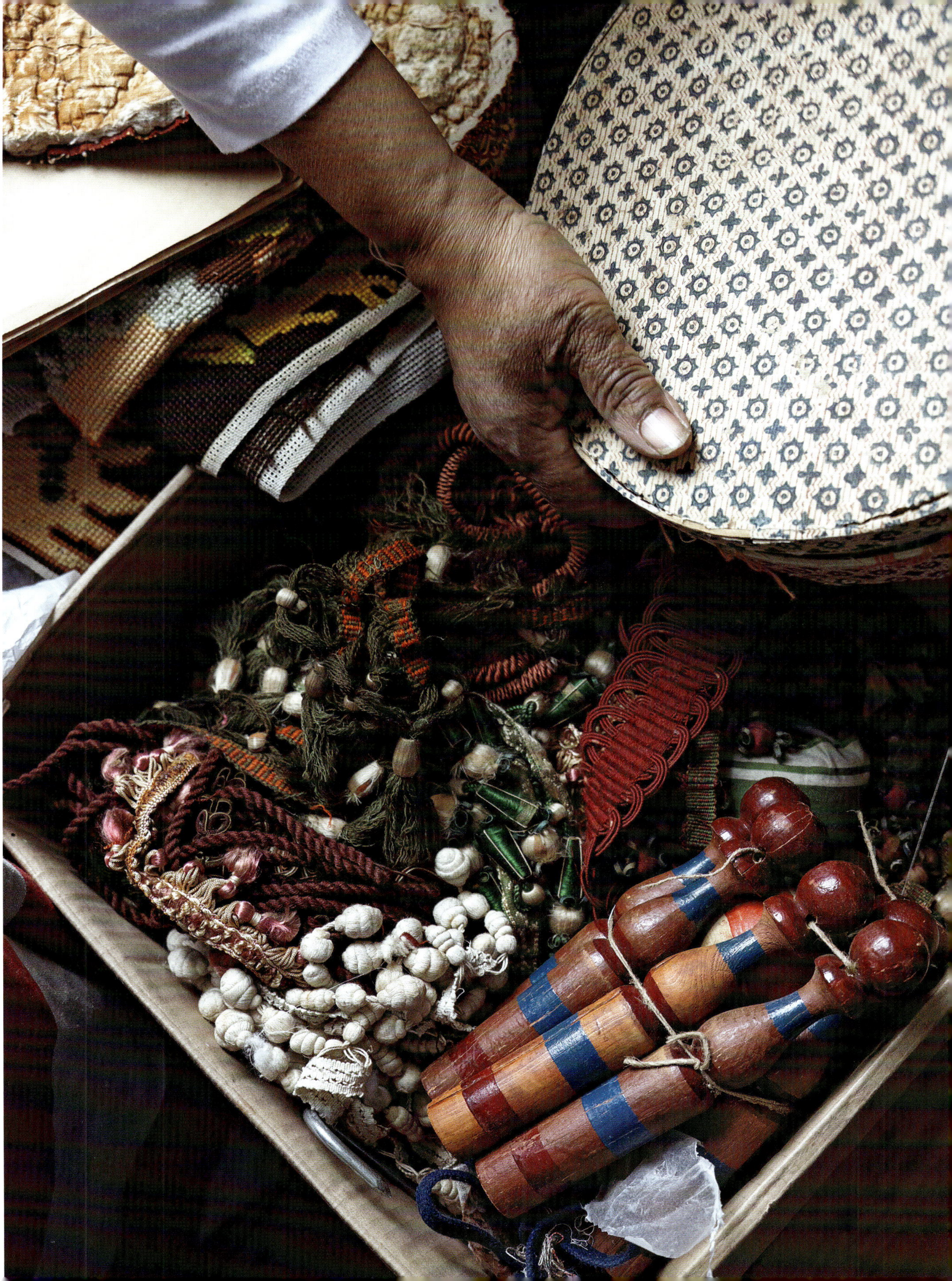

KATHARINE POLE

Katharine Pole, an antique textile collector and expert, has been involved with textiles in one way or another all of her adult life. Originally, Katharine thought she would study fashion, but she quickly turned her attention to textiles. She worked as a textile designer and eventually began to amass a large collection of vintage textiles. Then she pivoted and began selling these textiles and using them for the cushions she has become well-known for. Nestled in her home in one room is her impressive collection of primarily French textiles from the eighteenth and nineteenth centuries. She is an example of someone who has made a career out of her passion. Here she shares some helpful tips for anyone that wants to add textiles to their home.

THE ESSENTIALS

Opposite: Katharine in her design studio in London. Above: The plethora of pattern, color, and texture that Katharine houses in her studio.

BRITISH TEXTILES
Textile Classics

THE HULLS COVER,
Near Monk's House.
100 LOTS
POLES

> *"First of all, to buy what you love is probably the best way, as the collection can be an extension of one's hobbies and interests."*
>
> —KATHARINE POLE

1 How can textiles add depth to a home's design?
Antique textiles can be the vital ingredient of any interior. Natural dyes and colors, such as indigo, bleu de pastel, woad, saffron yellow, madder red, cochineal, etc., were used before the 1850s invention of the first synthetic dyes and will often have aged beautifully into incredibly rich colors, which have grown in depth and subtlety over the years. For example, a late eighteenth- or early nineteenth-century quilt of bourette de soie, a beautifully textured silk, can be used in a bedroom to create a pool of light and a focal point.

2 How can textiles help add personality to your home?
Textiles can tell a story and express the things in life that you are drawn to. If like me you have a passion for eighteenth-century life, imagine dressing a bed in that style, perhaps with a canopy and bed hangings of toile de Jouy, an arborescent indienne, or a block-printed indigo resist. And in a modern contemporary home with a more minimalist style, just one beautiful antique textile, in the form of a cushion, wall hanging, or throw on a sofa, can create a beautiful note with a splash of color, providing contrast and depth.

3 Can you suggest some ways in which textiles can be layered to make a home a more multidimensional environment?
To create a layered look, textiles offer many ingredients: everything from cushions, curtains, and throws to quilts and upholstery. A small embroidered piece or printed textile can look wonderful framed, and you can build a collection to make a focal point in a room. It is rare to find enough of one antique textile to provide a complete scheme for the different layers of an interior, but if you make careful choices, complementary pieces can provide a visual theme uniting curtains, cushions, and upholstery.

4 How can we begin a textile collection?
First of all, to buy what you love is probably the best way, as the collection can be an extension of one's hobbies and interests. Then try and read around the subject, go and visit museums and exhibitions, and get out there to see and touch—everywhere from junk shops and flea markets to antique fairs can be inspiring and spark your journey. Let things evolve as your eye develops and your taste is refined.

WORKING ELEMENTS

90

COLOR

Opposite: A great way to see how your potential project choices may look together is to place them on a mood board.

One of the most exciting parts of designing your home is figuring out the colors and patterns you want to include. Preferences are very personal in this category. Think about how different colors make you feel, and look at rooms you are inspired by. Are you attracted to mixing patterns in a room, or do you prefer solid color?

Colors and patterns can set the mood and have a huge impact on a room. Here are crucial things to consider:

TRENDS OR TIMELESS COLORS There is no question that color is affected by trends in both interior design and fashion. Just remember when you choose a color that is popular that it will also feel outdated as quickly as it started trending. A combination of colors that are hot at the moment with ones that are more traditional can make your choices last longer.

COORDINATION Matching everything perfectly isn't necessarily the best choice, but do make sure colors flow from one room to another. It is always nice to feel continuity between spaces. For example, you may have a terra-cotta tone in your kitchen. You probably don't want the entire home in terra-cotta, but finding a way to introduce it in another room with a painting or a throw pillow can help the flow between rooms.

PSYCHOLOGY OF COLOR Certain colors have an effect on how we feel. Cool colors, such as blue and green, can be calming. Warmer colors—red, yellow, and orange—can call to mind energy and excitement. Neutral choices—white, beige, and gray—can complement your color choices.

USE OF LIGHT Both natural and artificial light, and the things the light filters through before it reaches the interior of your house, can have an impact on how a color looks. For example, greenery that is close to windows will cast a green light onto the walls. It's vital to try out a color of paint or any other wall covering in the actual space and observe it at different times of day before making your choice.

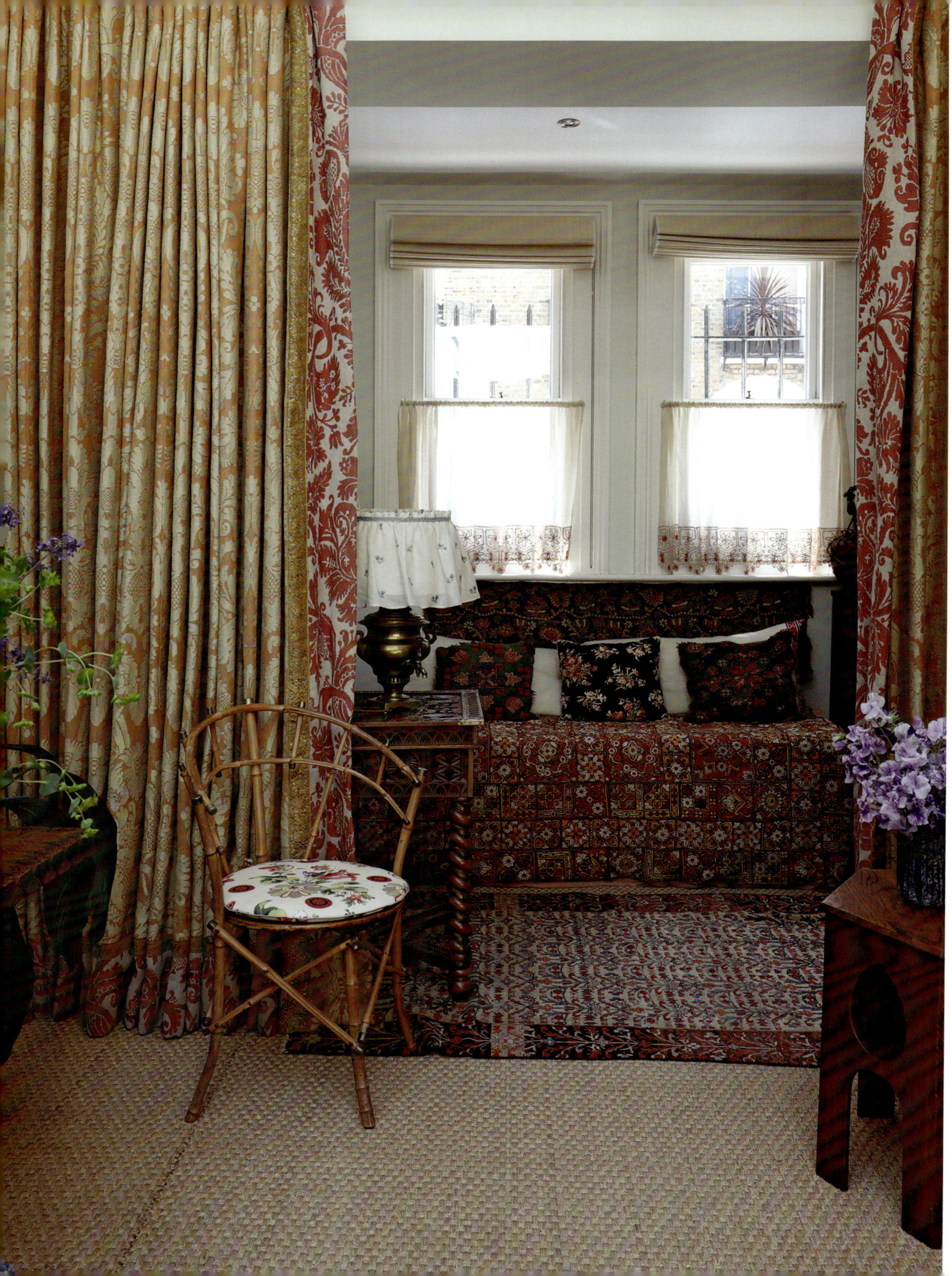

Opposite: Nathalie Farman-Farma created a nook in one of the corners of her studio in London and added curtains to distinguish the space. Patterns and colors live happily together. Right: The guest room in Charlotte Boundy's home layers red patterns together beautifully.

THE ESSENTIALS

HEIDI CAILLIER

Heidi Caillier is known as an interior designer who creates rooms with intimacy and yet also reinvents traditional design. She embraces both color and pattern in unique and authentic ways. Heidi is based in Seattle, Washington, and has projects throughout the United States and abroad. Heidi shares her insights on not being afraid to think outside the box in the way she uses both color and pattern in her design projects.

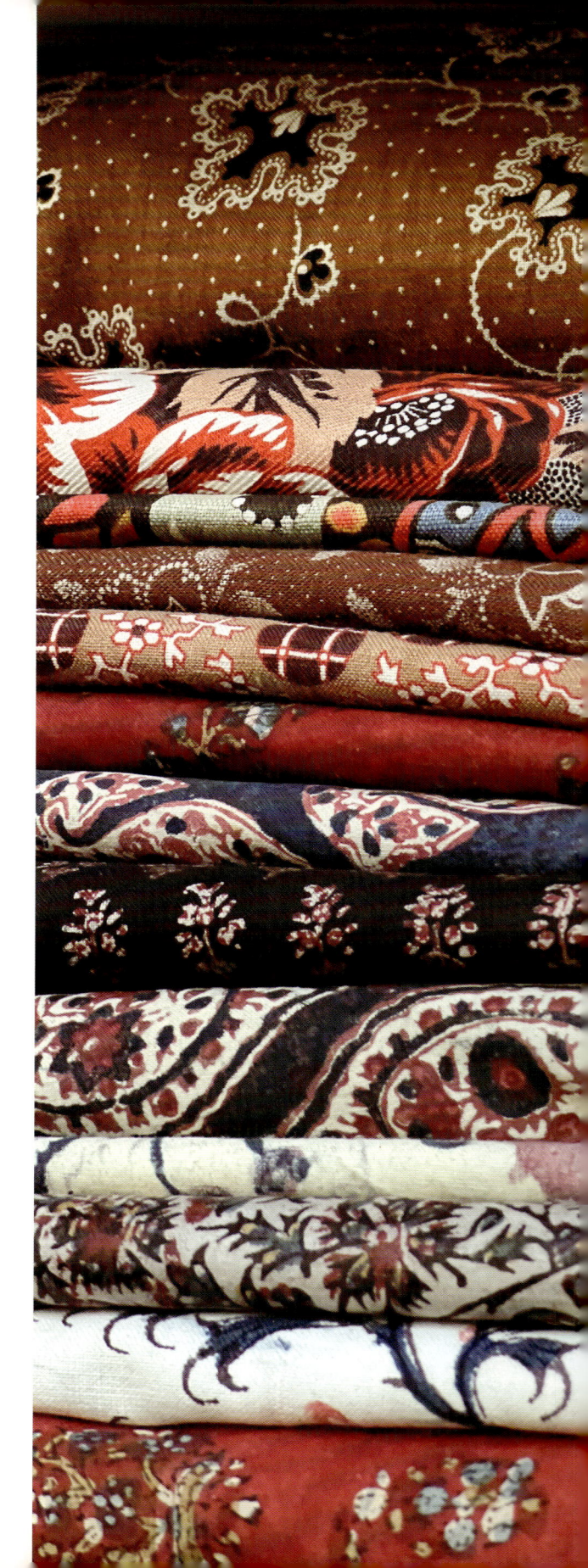

THE ESSENTIALS

"It's all about mixing colors—different shades, tones, qualities—and then also mixing scale, pattern, and vibe."

—HEIDI CAILLIER

1 You seamlessly use color and pattern in your design work. How do you manage to do this without making a home appear "too matchy"? I never want a home to feel too designed. I want things to feel collected and layered—like it's been added to over time. I also value tension and think it's important for there to be something off to create that. I love mixing vintage textiles with designer fabrics. I find that the designer fabrics tend to be recognizable, and I want something that feels a bit weirder to pair with them. It's all about mixing colors—different shades, tones, qualities—and then also mixing scale, pattern, and vibe. I think there is a way for all of the colors to play harmoniously if used right.

2 Which spaces work well for a more moody or darker use of color? I love to use moodier tones in small rooms to really lean into that coziness. But a very large room can also be a good candidate for an all-over pattern because it helps to bring the scale down and make it feel more livable.

3 What colors have you been recently gravitating toward? All of them! I love color, and I love to use it in unexpected ways. I have been loving red and yellow lately.

4 Can you recommend ways to incorporate patterns into your home? I like to use patterns in significant ways. I prefer to think big—walls, window treatments, upholstery. They can bring so much joy, and I just don't get as much happiness from using them on just pillows or smaller pieces. I want to be immersed.

5 When is wallpaper a good idea? Always!

6 Do you use special finishes for walls? What are some treatments you like? We have been using lime wash a decent amount, and I love plaster as well. We do a lot of paneling, applied moldings, and detailing on walls and ceilings. It is so crucial to bringing charm and architectural interest.

WORKING ELEMENTS

96

LIGHTING

Opposite: Lampshades and their bases in Tamsin Saunders's studio reflect the various hues and patterns that can augment a room's design.

Lighting has a significant impact on your home, affecting its atmosphere—what it feels like to inhabit the spaces—more than almost anything else does. Not only is it important to find lighting that functions for the activities you plan to do in each area of the space, your lighting also should resonate with your home's overall style. Here are the primary types of lighting you should take into consideration.

NATURAL LIGHT One of the most important sources of light is the sunlight that enters your home through glass windows, doors, and skylights. If you are building a home, consider the movement of the sun and how it falls in the space throughout different days and seasons. Where you place your windows can have a large impact on how you'll be able to enjoy and use natural light.

AMBIENT LIGHTING Ambient lighting is the primary lighting of the room, providing the overall illumination and setting a tone for the space. It is usually achieved through an overhead light or recessed lighting. Consider a ceiling-mounted fixture for lower ceilings, and chandeliers for higher ceilings. Wall sconces are ideal for lighting a portion of a room and are ideal for places like a bedroom or living room where you are looking to create a cozy atmosphere. However, for almost any space, we prefer the ambient light in our homes to be a more diffused, softer light, which is much more inviting than harsh, brightly lit rooms.

THE ESSENTIALS

TASK LIGHTING Sometimes you need more direct, focused lighting; for example, a desk lamp for paperwork or studying, recessed lighting under cabinets to illuminate countertops in your kitchen, or a floor lamp next to a chair you gravitate toward when you want to read a book. Think about how you use your home when deciding on task lighting.

ACCENT LIGHTING Accent lighting can be used to highlight artwork or a particular architectural feature of the home. For example, in some libraries, lights are attached to the bookshelves to illuminate them.

TABLE LAMPS We are big believers in table lamps. They not only add a soft light, but they can become a part of the decor. Consider vintage lamp bases. You can find such a variety—from alabaster lamp bases to unique pottery in a variety of shapes and sizes. You'll also want to put the time into finding the right lampshades. Pleated lampshades can diffuse the light and cast a soft glow. You can have lampshades made with a patterned textile. You can choose wicker lampshades to add texture to a room.

Above and opposite: Lighting not only helps to create atmosphere, it offers focal points that can tie the design together.

THE ESSENTIALS

WORKING ELEMENTS

TAMSIN SAUNDERS

Tamsin Saunders comes from a family who appreciate beauty and craftsmanship. Her great-grandfather was a builder, and both her father and grandfather favored restoration in their work as architects. Her mother, an avid gardener and antiquer, encouraged Tamsin's love of nature and appreciation of the beauty of things made by hand. Tamsin's West London studio, which she founded in 2012, is home to her architectural design practice, Home and Found. The studio is furnished with an ever-changing collection of antique furniture, one-off finds, and unique vintage lamps, which she uses to create the effortlessly relaxed, elegant homes that are her hallmark. Tamsin advises how lighting, an often overlooked aspect of a home, is key to creating beautiful, comfortable, original homes.

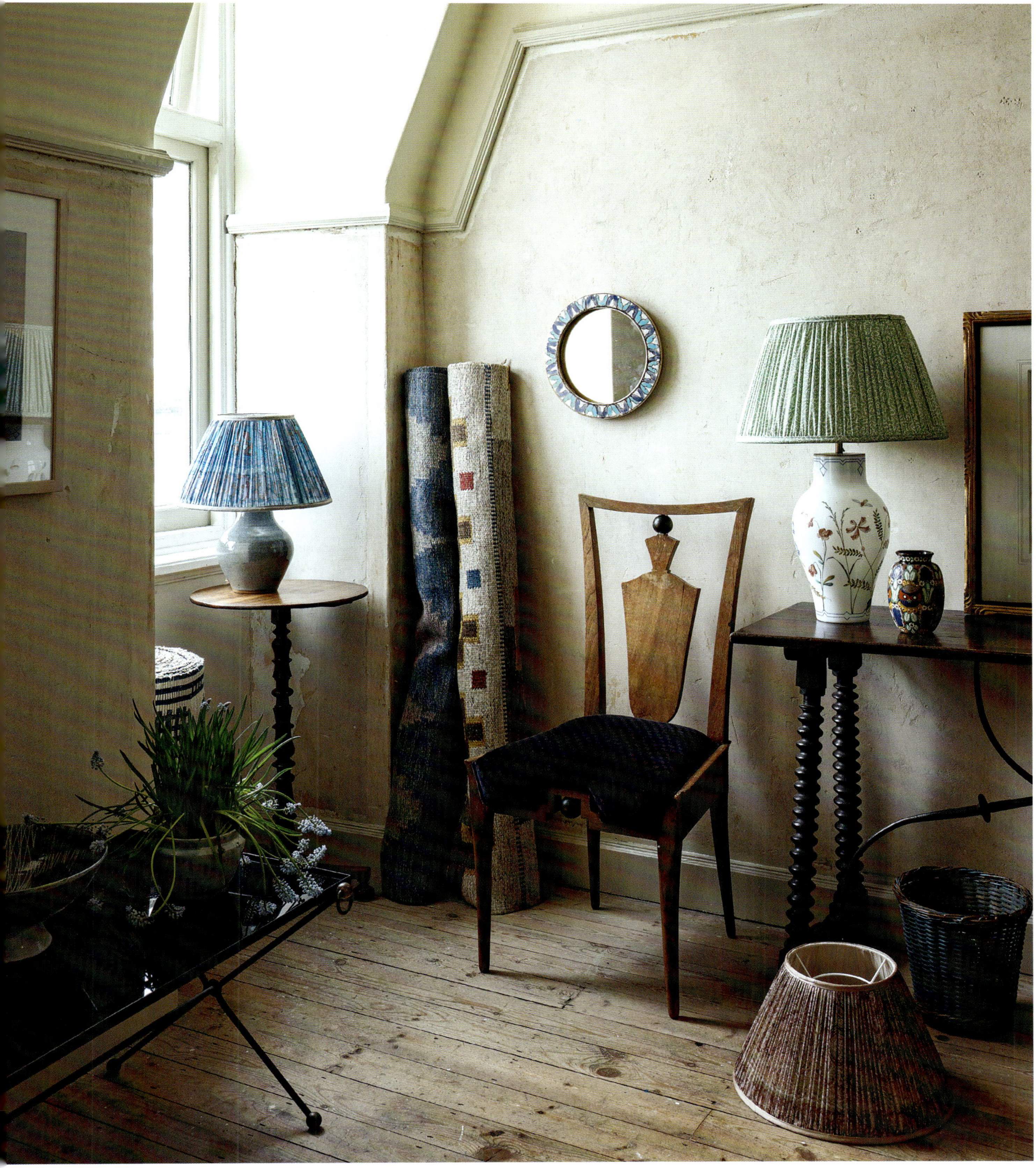

1 Why is it important to carefully consider lighting in your design? Home is a feeling. How well a home is designed is determined not by how it looks in a photograph but by how it feels to be in it. Consider how the space is going to be used at different times of day and throughout the year—lamps can help you transform a dingy nook into a cozy corner; equally, it can shape and zone an otherwise open-plan, potentially cavernous space. Lighting is the benchmark of good design; it can literally make or break it. Too bright and there's no atmosphere, or too boring, too bling, too predictable and a room becomes sterile and soulless. Get the lighting wrong and, I would argue, all else counts for nothing. The gentle, warm glow of a beautiful, interesting lamp is transformative—on and off. Good lighting always has something interesting to say but never dominates or shouts for attention. It is like the bass note in music—the deep sonorous richness that lifts your spirit, soothes your soul, or gets your foot tapping.

2 Choosing the lighting in a home can feel like an overwhelming task. Can you give us a list of your top ways to cut through noise and make good decisions? Embrace the random and unexpected. I love to see the irregularities and imperfections of things made by hand. One-off vintage lighting (lamps, pendants, and wall lights) that celebrate texture, pattern, color, shape, and form, and which were clearly made with care and attention by hand rather than mass-produced by machines, will give your home a feeling of looseness and freedom that I believe is key.

Zone different areas on separate dimmer switches so that the lighting can be adjusted to create the mood or atmosphere desired. You will need good, brighter lighting in a bathroom and in a kitchen to work by, but then you also want to be able to tone it down so you can lie in the bath and relax, and sit around the table and forget about the mess on the kitchen island. They are not interrogation rooms!

Avoid anything new or that you've seen before, and avoid spotlights.

Always mix it up: Use lighting as a way of introducing a different style, color, shape, or texture. The way you put things together is what will make your home unique.

Less is always more. The trick is to allow things space to breathe and be seen.

I trust my eye and actively try and avoid what anyone else is doing. Choose a lamp because you like it, and remember, it is an investment not just in your home but in you. It will determine not only how your home looks but how you feel living in it. My mantra is "Do it once and do it properly—buy what you love, love it, treasure it, and pass it on."

THE ESSENTIALS

3 What role does natural light play in a room? Nature is key to creating a sense of well-being. I always think about when the light falls into a room—and where. It's not necessarily about maximizing natural light but positioning and using it. If possible, try and capture the natural light from other rooms by positioning doorways so that you can see out through a window when you look into an adjacent room. It will make a home feel freer, more relaxed and spacious, fresher, more natural, and less enclosed. Muslin on windows also helps create a beautiful light in a room.

4 How can you combine aspects of functionality with aesthetics in your lighting? Lighting is not only an opportunity to add something new to the conversation—a different style or texture, an element of surprise—but it is vital to developing a sense of mood and creating atmosphere and nurturing a feeling of well-being, of sanctuary and retreat. Think about how you are going to use and live in your home: how you feel walking into it, the dynamics of passing through it, the cadence of moving from one room to the next, how each room relates to and informs another, how your use of the space will change with the seasons and how lighting will affect it. Beautiful, gentle lighting affects how a home feels, creating a reassuring sense of comfort, containment, and connection in even larger, more sparsely decorated spaces. Carefully considered lighting is a uniquely understated way of making a big impact. A little silver art deco lamp on a shelf or mantlepiece, a large mid-century studio pottery lamp beside a sofa, or two different but complementary lamps on either side of a bed—these are all so much more interesting, and aesthetically and ethically, they are far more satisfying than anything mass-produced.

5 Why do you prefer vintage lamps over new ones?
There is an unfathomable amount of waste and pollution in the building and design industry, not to mention reproduction, regurgitation, and repetition. I think it's important to make use of what is already out there and to treasure the unique beauty and craftsmanship of the past. I buy what I like, things that move me in some way, which you can tell were made with love and care and which I know will add interest and originality to a home. I like homes that tell me about the lives, loves, values, and interests of the people who live there. Lighting is an opportunity to have fun, to be a bit more adventurous, and to introduce something slightly random, unexpected, and truly individual. It is always so refreshing to walk into a room and not see anything you've ever seen before. Good design never dates; it's all in the mix. Not just where you put it, but what you put with it—the color, shape, style, scale, and finish of a lamp and the shade you use with it will completely change how a room looks and feels.

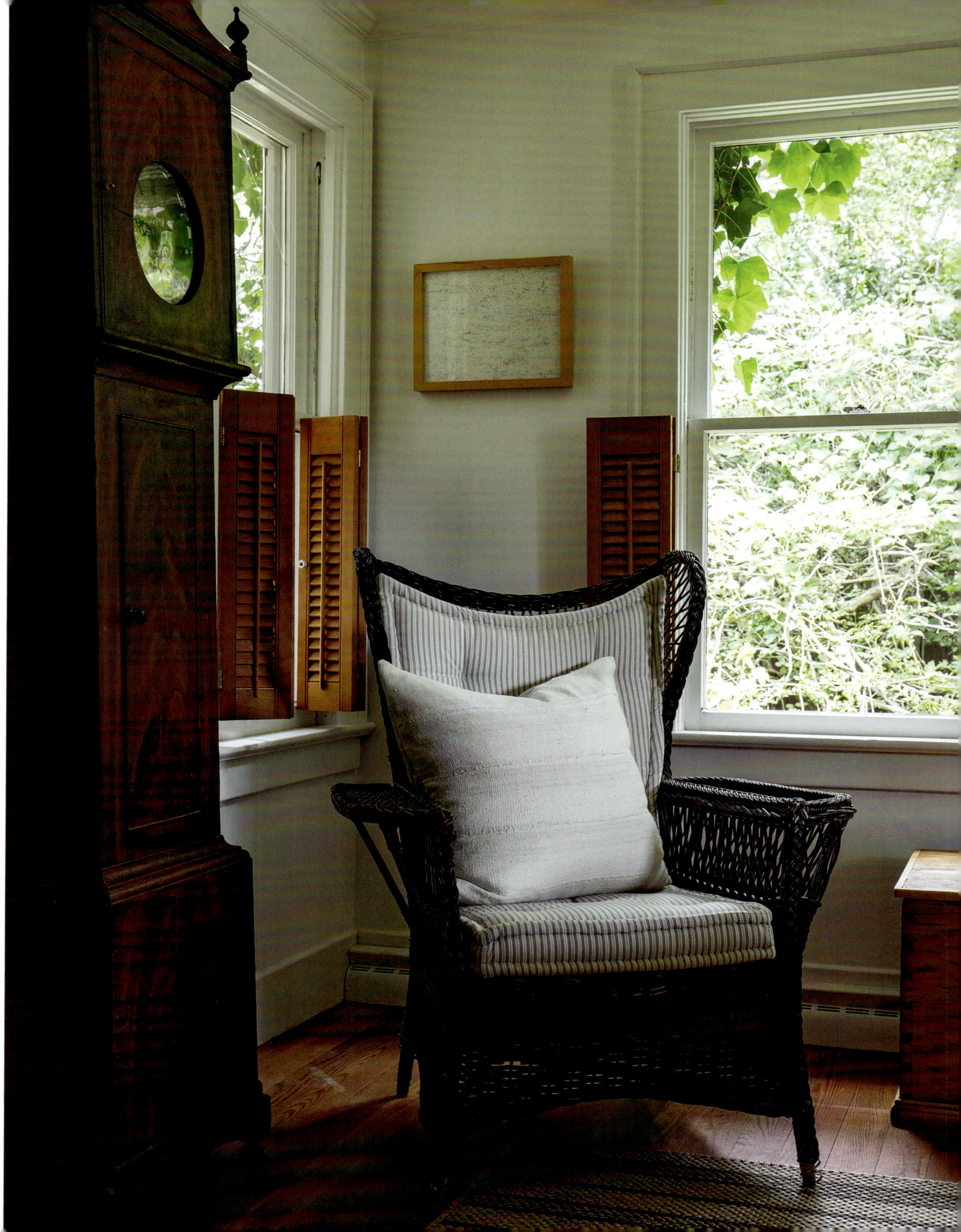

FURNITURE

Other than your home itself, furniture can be one of the most expensive things you invest in. It will also determine how you enjoy a space and how comfortable you are spending time there. Here are a few things to take into consideration before making any big commitments:

Using antique furniture can bring a sense of the past to a room and help to ground it. Consider visiting antique shops where you hone your eye and decide what type of furniture resonates with you. With practice and patience, you will be able to identify pieces of high quality and know what you would like in your own home. Spending time browsing in these shops can also help you to understand good (and bad) craftsmanship.

Using antique furniture in your home is a more sustainable practice, giving a new lease on life to an older item, and this means you don't have to purchase something new. When you buy a piece of antique wooden furniture, such as a cabinet or chest of drawers, the wood itself is a thing of beauty, and the patina just can't be replicated. Additionally, a good piece of furniture can be reupholstered many times.

If you prefer new furniture, do your homework on where to buy it from. Consider the materials used in their production. Are they safe? What kind of chemicals, glue, and wood are used to make them?

For furniture, we have two experts offering advice: First, celebrity interior designer Nate Berkus, who is known for his use of antique furnishings in a fresh and modern way, and Lulu Lytle, who has transformed interior design in the United Kingdom by growing a community of craftspeople to make well-designed furniture. Lulu's company, Soane, now collaborates with more than forty independent workshops across Britain, bringing together rattan weavers, ceramicists, blacksmiths, cabinetmakers, and more. What both Nate and Lulu have in common is the belief in using quality pieces in our homes instead of the inexpensive alternatives that continue to end up in our landfills. Their words of wisdom resonate with our design ethos. Having less but intentionally choosing items of better quality will also help our fragile planet.

Opposite: Furniture is a key element in defining the space, establishing its purpose and enhancing the aesthetic. This corner of Glenn Ban's dining room is a perfect spot for a quiet moment with a book.

THE ESSENTIALS

"Rooms with exclusively new things simply can't achieve the same layers and depth as when there are pieces with age, history, and patina."

—NATE BERKUS

NATE BERKUS

1 Why is it beneficial to combine antiques with new furniture in a space? Two elements that are deeply important to me when creating a space are layers and depth. Vintage pieces and antiques bring these qualities in beautifully. Rooms with exclusively new things simply can't achieve the same layers and depth as when there are pieces with age, history, and patina.

2 What do you recommend as ways to learn more about investing in antiques? Smart investment in antiques is all about the knowledge you have before you start buying pieces—because you'll want to have these things for years, if not for life. Start by researching online, which will help you identify a style or era that you like. Then find out as much as you can about it: who were the best makers at the time, materials that were used with great effect, etc. If you can, talk with the antiques shops in your town, ask them what they know, and get key words to help you search online and beyond to auction houses and dealers. Once you've researched and learned all you can about how to know if something is real, you'll be ready for whatever you might stumble upon at an estate sale or flea market.

3 How do you keep a home from looking too "grandma" when using antiques? There are two antidotes to "grandma" antiquing: one, mix the antiques with modern upholstery, or contemporary art, or modern lamps and lighting; and two, avoid accessory overload (doilies, figurines, anything ever sold by the Franklin Mint, souvenirs, kitsch). Limit the number of things on your tabletops and bookshelves.

4 What periods of furniture are you drawn to? Swedish/Gustavian: I'm drawn to the original painted finishes and love bringing this into a space that needs something soft and pretty. The carvings and chalky paleness of this era can really balance a space. I'm thinking of chests of drawers with old stone tops and classic oval dining tables.

French 1950s: This is one of the easiest periods to layer into a mix. You'll always find it in my interiors. I'm attracted to the architectural shapes and the mix of materials like iron and leather, bronze and mirror, as well as limed oak finishes. These pieces can really be a highlight in a room, such as a pair of lamps or a special side table.

5 What is the one piece of antique furniture you would tell someone to start with if they are new to collecting antiques? A gilded wall mirror: French or Italian from the nineteenth century up to 1940. I have several of varying quality and age, and they always find places in our home, despite the fact we have moved ten times over ten years.

Above: Nate is well known for his talent for mixing antiques with contemporary furniture in a fresh and modern way.

Above: The dining room of Glenn Ban serves many purposes; with a daybed in one corner, it is often a spot for a nap or to read a book. Opposite: The living room of Nate Berkus and Jeremiah Brent in Montauk, New York, is a study in refined simplicity.

THE ESSENTIALS

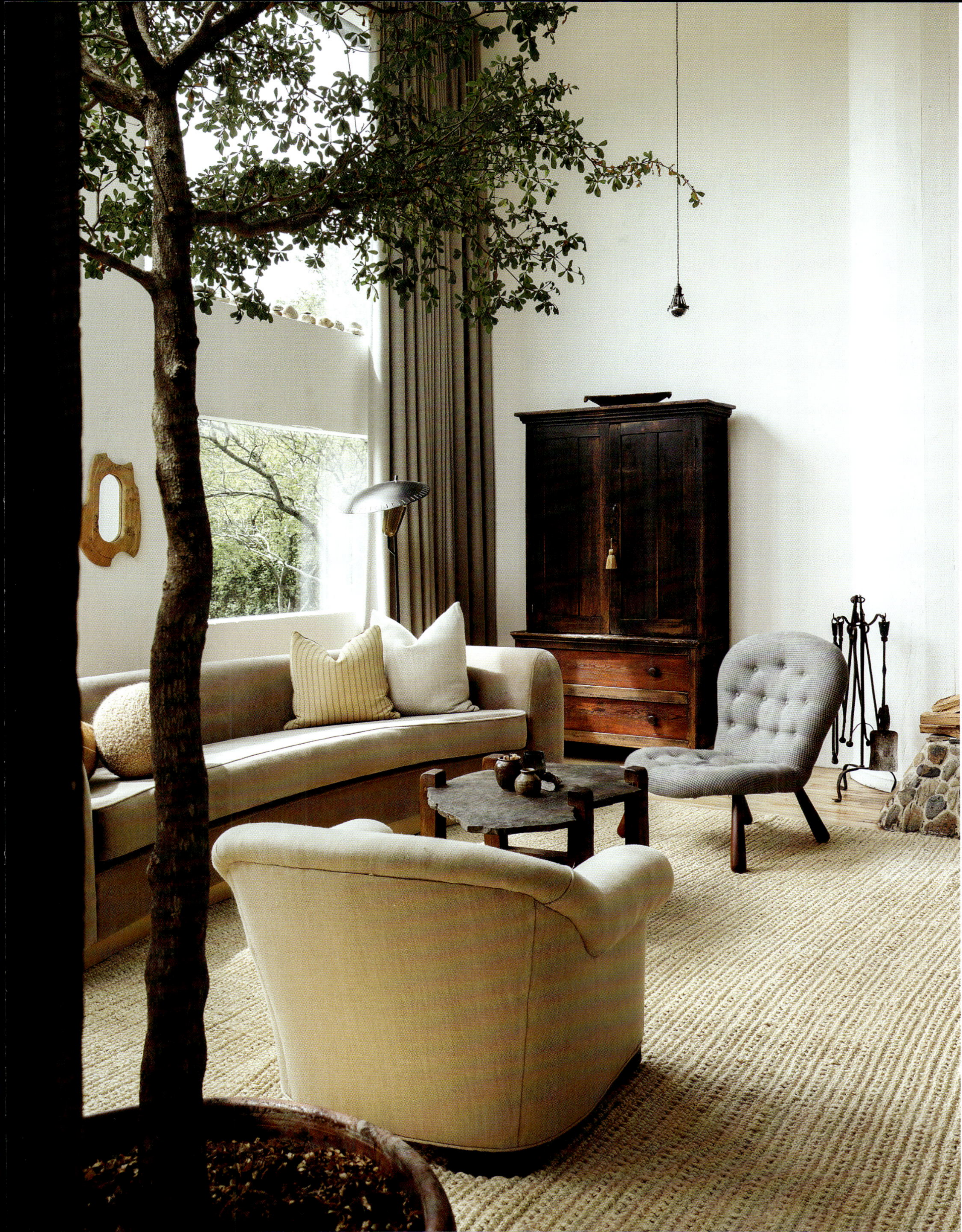

Above: Lulu, who is a great believer in buying well and buying once, relaxes in her rattan workspace.

"If we all have the 'buy once, buy well' approach to everything, then the logic follows that restoration offers much greater value than replacement."

—LULU LYTLE

LULU LYTLE

1 Why does transparency in the supply chain matter for all of us? Transparency around how, where, and by whom things are made should be absolutely standard. Without it we stand little chance of making urgent improvements to our relationships with nature and people. There is a pressing need to make less, better, and I believe we have a responsibility to initiate the conversations around integrity of craftsmanship, modes of production, sustainable materials, etc. and to encourage curiosity in the provenance of every single thing we buy.

Of course, we should be able to trust the information companies give us around supply chains, knowing every step of production from sourcing of raw materials through every element of the making process, and right down to how we dispose of manufacturing waste. People are at the heart of this whole subject, acknowledging their skill and commitment and paying them fair wages. When clients visit our workshops to see Soane's designs being made and talk to the craftspeople, only then do they really understand what goes into every single piece. The makers' attention to detail and obsessive perfectionism encapsulate true craftsmanship for me. In both home furnishings and fashion, there is a real urgency to discuss these thorny issues and consider the hypocrisy at play: the companies prioritizing profit over people.

2 How can handcrafted items enhance the authenticity of a home? By their very nature, pieces made by hand add soul to a home because thought, effort, and skill have been invested in their making. I realized that nearly all of the things I particularly treasure—be they paintings, textiles, ceramics, clothes, or furniture—have been made by hand, which I find very comforting.

3 Why should you consider reupholstering an older piece in place of buying new? If we all have the "buy once, buy well" approach to everything, then the logic follows that restoration offers much greater value than replacement. We are far more likely to value something in which we are both financially and emotionally invested rather than [one acquired by] a less-considered impulse buy.

4 Could you explain to us the concept of your makers' village? For many years we have had an ambition to see our craftspeople working side by side on one large site of purpose-built workshops, which we have referred to rather boldly as a "makers' village." The aim is to foster a community of makers working collaboratively, drawing on each other's skills, and with access to shared tools and machinery, making technological developments more accessible. We have plans for a library and a canteen as well as a small museum to show our extensive rattan archive of designs, dating back to the nineteenth century. It has huge potential as we identify a more diverse group of makers and skills. We appreciate it is a very ambitious plan, which will take anywhere between five and ten years to bring to reality.

Above: The vintage Thonet bench from France creates a welcoming entryway.
Opposite: A hand-crafted table and cabinet paired with Baumann Fourmi chairs refine the dining room. Both spaces were designed by Caitlin Flemming.

THE ESSENTIALS

WORKING ELEMENTS 113

WORKING ELEMENTS

114

ART

Opposite: In the basement of Josh Young's Washington, DC, home, you will find his art workshop. It is an inspiring space, where his creative ideas come alive.

Including art in your rooms is one of the most important ways to put your own personal stamp on your home, adding depth and meaning. We strongly believe art, along with accessories (see pages 147–151), can provide a glimpse of who you are to those who visit. What's more, it has the power to improve your mood and remind you of the things you love. We steer away from putting up "filler art" until you find the right thing. Better to have a blank wall than to place items there that you feel no connection to. Collecting art is something you should do slowly over a lifetime.

Art brings many benefits to your home, including:

SELF-EXPRESSION Art permits you to share your personality, tastes, and interests. The artwork you choose should reveal something about who you are. Collect what you are drawn to—including photographs, paintings, sculpture, ceramics, basketry, textiles, and mixed-media pieces.

EMOTIONS Art has the power to change the mood of a space. Think about how you want to feel in a room, whether you want to relax or be energized, and what you hope to achieve with a piece of art. How does it make you feel? How do the colors speak to you?

AESTHETICS Art adds visual interest—color, texture, and dimension—to a room in a direct way, an effect that can be difficult to match with furniture alone.

CULTURE Art is often the reflection of a cultural heritage, a historical moment, or a community. Art from a variety of time periods can provide an understanding of where we are from and where we have been.

VERSATILITY Art is one of the easiest things to change in a home. You can change its location with relative ease. Rearranging your art can keep it fresh and allow you to see it in a new light.

APPRECIATION Over time, art often increases in value. Not only does it bring beauty to your home, but collecting it can also have financial returns.

Above: Carving out a space for your creative endeavors is important. Having it pleasing to the eye can also spark your ideas. Opposite: A display of art supplies tells a story, becoming a form of art in itself.

THE ESSENTIALS

WORKING ELEMENTS
117

JOSH YOUNG

Josh Young, an artist known for his avant-garde approach to classical portraits, has a deep admiration for the past, a passion that is reflected in both his home (see pages 226–241) and his artwork. He was kind enough to answer a few questions about how we can start to collect art and use it in the design of our homes, and he let us visit his art studio. Here he shares his sage advice.

1 How does someone new to the world of art begin to amass a collection? Tap into what speaks to you. What are you instantly and viscerally drawn to? What do you want to be surrounded by in your home—considering everything, from subject matter, to color palette, to texture, to the overall motif and style of a piece? It goes beyond reacting; instead identify that common thread between everything you are curating. Oftentimes I find that once you build a large enough collection of anything, you will be able to step back and the throughline becomes evident. Doing so can help you home in on what you are looking for as you continue to grow your collection. It's about forming and establishing your own artistic point of view from a collector's standpoint.

2 How does art enhance the aesthetics of a home?
Since art is such a personal extension of oneself, it becomes a direct reflection of an individual's style and taste within a space. The curation of the artwork featured in a home is what will offer personality and depth. Artwork allows you flexibility to play with different styles, whether it be abstract paintings, photography, or installation pieces. Adding art to a space truly lets you have the freedom to have fun without too much restriction. You may have a very traditional and subdued room and yet allow space for bolder and statement-like pieces of art. Art can tie together different elements within a space, creating a greater sense of cohesion and ultimately elevating the overall aesthetic of a home.

Above: Josh finds inspiration in his Washington, DC, art studio.

WHITE
WHITE
WHITE
WHITE
WHITE
SYCAMORE HOUSE
ARTFUL HOME JOSH YOUNG

3 For the novice, can you explain the importance of scale and proportion? It's about finding the right balance so that everything in a design feels harmonious and visually pleasing. Proportion helps create coherence and unity in a design, guiding the eye and creating a sense of order. One person may appreciate a small piece on a wall, allowing for more negative space. On the other hand, someone who is bolder and braver when it comes to scale and appreciates drama may want larger pieces that have more visual weight on a wall. It comes down to your personal preference and overall aesthetic. There is no true formula; it is about finding the right balance and scale of the art's interaction with the other pieces in a room, such as furniture, decor, etc. in order to build a harmonious design.

4 How does art have the power to evoke emotions and inspire your creativity? You may find that a color palette or subject matter evokes feelings of joy, nostalgia, or sadness. This is why it's so important to intentionally curate what surrounds you in your home. For me, when I go to a museum or exhibit and I see an artist's work that I resonate with, there may be techniques or qualities used that inspire me to explore and experiment in my own work. I always find it so interesting going through an entire museum; there may be countless pieces that I admire, but there are usually one or two pieces that I cannot stop thinking about, and it's because they sparked a level of emotion within me.

5 Could you suggest how someone could learn more about art? Take every opportunity to visit museums and galleries. Specifically with museums, you gain firsthand experience of a variety of styles and periods—from modern art, to classical, to abstract, to photography. Once you discover a specific style or artist you're interested in, I would advise turning to books supporting this subject. I personally love reading about the artist behind the pieces that intrigue me. What influenced them, what inspired them, what life experiences helped shape their bodies of work? I find it so compelling to learn about the life of an artist. Documentaries are one of my favorite ways to take a deeper dive into this subject as well.

WORKING ELEMENTS

122

HANDCRAFTED ITEMS

Opposite: Deborah Needleman perfects the ancient art of basketry.

One great way to add a more personal feeling to a space is to include items that are handcrafted. They will bring interest, warmth, and, in many ways, soul to your space. There is a whole host of possibilities for you to choose from. We love pottery and baskets as they are not only beautiful, but they add texture. Handmade ironwork can look beautiful, especially in a Spanish-style home, even if it's just a pair of candlesticks or sconces. Additionally, it's fun to discover the artisans who live and work near where you live. Look out for fairs or sales in your area.

Handcrafted items can elevate your home by bringing the following:

QUALITY Handcrafted items are often made in small quantities with high-quality materials and with long-standing techniques.

MEANING When you add a handcrafted item to a space, you are recognizing and valuing the cultural heritage of artisans, adding both beauty and meaning to your home. It might be a handwoven textile or a vessel that is hand-thrown—whatever you choose, it will add a deeper dimension to your environment.

STORIES Often there are stories behind handcrafted items. For example, perhaps you purchased something directly from the maker and learned about the process of creating the item. Choosing to display objects with significance brings warmth and soul to your home.

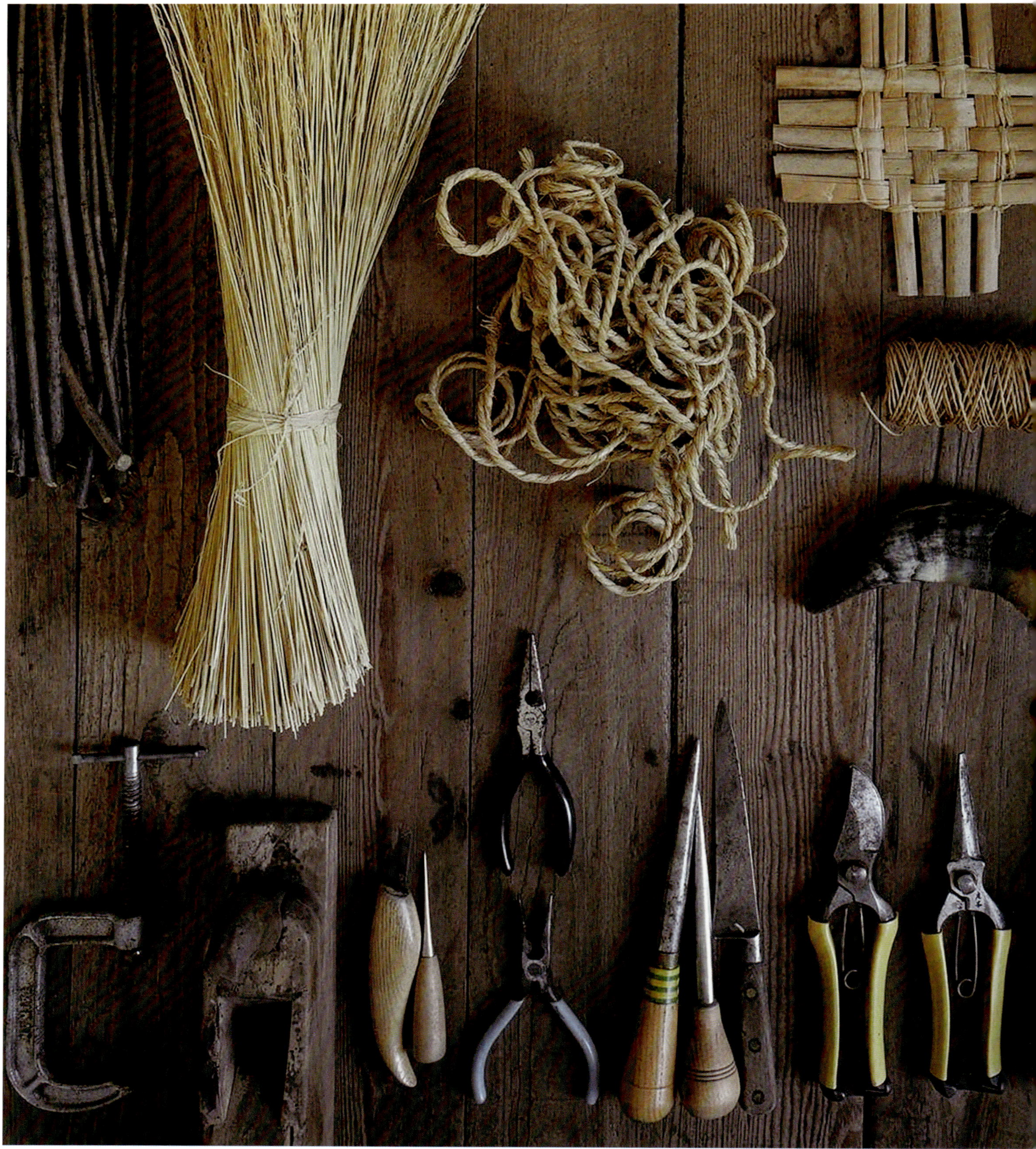

Left: The tools for creating baskets—artistic in their own right. Above: Deborah Needleman's workspace is an understated celebration of nature's bounty. Right: A finished basket adorns a small wooden bench.

DEBORAH NEEDLEMAN

Deborah Needleman had an impressive career as an editor and writer. She was the editor-in-chief of the *New York Times Style Magazine*; founder of the *Wall Street Journal's* weekend lifestyle section, "Off Duty"; and founding editor of *Domino* magazine. In 2016, Deborah made the decision to leave the frenzy of journalism and work with her hands instead. Since then, she has been fully immersed in the craft of basketmaking. Deborah shares her thoughts on her passion for handicrafts and how they can be used in home design.

1 How did you come to work in basketmaking? I've always been drawn to baskets as beautiful objects, and I also love useful things that are beautifully and thoughtfully made. I thought becoming a basket weaver would allow me to work in a new way, using my hands and body along with my head, after years as a writer and editor working only with my head. I also loved the way that being a basketmaker would organize my life and my days—working in tandem with nature and the seasons, listening closely to materials rather than, say, to other people in a meeting, and I loved the idea of the freedom that this kind of life would offer me, working on my own, using materials from the land. I have always gardened, and I've always been involved in the design world, so this new path also felt like an extension of my passion for trying to create beauty from nature's bountiful and beautiful materials. I also love the regional histories of the baskets themselves and the ancient and very human qualities of this craft.

2 How can handcrafted items add individuality to your home? Every handcrafted object has many stories to tell, even if you are unaware of any of them. I feel there is something animate or human that comes through in such objects. They are not perfect; they possess an imperfection that is perfectly human, which everyone can sense. Like a bunch of cut flowers in a home, handmade objects add an intangible but palpable sense of vitality and life to a home. Of course, the more you know about a handcrafted object, the richer this feeling is—if you know how the materials were gathered and processed or where the techniques or style were first derived, or what the utilitarian reasons for the design originally were. But this is not necessary to the enjoyment of craft, because the sense of the hand (and perhaps the heart) is palpable in the objects and in a space that contains these objects.

3 Where can you learn about where to find handcrafted items? Instagram, for all its downsides, is a wonderful way to discover artisans, and it allows artisans, perhaps for the first time in history, to sell directly, without a middleman, to customers, and so to earn an almost living wage. Craftspeople are no longer bound by their physical location or that of their retailers.

4 Are there any items you collect? I am not a collector by nature, but I am a gatherer of things I love. I love to have well-crafted items around me, and I prefer things made by a single person or a collective rather than things that are not individual (i.e., mass-produced). This goes for clothing and jewelry as well—I don't like to buy things from big luxury companies, where you are paying for their marketing and advertising campaigns, their celebrity wrangling or event production. I prefer small companies that have a smaller and more passionate footprint on the economy and the world. This preference is partly because of the beauty and passion I can sense in these objects, and because I don't like the big-footed power or the homogenizing quality that luxury conglomerates have on the fabric of our lives.

Opposite: The bundles waiting to be made into baskets lend a sculptural element to the space. Above: Deborah in her workspace.

Left: Baskets provide texture as well as function in a space. Opposite: Simplicity in its finest form. Handmade woven baskets by Deborah in a corner of her studio.

THE ESSENTIALS

128

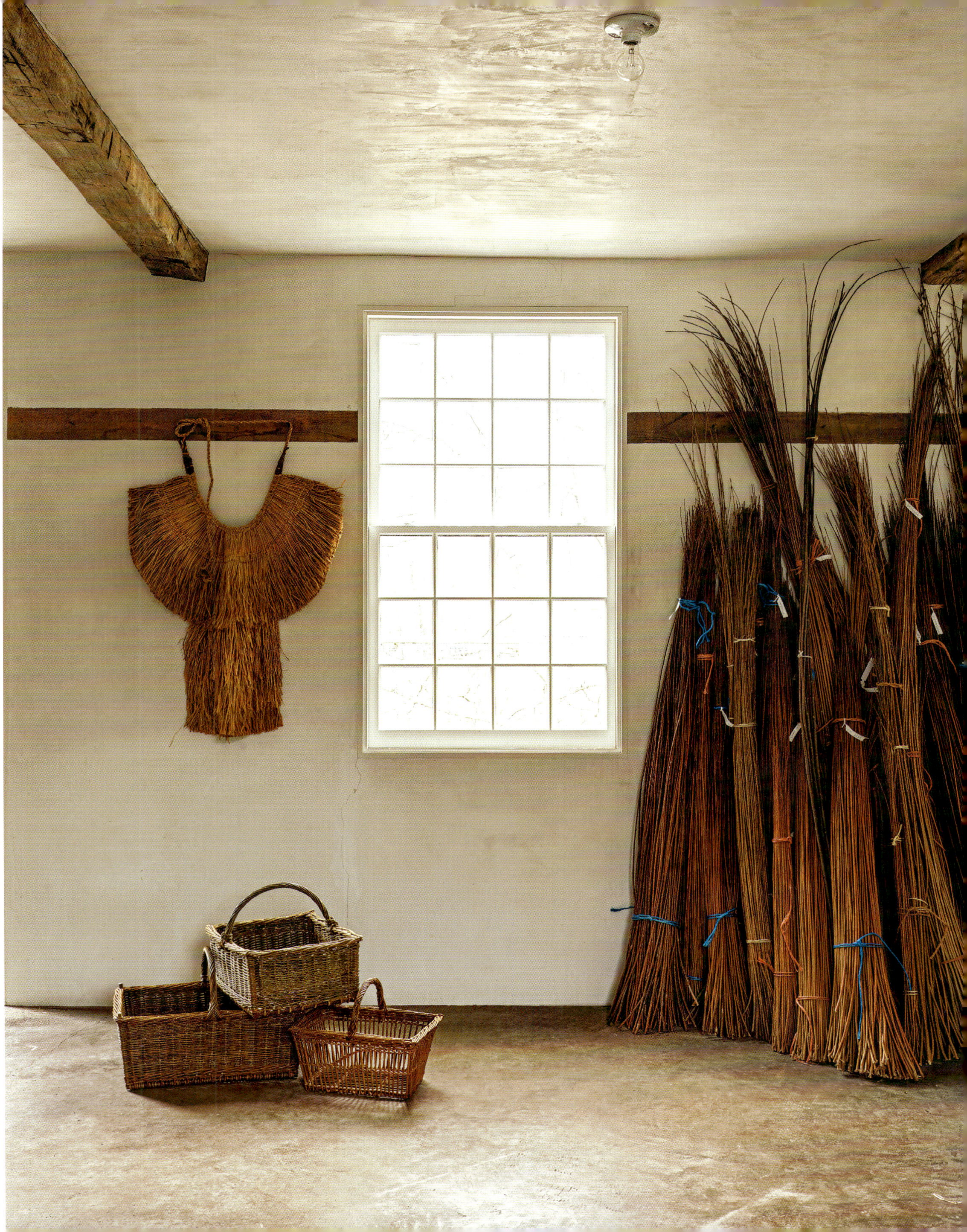

WORKING ELEMENTS

130

FLOORING

Opposite: In the dining room of a project by Caitlin Flemming, a simple natural-fiber rug adds texture to this soothing room.

The flooring you choose in your home can impact the look and feel of the space. In older homes, you can often resurrect the wood floors already there. Refinishing is always a great option and is less disruptive to the home than replacement. If you have experts sand and finish your floors, they will look fresh and polished but with a patina that only comes with age. Below, we hope to give you a brief understanding of many of the options you can choose. It's important not to rush this choice. Finding the right flooring can be key to making the space transform into your haven. Each option offers pros and cons, depending on how you plan to use a room. Here are some of the options.

HARDWOOD FLOORS Homes built prior to the 1980s often have hardwood floors. There are a variety of woods, finishes, and sizes of boards used. One main advantage of wood floors is the that they can be refinished numerous times. They are also warm, easy to clean, and very durable. We love installing antique wood floors as they have a patina from years of use that adds depth and soul to a room, which simply can't be replicated.

AREA RUGS We use area rugs on our hardwood and tile floors to add warmth, texture, and pattern. There are so many choices—including vintage (our favorite), handmade wool, or a variety of modern possibilities.

ENGINEERED WOOD FLOORS Engineered wood floors are made of layers of wood veneer bonded together and finished with a veneer top layer. Ideal for basements or converted garages, this is a good alternative to hardwoods when you need to consider moisture or temperature fluctuations. Where possible, we prefer hardwood floors over engineered floors, but there are some very good ones on the market recently.

TILE FLOORS Tile floors are primarily used in bathrooms and kitchens, although in warmer climates they can be found throughout a home. They can be of ceramic, porcelain, or natural stone. There are a multitude of tile shapes: square, rectangular, octagon, and even circles. Antique tiles can also be used to add patina to a home that you won't get from new tiles. A sunroom can be transformed with a floor of natural honed marble in a checkerboard layout.

CARPET Wall-to-wall carpeting can add warmth and make a room more comfortable for some. In particularly cold climates, upstairs bedrooms can benefit from the added warmth, texture, and softness of carpet. Consider natural fibers—wool and sisal are two of our favorites.

Above, from left: Many designers begin their projects with a rug. For these rooms, Caitlin Flemming chose vintage rugs to provide depth and color.

THE ESSENTIALS

"I always try to include a beautiful rug, often vintage, to anchor the room and bring an added level of texture."

—AMBER LEWIS

BAMBOO OR CORK FLOORS Two other floor alternatives are bamboo or cork. Cork, made from the bark of cork oak trees, is hypoallergenic and antimicrobial, making it ideal for those suffering from allergies. Additionally, it is known for its softness and natural sound insulation. Bamboo is harder and more scratch-resistant, although sensitive to moisture. Both are considered environmentally friendly options due to the renewable nature of both materials. Overall, cork needs more maintenance compared to bamboo.

AMBER LEWIS

Amber Lewis is the principal designer and founder of Amber Interior Design, a California-based interior design studio. Amber has vast experience in both residential as well as commercial projects. Her work is current, approachable, and timeless. Amber has collaborated with Loloi Rugs and with many other brands. Amber is also the owner of a growing retail business, Shoppe Amber Interiors. She has written two design books, *Call It Home* and *Made for Living*. Amber shared her thoughts about flooring with us.

THE ESSENTIALS

1 How do you decide what kind of flooring to use in a home? So many factors come into play—everything from the size and scale, the natural and installed lighting [in the space], and of course how each space will be utilized.

2 Currently, what are your favorite materials to use in your designs? There isn't one medium I use when designing a space, but I have been incorporating some brick in projects, particularly kitchens and mudrooms. I love the juxtaposition of brick next to a material like an oak hardwood. I always try to include a beautiful rug, often vintage, to anchor the room and bring an added level of texture.

3 Do you ever use antique flooring? If so, what is the advantage to using it? I love using reclaimed antique flooring, particularly stone, terra-cotta, and wood. The unique patina, the story, and the texture bring an unmatched element of vintage that you can only find with antiques.

WORKING ELEMENTS

136

WINDOW TREATMENTS

Opposite: The curtains in Courtnay Daniels's home were made of a pattern by Lee Jofa that had been discontinued. She had it brought back to have the drapes made in her living room.

Window treatments are equally about form and function. In a bedroom, they can block out light to keep it from interrupting your sleep. Depending on where and how your house is set, window treatments can also provide privacy to rooms. In older homes in colder climates, they can also give much-needed insulation to a room. But beyond that, window treatments can transform a cold, sterile room into a warm and inviting space. They can add color, texture, as well as pattern to a room. That being said, if you asked ten different interior designers how to dress a window, you would probably get ten different opinions.

There are many versions of window treatments, and it's important to figure out what your needs are before you make any purchases. The size of your windows, the climate you live in, and how you use your home should all play a role in what you decide to use. After all, wool-lined curtains might be perfect for the English countryside to keep cold drafts out in the winter, but they would be out of place in a warmer climate.

In this section, we introduce you to some of the options for window treatments and discuss where they work well.

HOW TO MEASURE FOR CURTAINS

We suggest hanging curtains starting 4 to 6 inches (10 to 15 cm) above the window frame, as a rule. The width of the curtains should extend 6 to 10 inches (15 cm) beyond the frames of the windows to allow more light to enter when the curtains are open and to block more light when they are closed. Hanging your curtains higher and wider often can make your space look bigger and make the curtains themselves more impactful.

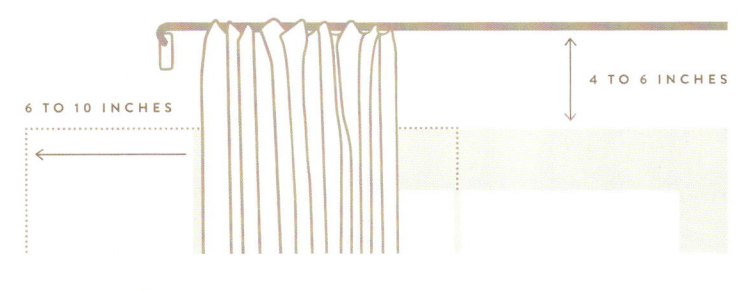

6 TO 10 INCHES

4 TO 6 INCHES

THE ESSENTIALS

CURTAINS

The four most common styles of curtains: pinch pleat, gathered, single pleat, café curtain.

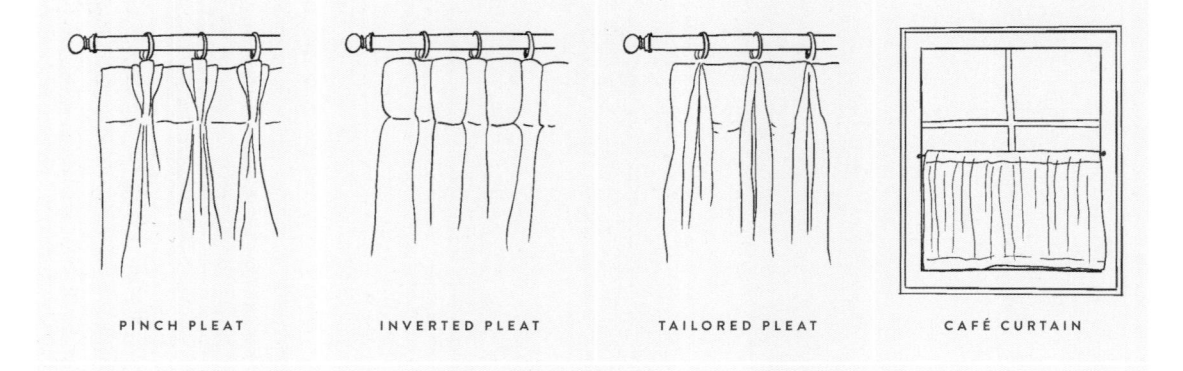

PINCH PLEAT   INVERTED PLEAT   TAILORED PLEAT   CAFÉ CURTAIN

OTHER THINGS YOU MIGHT CONSIDER FOR CURTAINS

1 If you hang curtains almost to the ceiling, the ceiling will look higher.

2 Sunlight can be hard on fabric, especially in a sunny climate, causing it to decompose and fade quickly. We recommend lining your curtains. They will hang better and will also last longer. The only time we suggest not lining them is when you want the sunlight to peek through.

3 For curtains that may be a little difficult to reach, consider hanging them on rings so they can easily slide along a rod when you want to open and close them.

4 Something we have seen frequently in the United Kingdom are heavy curtains that can be pulled across the front or back door. Oftentimes they are long enough to pool on the floor. These help regulate the temperature in the home, provide privacy if there are windows in the door, and can offer a pop of color and pattern to the space. In addition, they often have a fun, different print on the back side of them (the lining) since the back of the curtain can be seen through any windows that are in the door when drawn.

Opposite: In the laundry room of a home Patricia Giffen designed for Julie Forrest, she created a curtain to pull across the laundry area when needing to hide certain messes.

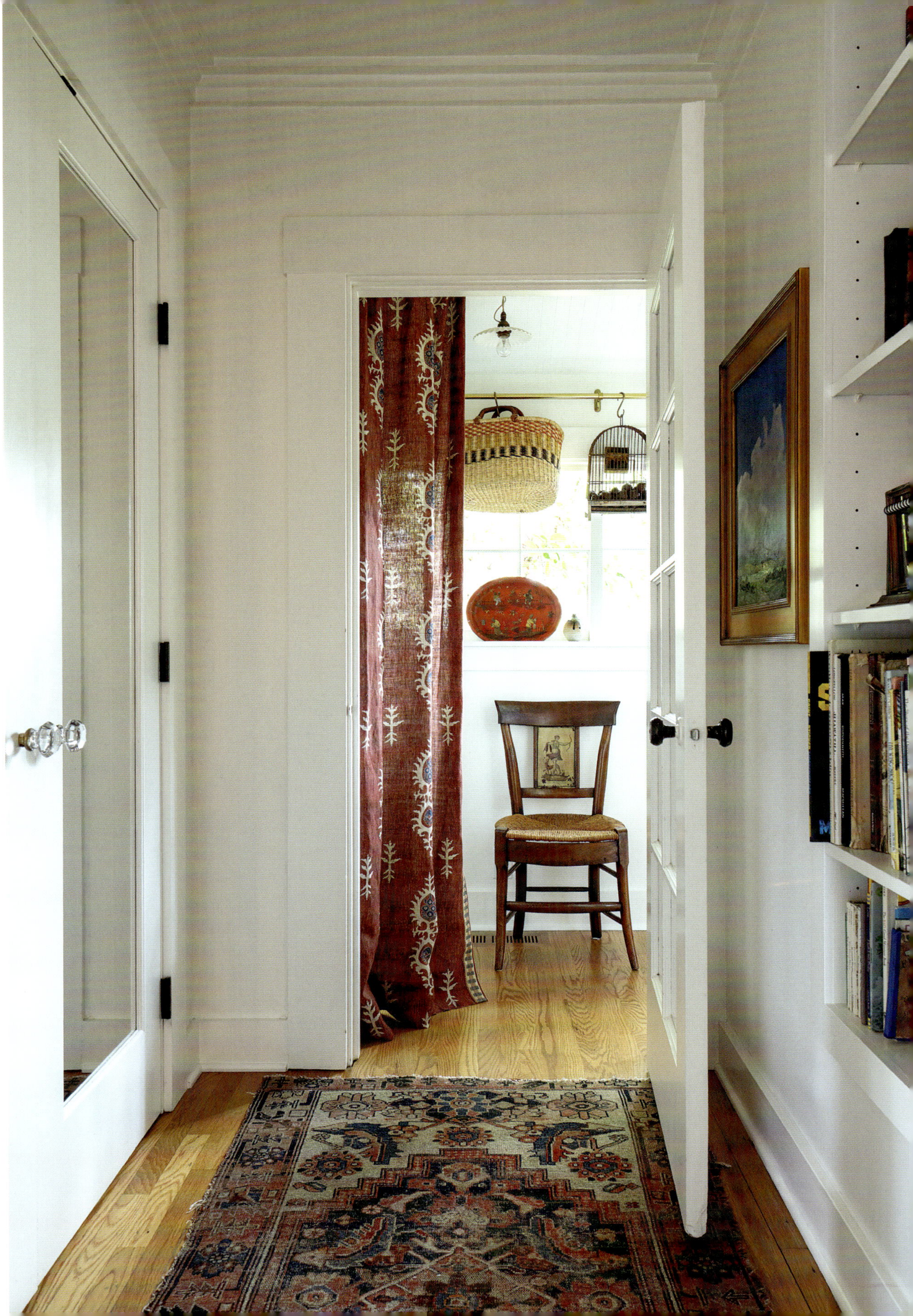

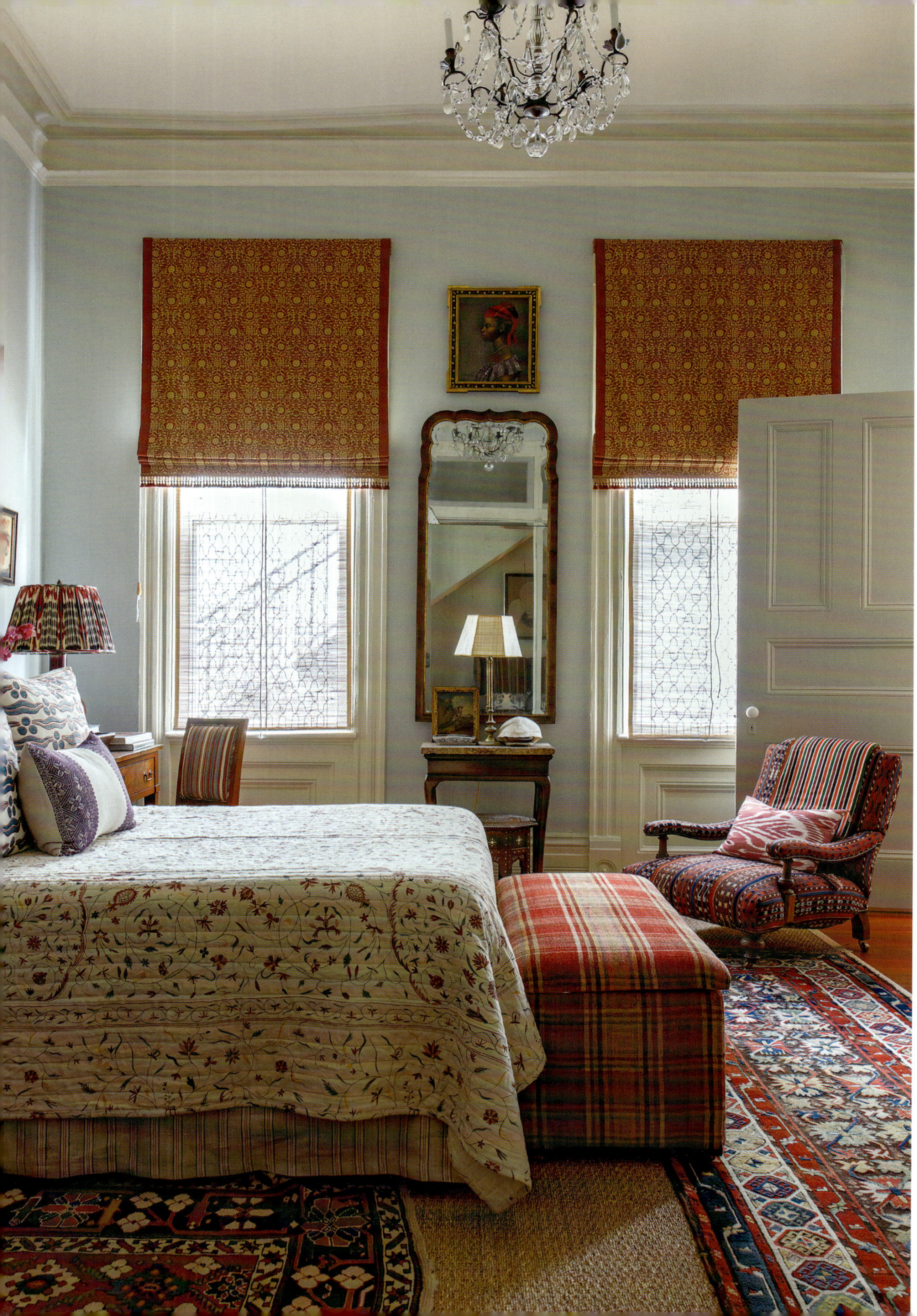

*"Sourcing the right fabric can make all
the difference for drapery and roman shades."*
—DAVINA OGILVIE

SHADES AND SHUTTERS

Shades can be mounted inside or outside of the window frame. For a shade to block light completely, an outside mount is the most effective. For a window with beautiful casings and moldings, it might be better to mount the shade inside the frame so you can show off the architectural details. If you want to add texture to a room, consider adding rattan shades. They are good for semiprivate needs and also filter the sunlight. They are often an economical alternative. If you live in a warm climate, shutters can allow you to open your windows so that air can flow through the space without obstruction, and they will still provide privacy when they are closed.

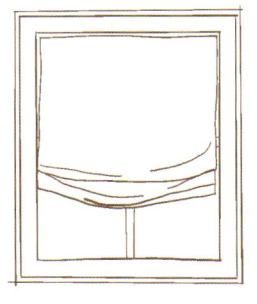

RELAXED / EUROPEAN ROMAN

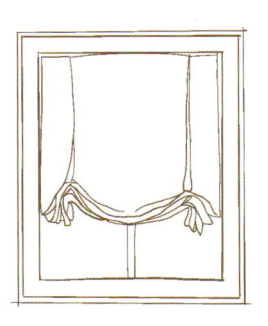

SWAG / TIED ROMAN

FLAT ROMAN

SHUTTERS

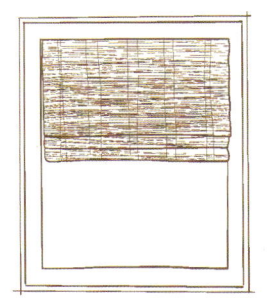

WOVEN WOOD ROMAN

Opposite: The custom roman shades in this bedroom, designed by Katie Koch and Calhoun Sumrall, were mounted on the outside of the window frame.

DAVINA OGILVIE

Davina Ogilvie has been recognized nationally for her innovative approach to bringing custom window treatments online. After graduating from Harvard and having more than fifteen years of experience in the fashion industry, Davina realized the progress being made in e-commerce. While renovating her own home, she saw the need for an online alternative for high-quality curtains, shades, and hardware, and she turned that insight into a business. In 2019, Davina launched Wovn Home and has cultivated a loyal clientele. Davina shares a few of her secrets to selecting window treatments.

THE ESSENTIALS

Above: Curtains across a front door, as in this room in the home of Julie Forrest, designed by Patricia Giffen, are especially good in cold climates. They soften the room but also provide much-needed insulation.

1 What are ways to narrow down the options of types of window treatments you use in a room? I always first consider the size of the window. I find large windows look best with curtain panels flanked on either side. The proportions of full-length drapery work well with the scale of larger windows and add a touch of formality, which is often why I recommend them for living and dining rooms. Smaller windows tend to look best with either tailored or looser, relaxed Roman shade styles.

2 How can the right window treatment help to elevate a room? Custom window treatments are the ultimate finishing touch when it comes to the design of a room. The softness of fabric window treatments helps create a warm and inviting space and adds a layer of texture. The right fabric color or pattern selection can work in concert with the overall color scheme to help unify the room's palette as well. Best of all, window treatments can be used to either highlight beautiful architectural details in the space, like plaster moldings, or disguise unsightly elements you might not want to see.

3 Do you have any advice for how to avoid some common mistakes that novices make when ordering custom window treatments? When creating custom drapery and shades, I get to see so many beautiful installations. I have also seen my fair share of mistakes, so I always share these tips with my clients to avoid some common pitfalls.

❧ CONSIDER YOUR CURTAIN ROD PLACEMENT

Lately, everyone wants to hang their curtains as high as possible, just under the ceiling. That can be a beautiful way to install your curtains as it draws the eye up, creating the illusion of a taller ceiling. But I always recommend looking at the distance between the top of the window and the ceiling before making that call. If there was 2 feet (60 cm) of space above the window, for example, I like to apply the rule of thirds, installing the hardware two-thirds [of the way up] from the top of the window. The curtain rod would then be placed 16 inches (40 cm) above the window.

THE ESSENTIALS

🌰 **KNOW YOUR STACK BACK** The drapery stack back is the amount of wall space your curtains will cover when they are open. I like to add at least 8 inches (20 cm) to each side for smaller and medium width windows and scale up from there. This helps you to have more window free of curtains when they are open.

🌰 **MEASURE TWICE, MAKE ONCE** Custom window treatments take time to fabricate, and getting the details right the first time will save you time and money. It may sound obvious, but I always double-check my measurements to ensure everything will fit perfectly when it comes time to install.

4 How do you decide on the right fabric for shades and curtains? Sourcing the right fabric can make all the difference for drapery and roman shades. I always look at the drape of a fabric to see how it falls when it is hanging, and I like to know how it feels to the hand. Linen and linen blends hang and gather beautifully when made into drapery or roman shades. When it comes to fabric color and pattern, I prefer window treatments to either blend in with the wall color or provide a contrast. A plain color fabric might work well with a patterned wall covering and really stand out. Alternatively, a coordinating pattern may be the way to go if you want your curtains to blend in.

WORKING ELEMENTS

146

ACCESSORIES

Opposite: In the nook of an entryway in a home Caitlin Flemming designed, the accessories are kept simple: a lamp, a bowl for keys, and a vase with trimmings from the garden.

Your life story can be told by the accessories you have collected. Accessories—the objects that you decide to display in your home, on a table or a shelf, drape on your sofa or your bed, or hang from walls and stack on the floor—are the frosting or final touches that can help show who you are. It's important to find things that speak to you, that hint at what makes you unique. When you infuse your interests into the design of a space, it becomes a reflection of who you are. For example, we love original botanical specimens, wicker, vintage silver, and a stack of design books.

Consider the following when you select accessories:

PERSONAL CONNECTION Many accessories call to mind memories you have from the past. We will always cherish our antique terra-cotta pots that we bought in Mexico when we lived there. It's important to include items that tell the stories of your life and the joy you have experienced.

CURATED COLLECTIONS When you focus on items you love, you can reflect your travel or other interests. For example, you might showcase family heirlooms that hold meaning for you.

FUNCTION Accessories also provide practical functions. Pillows on a sofa, rugs, lamps, mirrors, a throw blanket, wicker baskets, copper pots, and ceramic bowls all serve a purpose. You can choose items that have a function but also work within your chosen aesthetic.

BALANCE It is often the accessories that tie all of the elements of a room together. They can provide soul, even to a space that could look a little cold or impersonal without them. They add visual interest and bring the architectural elements together with the furniture so that the room feels complete.

The TULIP Anna Pavord
William Blake's Water-colours Illustrating the Poems of Thomas Gray
MODIGLIANI

Opposite: In a corner of Charlotte Boundy's home, a balance of items adorn the table: books, a bowl, a candle, and a potted geranium. Right: In the kitchen nook Caitlin Flemming designed, accessories are kept to a minimum so clients can utilize this area without too much clutter.

THE ESSENTIALS

CAITLIN FLEMMING

For Caitlin Flemming, San Francisco–based interior designer and coauthor of *Travel Home, Sense of Place*, and this book, accessories are a way to tell a story about the person living in a home. They help to make a home a reflection of its owners. Here, she provides key points on the value of accessories in your home.

1 How do accessories help create the soul of a home? There is no doubt in my mind that accessories play a huge role in making a house feel like the people that live inside it. The furniture creates the canvas for the accessories that tell stories. Your home should fully embody you and your family.

2 How can accessories tell the story of those who live in the home? I love when someone walks into our home and asks where pieces are from. Telling those stories about a local antique shop, flea market, or a trip can create the most meaningful conversations. I used to have a bowl of printed photos on our coffee table filled with images from travels and of family and friends. I loved when we had guests over and they started to look through them. It's these little things that can spark real connections and make you feel good in a space.

3 How do you keep a balance in the number of accessories you use? As a designer, I move pieces around our house weekly (well, actually, daily). It's the easiest way to make your house feel refreshed. Balancing the number of accessories is really a personal preference for the people living in the house, whether you like them to be minimal or have a more filled in aesthetic. My mom [coauthor Julie Goebel] always taught me to pair three objects together to make a little grouping—even if there are several vignettes on the same surface.

4 How do you find the right accessories for a space? My best advice is to collect over time. I'm constantly telling friends and clients that the best way to start a collection of accessories for your home is to start purchasing pieces you love when you see them—even if you don't think you have a spot for them. You might be surprised when you get home that they fit perfectly somewhere.

STYLING TIPS

How you arrange and display the functional objects like furniture in a space alongside the objects that you love and collect over time can make all the difference to your home.

- Play with scale and height when grouping pieces together.
- Add natural elements such as branches or plants.
- Allow negative space in your rooms and on your shelves and tables.
- Use mirrors to make a small space feel more spacious.
- Group accessories in a triangle.
- Bring in bits and bobs from travel that can tell a story.

Above: Caitlin has always believed that accessories should tell the story of those who inhabit the home.

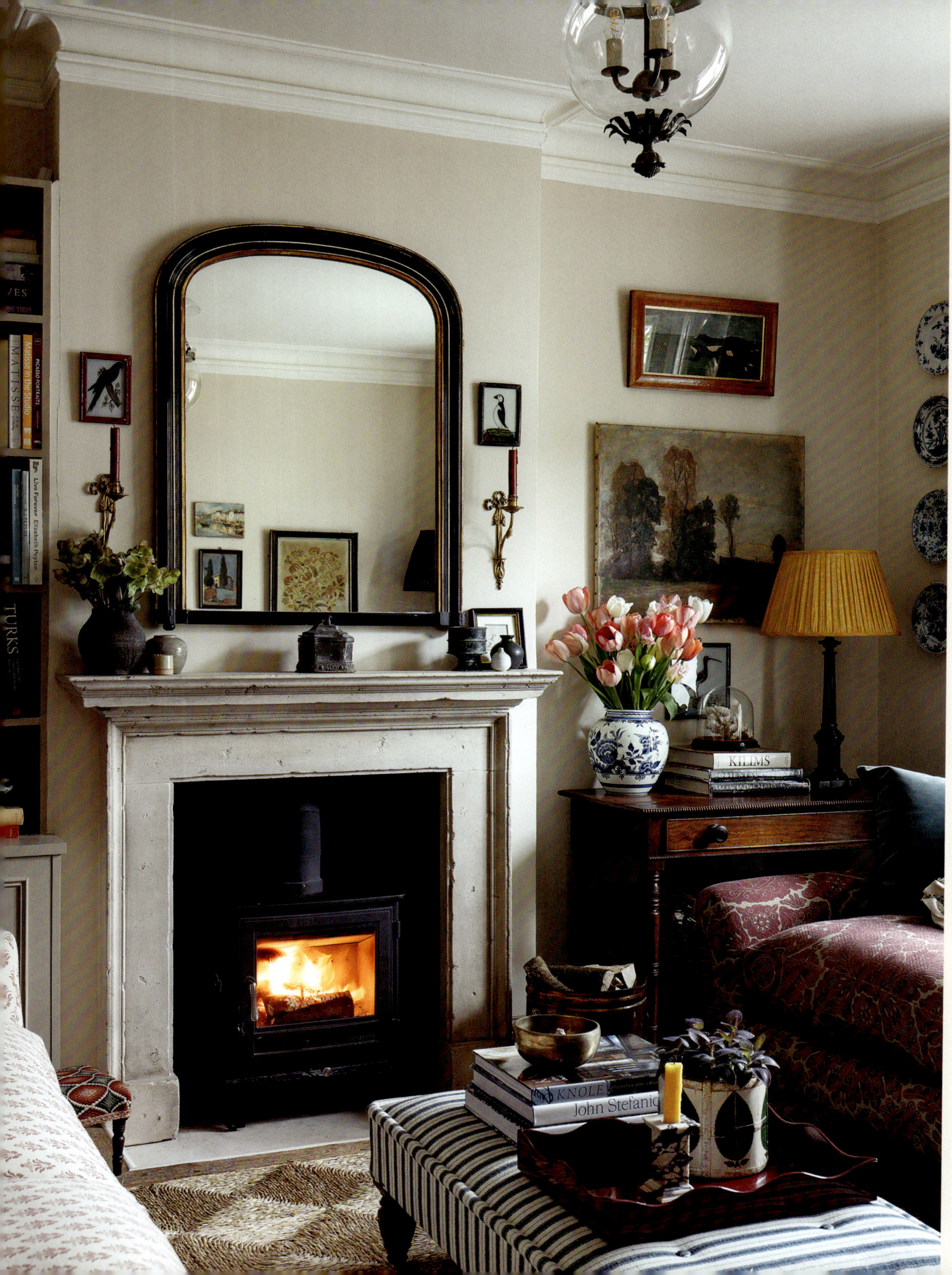

LONDON,
ENGLAND

3

NINE HOMES FOR INSPIRATION

MANHATTAN,
NEW YORK

Much of what we have hoped to teach you in the first two chapters of *The Essentials* can be seen here in our "Nine Homes for Inspiration" chapter. You will want to pay special attention to our captions, where we point out the ways you can see design in action and why the design is successful. We are presenting nine beautiful homes whose owners have mastered the art of home design.

We begin our tour with **CALHOUN SUMRALL**'s home, located in the Garden District of New Orleans, Louisiana. Calhoun excels in the art of layering, attributing it to his exposure to design around the world while working at Ralph Lauren. As we move to the home of **KRISTIN ELLEN HOCKMAN**, set outside of Charleston, South Carolina, we see how this fixer-upper was lovingly restored room by room. **RACHEL ALLEN**, an interior designer based in London, found herself in need of a home, but prices were too expensive. Instead, she had a barge built with reclaimed materials. Although the vessel is small, she loves her life on a barge in the Islington neighborhood. **CHARLOTTE BOUNDY**, also a resident of London, waited six months after buying her house before making any changes. She wanted the house to speak to her first. **GLENN BAN**, an interior designer who resides in East Hampton, New York, has slowly designed a perfectly imperfect house for himself and his son to call home. In the second home of **JOSH YOUNG** in Middleburg, Virginia, his reverence for the past is front and center. A collector extraordinaire, Josh has filled his home with treasures that resonate for him. **COURTNAY DANIELS** originally had a design firm in San Francisco but recently moved to New York. Her apartment is home to her vast photography collection and is her family retreat in a bustling metropolis. We visit **AMY MEIER**'s home in Rancho Santa Fe, near San Diego, California, where much of life revolves around the outdoors. **LAN JAENICKE**, who recently moved to a different house in San Francisco, describes how frequently changing each room and its use keeps it both fresh and also more useful. All of these individuals impart their sage advice and describe their experiences designing their homes. We think there are valuable lessons to learn from each of these talented designers.

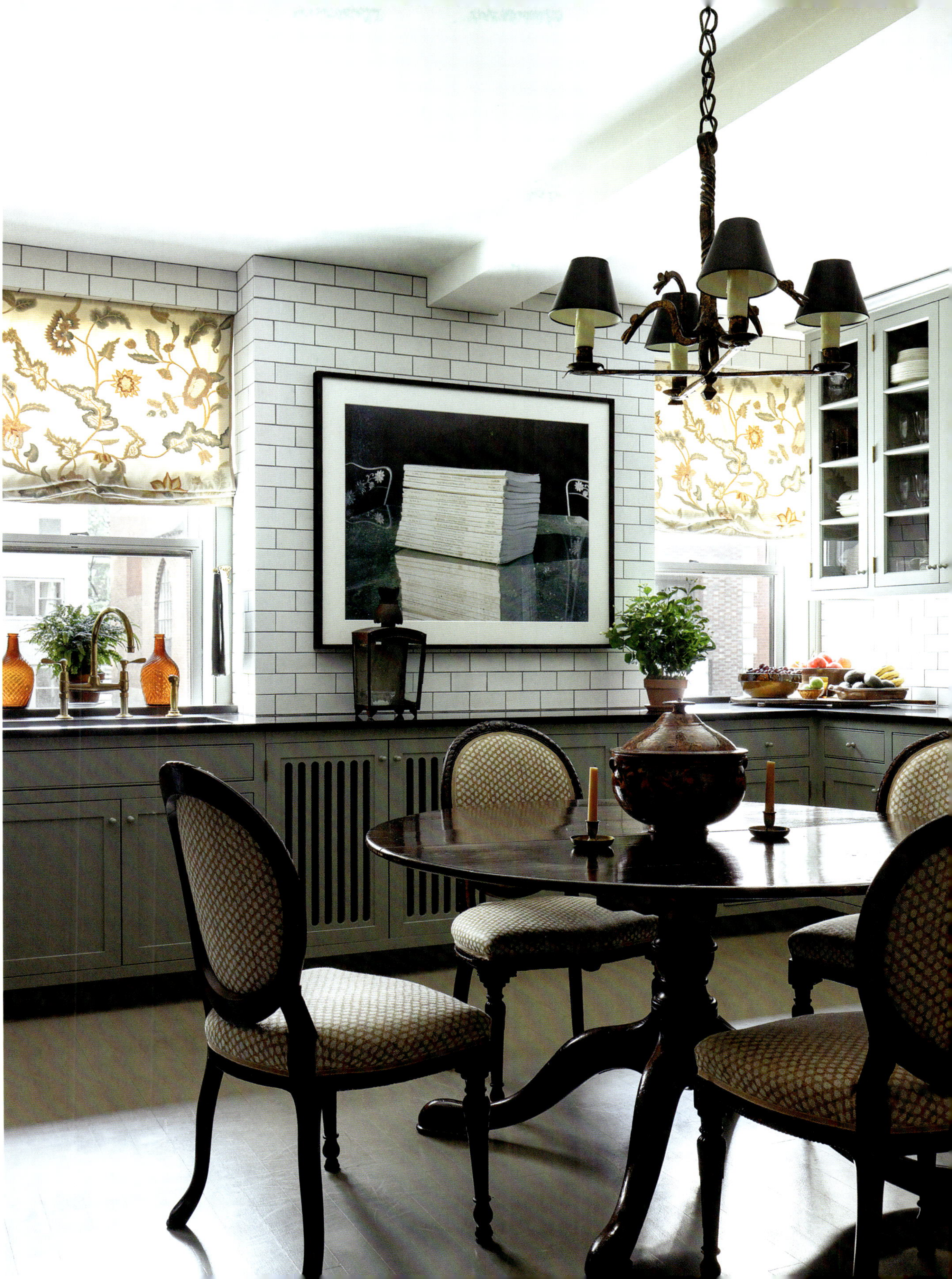

CALHOUN SUMRALL

NEW ORLEANS, LOUISIANA

Calhoun Sumrall grew up in Baton Rouge, Louisiana, but the day after graduating from college, he was on an airplane to New York City, where he worked in the fashion industry for thirty-six years. For the last sixteen he was at Ralph Lauren, a job that included extensive travel around the world twice a year. It was there he learned the value of the authentic. His work exposed him to extraordinary handmade and vintage textiles, where quality matters. "It wasn't the idea of tweed or plaid; it was the real thing," notes Calhoun. Both through the work at Ralph Lauren and from what he experienced during his work trips, his understanding and appreciation of quality and authenticity grew. He worked with artisans and craftsmen in Europe and Asia; these experiences trained his eye and helped him understand what he loved.

In 2017, Calhoun left Ralph Lauren as he wanted to find a slower pace and a less stressful lifestyle. He turned his creative energies to decorating his home in New York, with input from his friends of many years, Michael Trapp (see page 80) and Robert Kime. His home was applauded when it graced the pages of *Elle Decor*. He also practiced his hand on his second home in Sharon, Connecticut.

Above, from left: A barley-twist candlestick converted into a lamp pairs well with the other accessories. Calhoun, a native Louisianian, recently moved back after decades in New York. Right: Calhoun's home is the perfect harmony of color and pattern.

THE ESSENTIALS

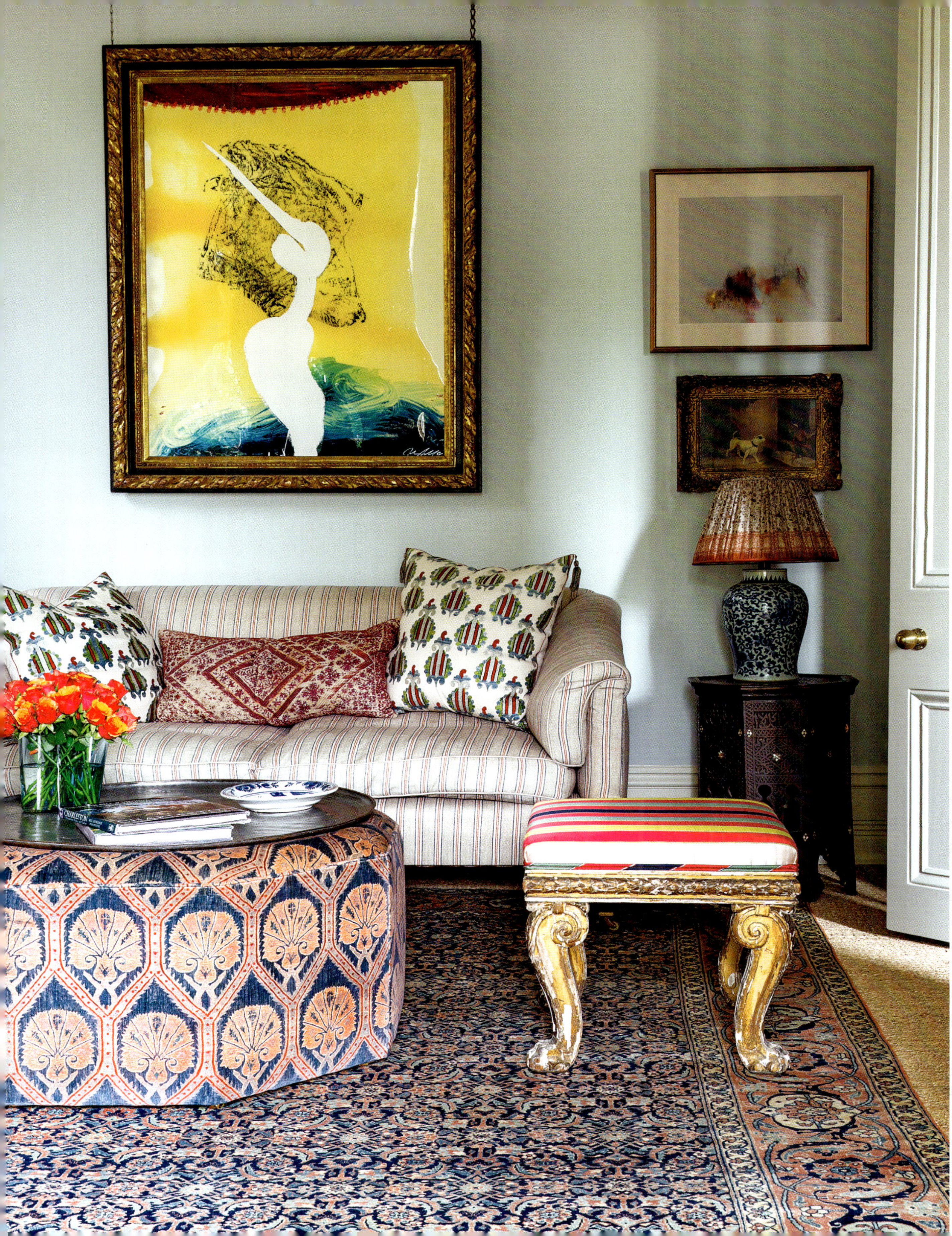

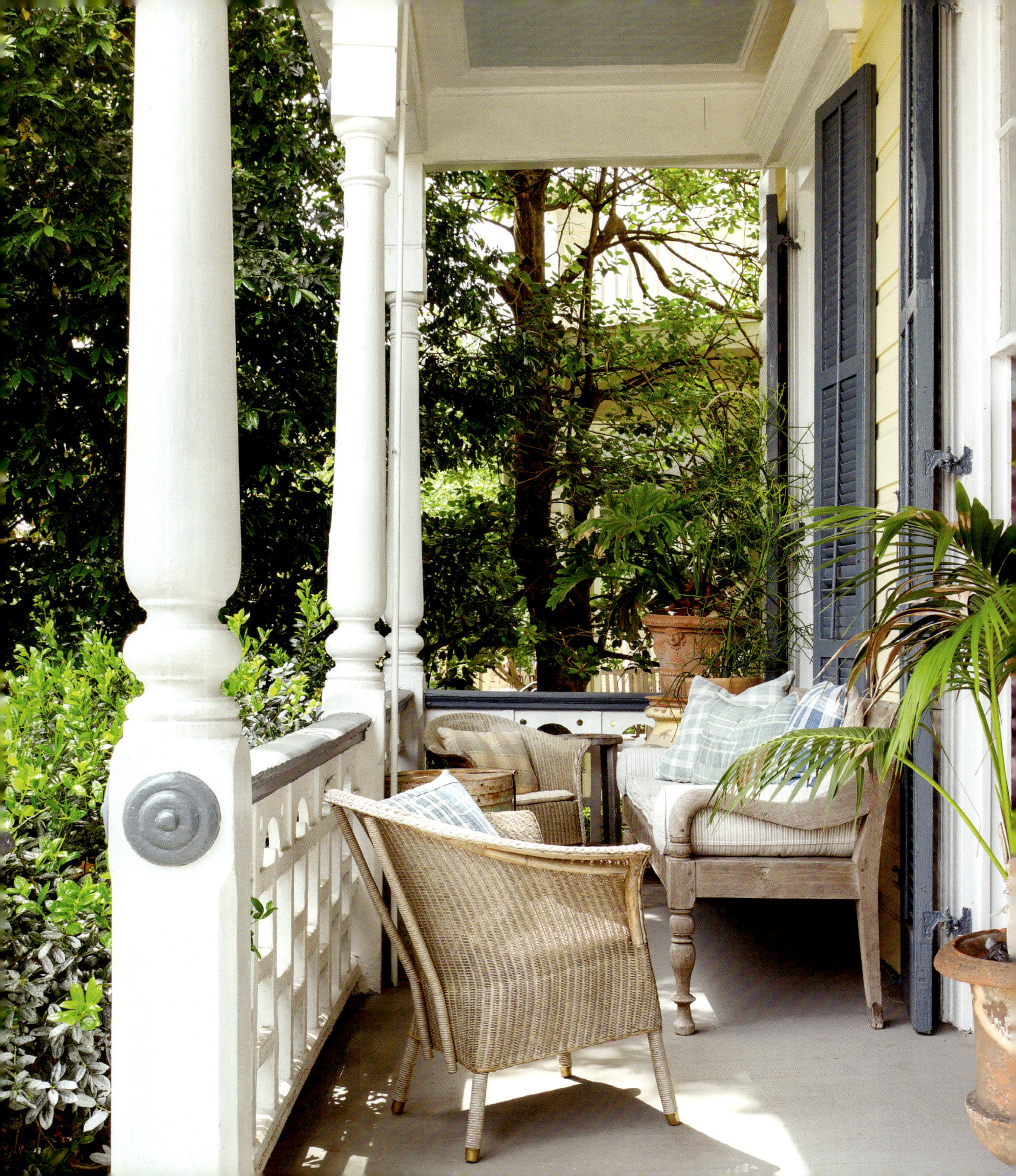

Opposite: In this inviting porch moment, Calhoun made another living space outdoors. Right: Utilizing every nook, the designer creates a catch-all space, including hooks for scarves and his go-to hat.

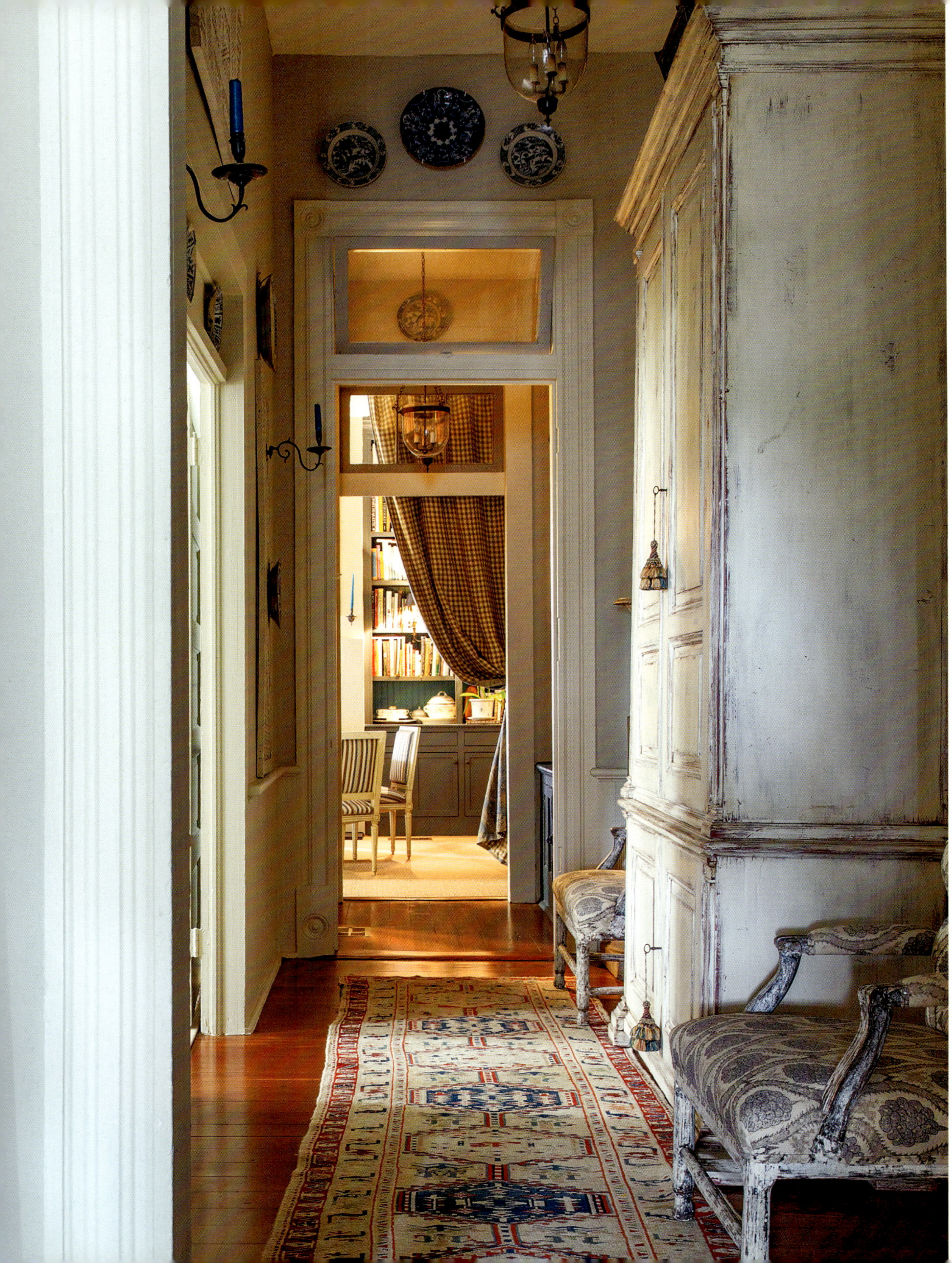

Opposite: No space in Calhoun's home is wasted. This hallway becomes another room, and a curtain on the door of the dining room announces that you are entering a cozy space. Above: Carefully curated items tell the story of Calhoun's life of traveling the world.

Calhoun then made the decision to move from New York to New Orleans, to be closer to family and live in an unhurried environment. "Life is definitely slower paced here. I drive five minutes to get to work. My sister lives next door. I have a real sense of family and friends here," he says.

Calhoun began helping Katie Koch, a skilled designer of fine window treatments who also owns a home decor shop. As business took off in the pandemic, Calhoun began assisting her in the retail side of her business and then started handling her interior design projects as well. He has enjoyed designing on this more personal level. There are no corporate decisions; he is simply working one-on-one with clients.

Calhoun's Queen Anne–style duplex home in the Garden District, built in the 1880s, boasts 13½-foot (4 m) ceilings and spacious rooms. There is a fireplace in every room. But when Calhoun moved into his home, it had been renovated to become essentially a white box with Home Depot ceiling fans in every room. Fortunately, the footprint of the home had remained untouched. "It took me a while to get the colors right and just create the layers of a curated environment with the things I've loved and always had." He experimented with colors for the walls and eventually landed on

THE ESSENTIALS

"It took me a while to get the colors right and just create the layers of a curated environment with the things I've loved and always had."

—CALHOUN SUMRALL

several Farrow & Ball shades. Over time, he added detail after detail to make home feel like his own. It is a warm, safe, and comforting environment where Calhoun enjoys having friends over and cooking dinners at home. "Basically, I like to hang out at home. Home is my happiness."

Much of what he has in his home came with him from New York and Connecticut. However, some pieces he had just didn't work and needed to be changed. "My Shaker bed looked like a child's bed with the high ceilings. Now I have a nine-foot-tall bed and it's perfect." He continues to enjoy his life and the relaxed pace of New Orleans. While he doesn't think he has room to acquire any more furniture, he says there will always be a spot for more art on the walls.

Above: In a perfect example of thinking outside the box, artwork is hung on a door and the wall of a cabinet. Opposite: Looking past the flowers on the fireplace mantel in the primary bedroom offers a glimpse into the guest room.

THE ESSENTIALS

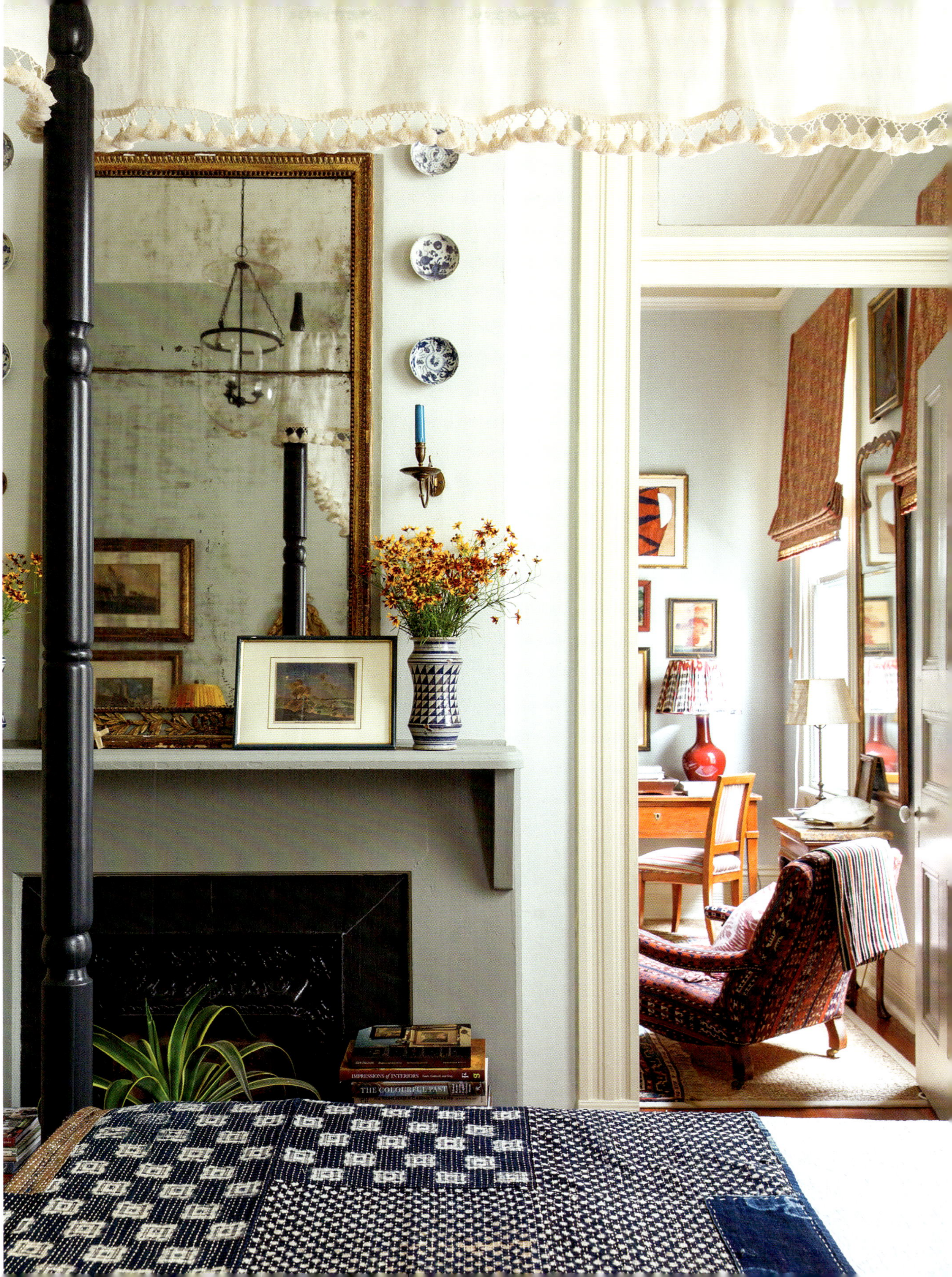
IMPRESSIONS of INTERIORS
THE COLOURFUL PAST

THE ESSENTIALS

Opposite: An antique chair is made fresh with striped upholstery, and artwork is found in surprising places—even above a door.
Above: The 13½-foot (4-m) ceilings can easily accommodate this Peter Dunham four-poster bed.

Left: No detail is overlooked: An ornate gold-leaf mirror sits on the mantel with a hand-painted vase and other keepsakes. Opposite: The symmetry of the two sconces along with the pair of porcelain lamps add an air of formality to the mix.

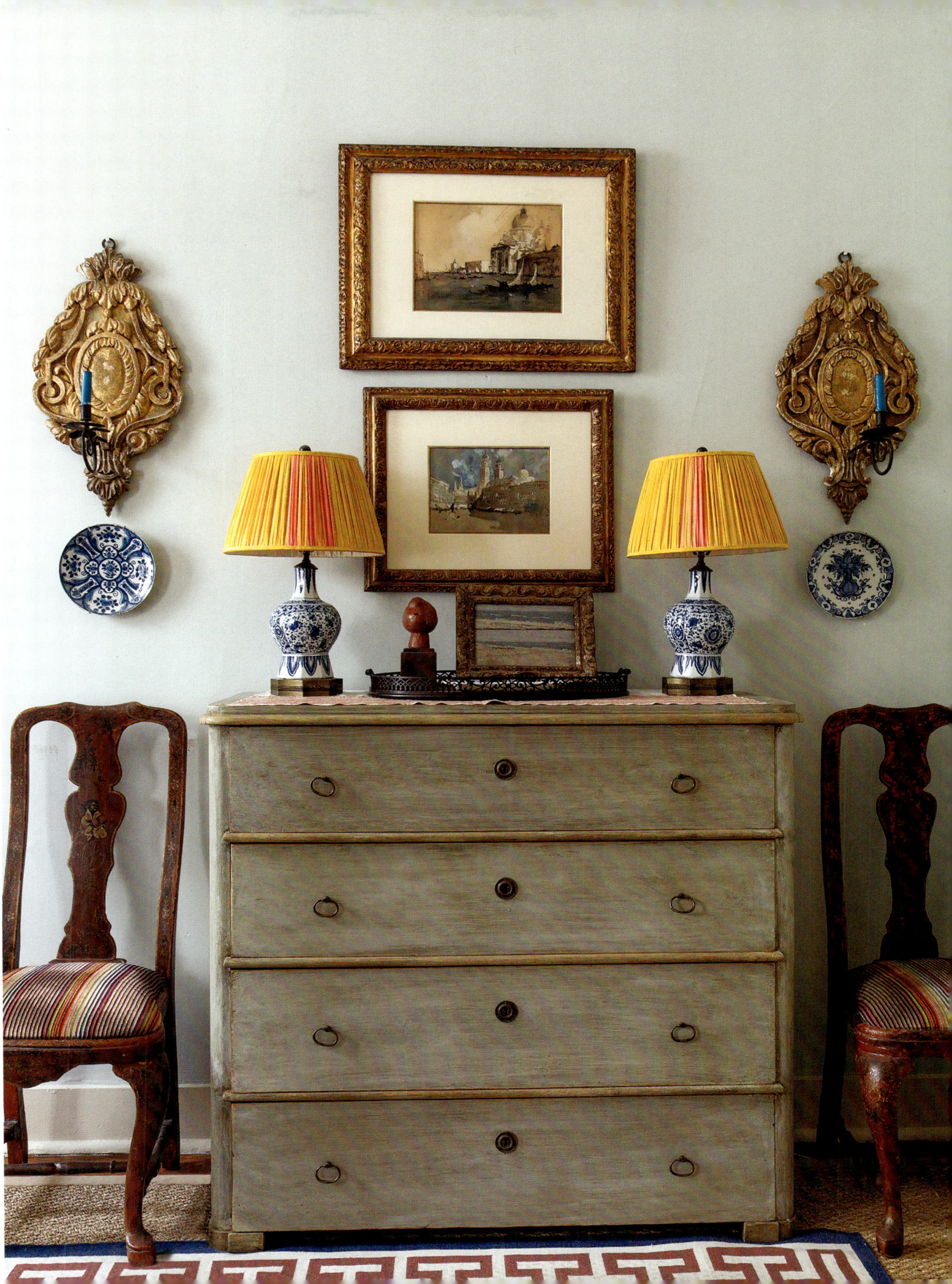

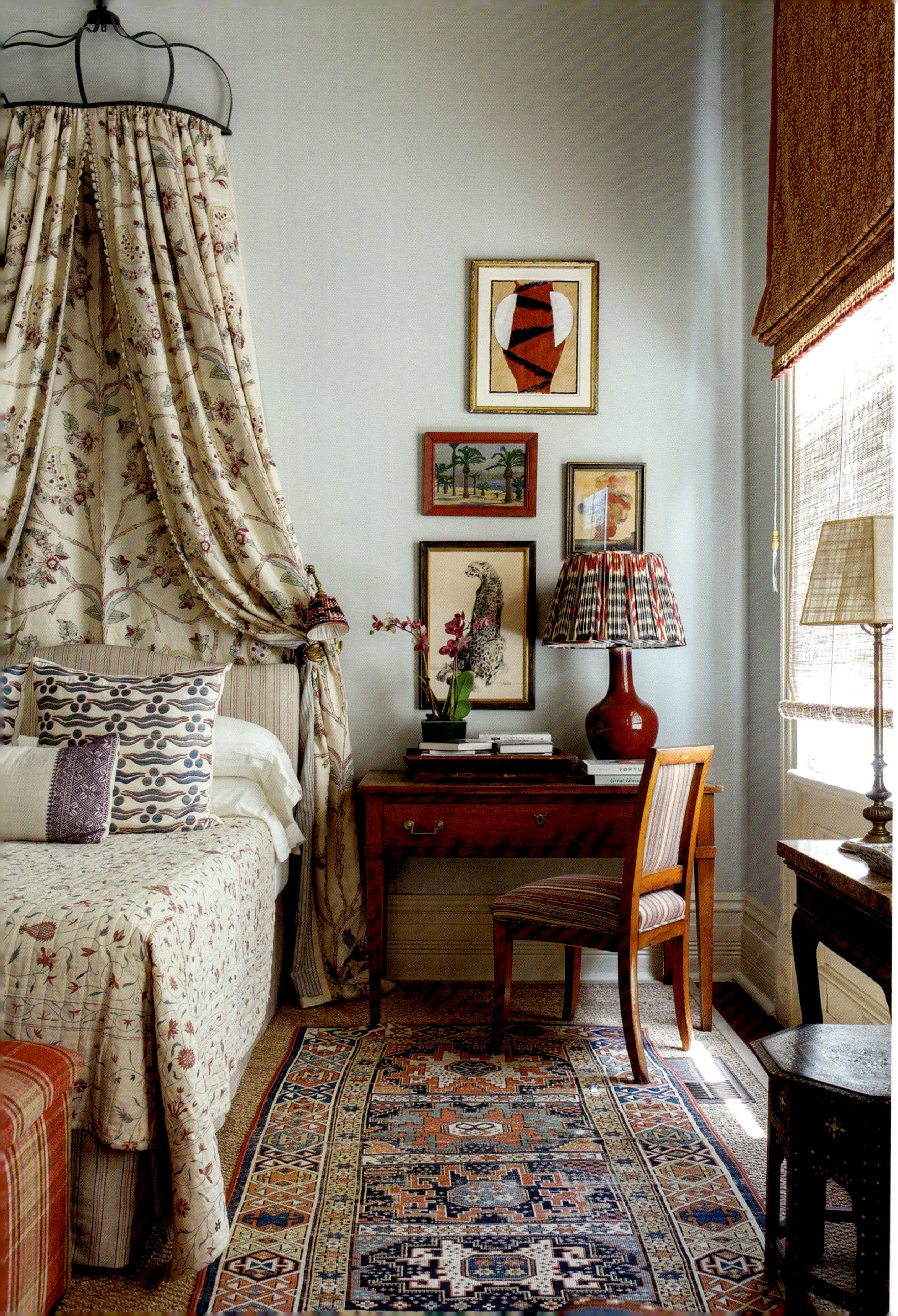

Opposite: The exquisite canopy above the bed was made by Katie Koch, considered a master designer of curtains. Above: Calhoun's vignettes demonstrate his love for details, and his artwork tells the stories of his many journeys. Custom lampshades can transform a room.

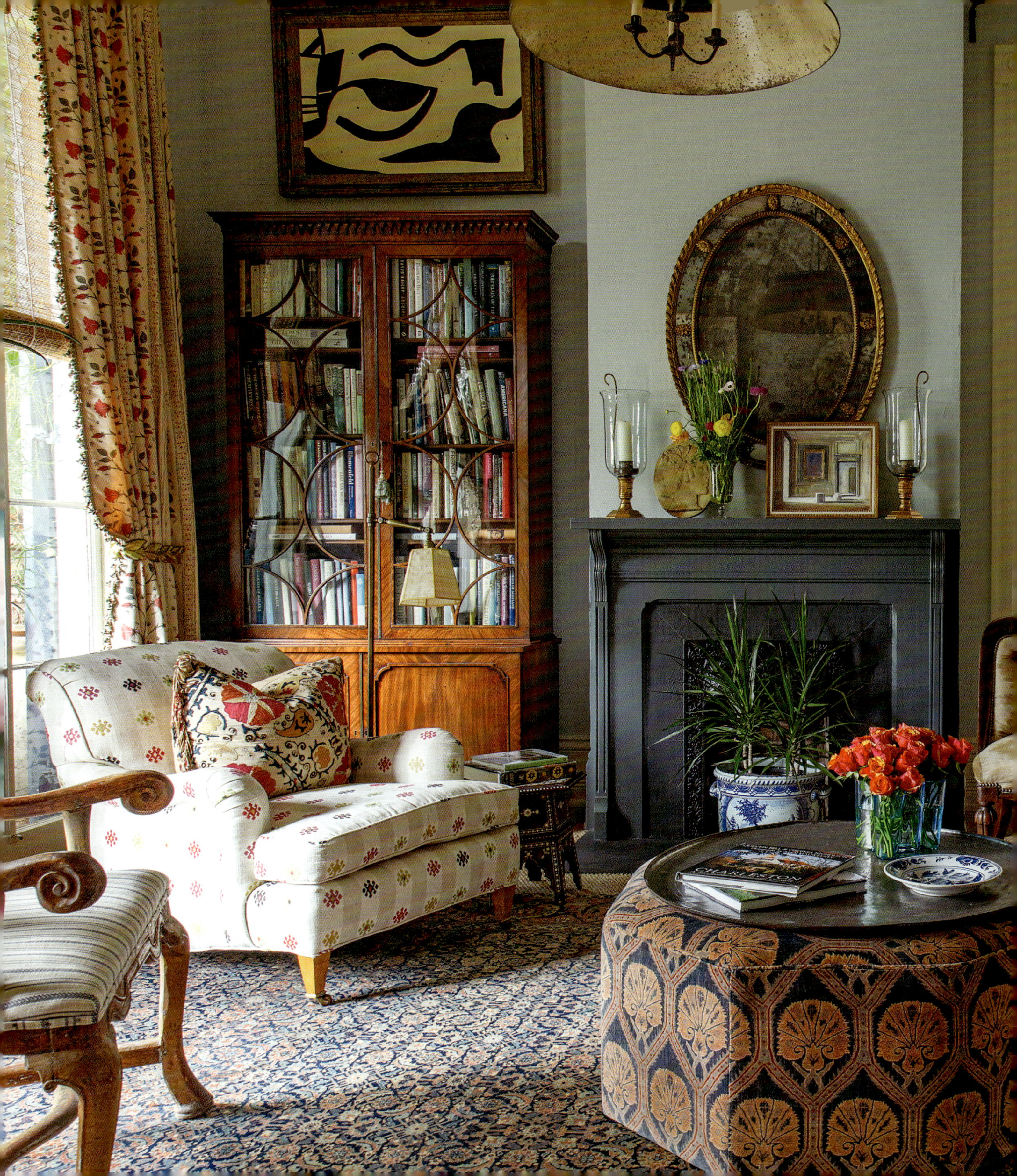
AMERICANA
CHARLESTON

The living room of Calhoun's home has a harmonious mix of colors and patterns in the floor coverings, curtains, pillows, and upholstery.

171

KRISTIN ELLEN HOCKMAN
BERKELEY COUNTY, SOUTH CAROLINA

Kristin Ellen Hockman has not always lived in South Carolina. After a particularly stressful week at work as an interior designer in New York, Kristin booked a weekend getaway trip to Charleston, South Carolina, with her husband. They loved how walkable the neighborhoods are and the easy access to good restaurants and shops. The striking beauty of the gardens and architecture made them never want to leave. They returned to New York, quit their jobs, and moved to Charleston. A few years later, in 2018, they purchased their home—a fixer-upper that had been vacant for many years. Finally, Kristin had a home of her own to practice her interior design talents. She had always leaned more toward modern design, but the home they bought, brought her to love a more traditional approach with fresh, forward-looking accents. She suddenly found herself buying antiques and scanning auctions for items. The style she has moved toward has gained her attention, and in 2024, she was one of *Frederic* magazines "It Designers."

Gippy Plantation, a Greek Revival with a four-column gable pediment at the center of the facade, was built in 1852 when the original house burned down.

Above, left to right: Beekeeping suits hang by the door, including one for Kristin's daughter, Astrid. The family enjoys time spent together in the light and airy sunroom. Right: The imposing entryway of the Gippy Plantation as seen from the garden.

THE ESSENTIALS

NINE HOMES FOR INSPIRATION

173

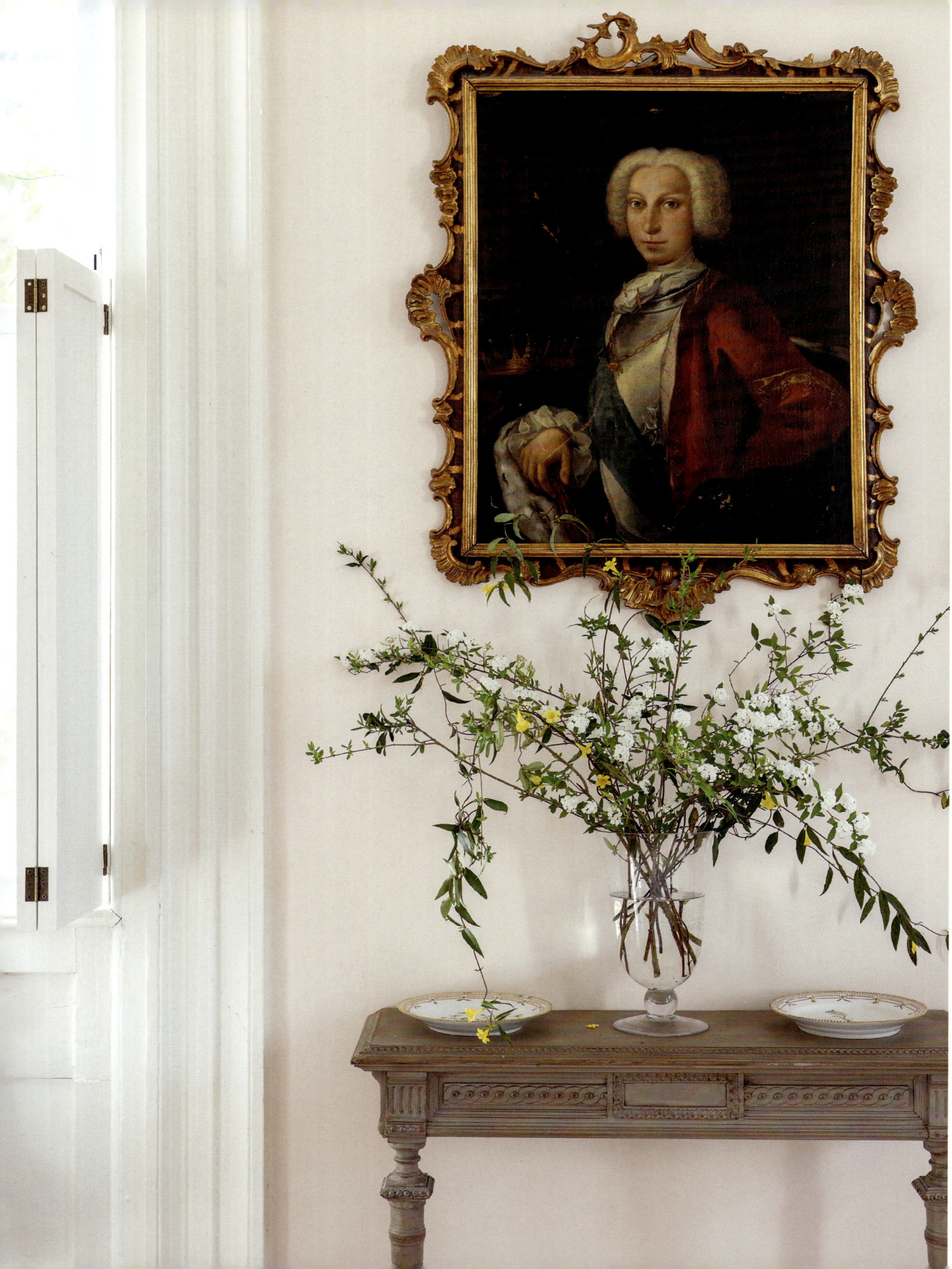

Opposite and right: Kristin had always preferred modern furniture, but since moving, her style has veered to a more traditional aesthetic, including the use of antiques and portraits.

Formerly a rice plantation, the property has a tangled past. The house was built by enslaved people, and the surrounding 18,000 acres (7,284 hectares) were tended by them. In 1927, Nicolas Roosevelt, cousin to Franklin D. Roosevelt, purchased it as his hunting lodge and later turned it into a dairy farm, which provided much of the milk to the Charleston area. The last owner was an antiques dealer who used it as a second home. "We don't want to sweep the history of this place under the rug," states Kristin, who educates visitors about the home's past. During the renovation, any features, such as the flooring, moldings, and fireplaces, that were built with enslaved labor were preserved to honor the people who built the home. Descendants of an enslaved couple from the property have held reunions and on occasion have visited the home.

THE ESSENTIALS

Above: The dining room, with Swedish chairs and custom blue gingham skirts, is a calm and restrained room.

The house, thirty minutes outside Charleston in Berkeley County, now sits on a plot of almost 5 acres (2 hectares), and the setting is decidedly rural, an ideal home for the ducks, chickens, rabbits, two golden retrievers, and three cats that the family cares for. "We couldn't have all of the animals we have if we lived closer to town." Their latest addition is a beehive. Even their two-year-old daughter, Astrid, participates in taking care of the bees. The former washhouse, a small structure separate from the main home, is now used to store gardening supplies and as a home for the rabbits.

The house itself is a work in progress. One of the first rooms Kristin and her husband tackled was the kitchen, which is a long galley at the back of the home. "We kept the same floor plan. We just updated it to make it more functional," says Kristin. From there, they moved on to a bathroom upstairs and then the sunroom, where they discovered original parquet floors under the carpeting. This has become the room the family spends their time in.

THE ESSENTIALS

Kristin had always gravitated to more modern design, but after moving in, she began to understand that this home needed more traditional furnishings. "It was living in the house and realizing that it needed to be honored, and the past needed to be recognized," that brought forth this realization, she noted. Kristin has brought in antiques, but nothing too precious, often using antiques that are not in perfect condition. She loves thinking about the stories behind the pieces: Who else sat at the dining table? What were the conversations they had? Why is a big chunk of a chair missing? The couple will continue to add to what they have and collect the stories.

Although Kristin and her husband have chosen a more traditional design, there is still an air of freshness, with light and splashes of color in their work. "I want the house to feel like a home for Astrid. I don't want it to feel stuffy or like a museum," states Kristin. A nod to the past is seen in portraits on the walls and in the style of the furniture, but there is also a modern restraint. With gingham chairs, bright and happy yellow walls, and bouquets of flowers cut from the garden, Kristin has succeeded in creating a warm home for her daughter.

Above, from left: The kitchen was the first project they tackled when they moved in. While they kept the same footprint of the original kitchen, they have updated it with a new design more in keeping with the home's aesthetic. Right: Their chickens make a visit to the kitchen.

THE ESSENTIALS

NINE HOMES FOR INSPIRATION

The primary bedroom is kept simple and serene: a linen bed cover, simple linen curtains, and a few portrait paintings.

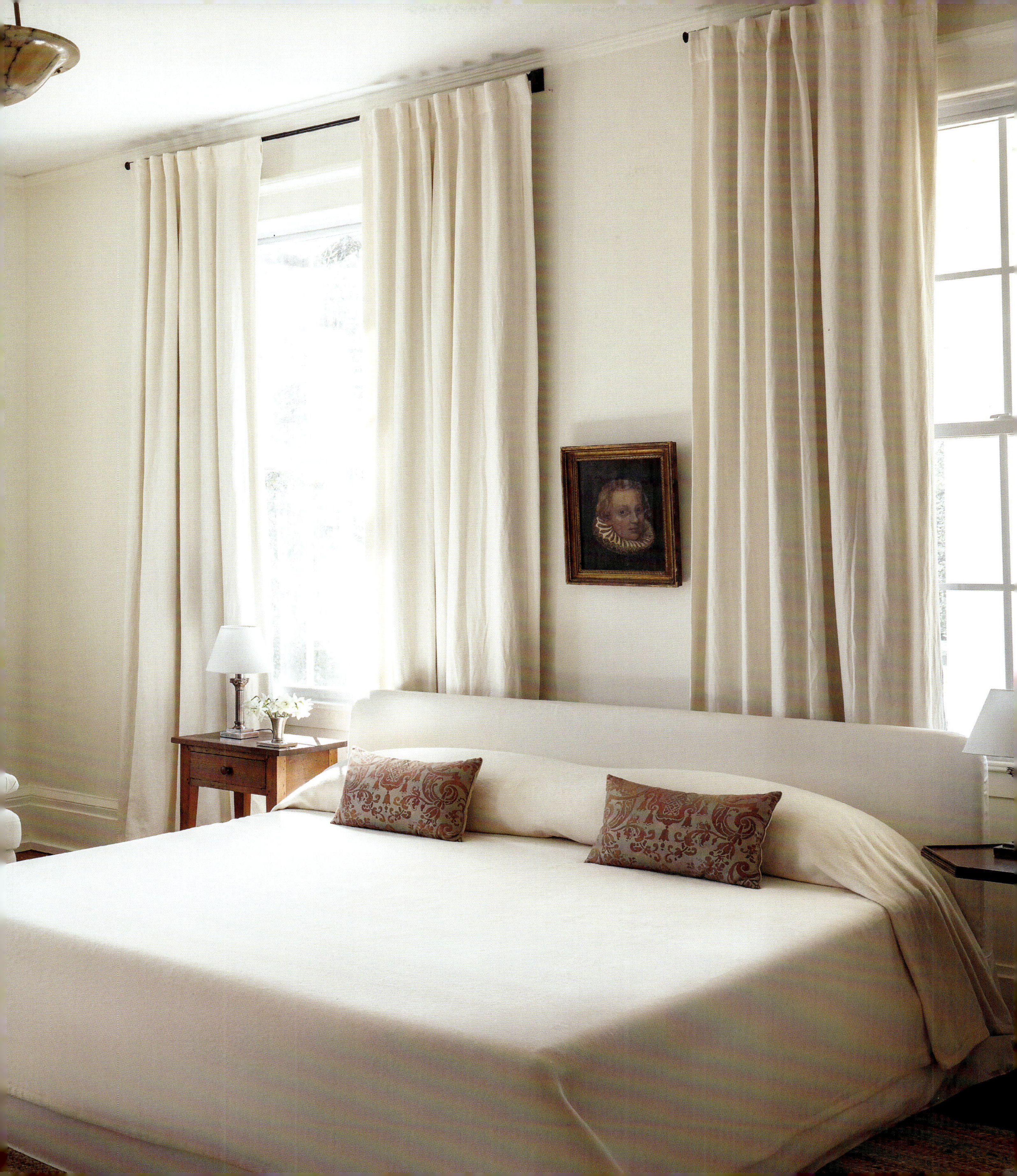

> "It was living in the house and realizing that it needed to be honored, and the past needed to be recognized."
> —KRISTIN ELLEN HOCKMAN

Above from left: Kristin's daughter, Astrid, has a whimsical bedroom with life-size stuffed animals and a striped tent that Kristin made. Opposite: Astrid's bed is draped with a simple gingham canopy.

THE ESSENTIALS

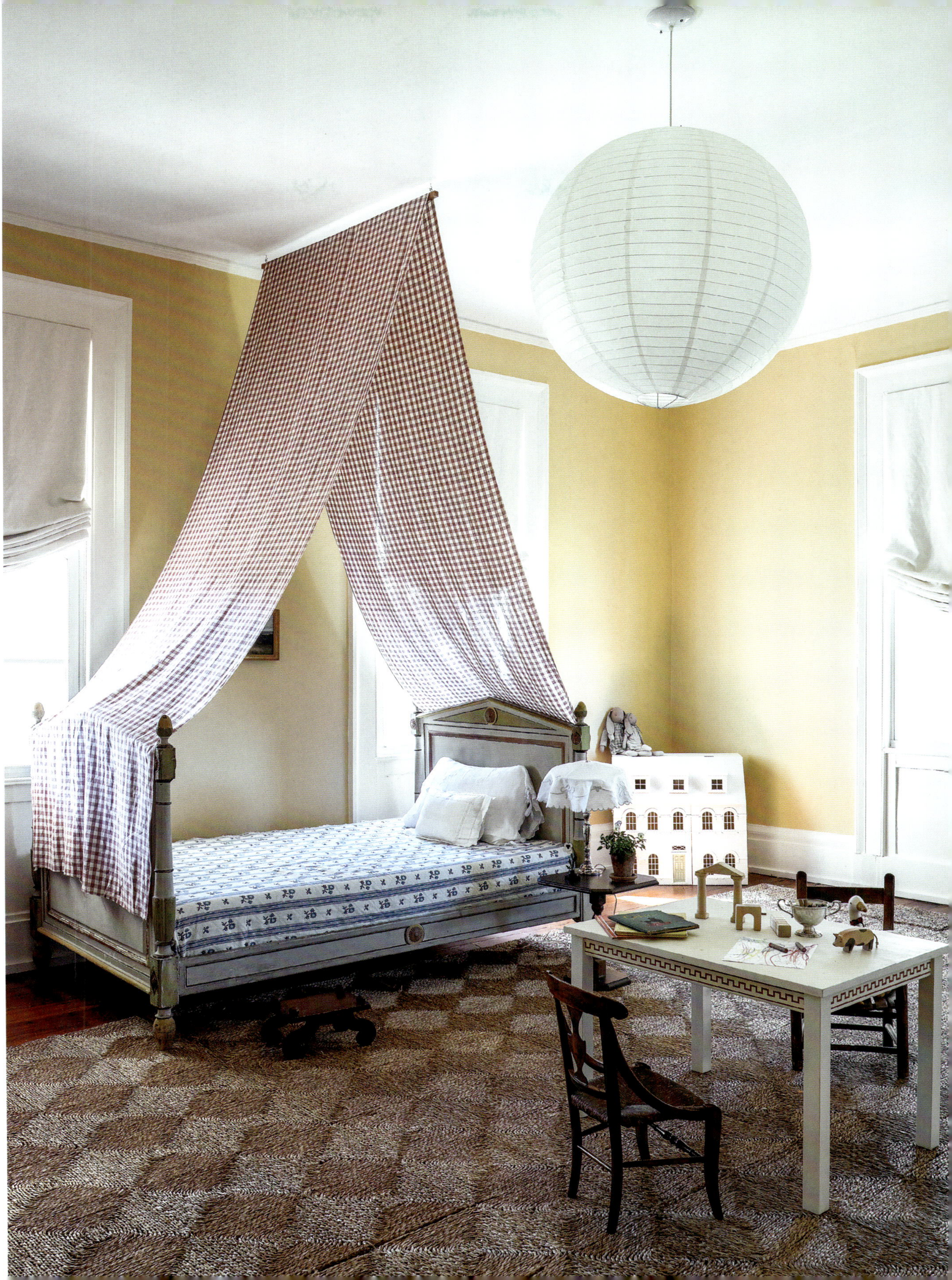

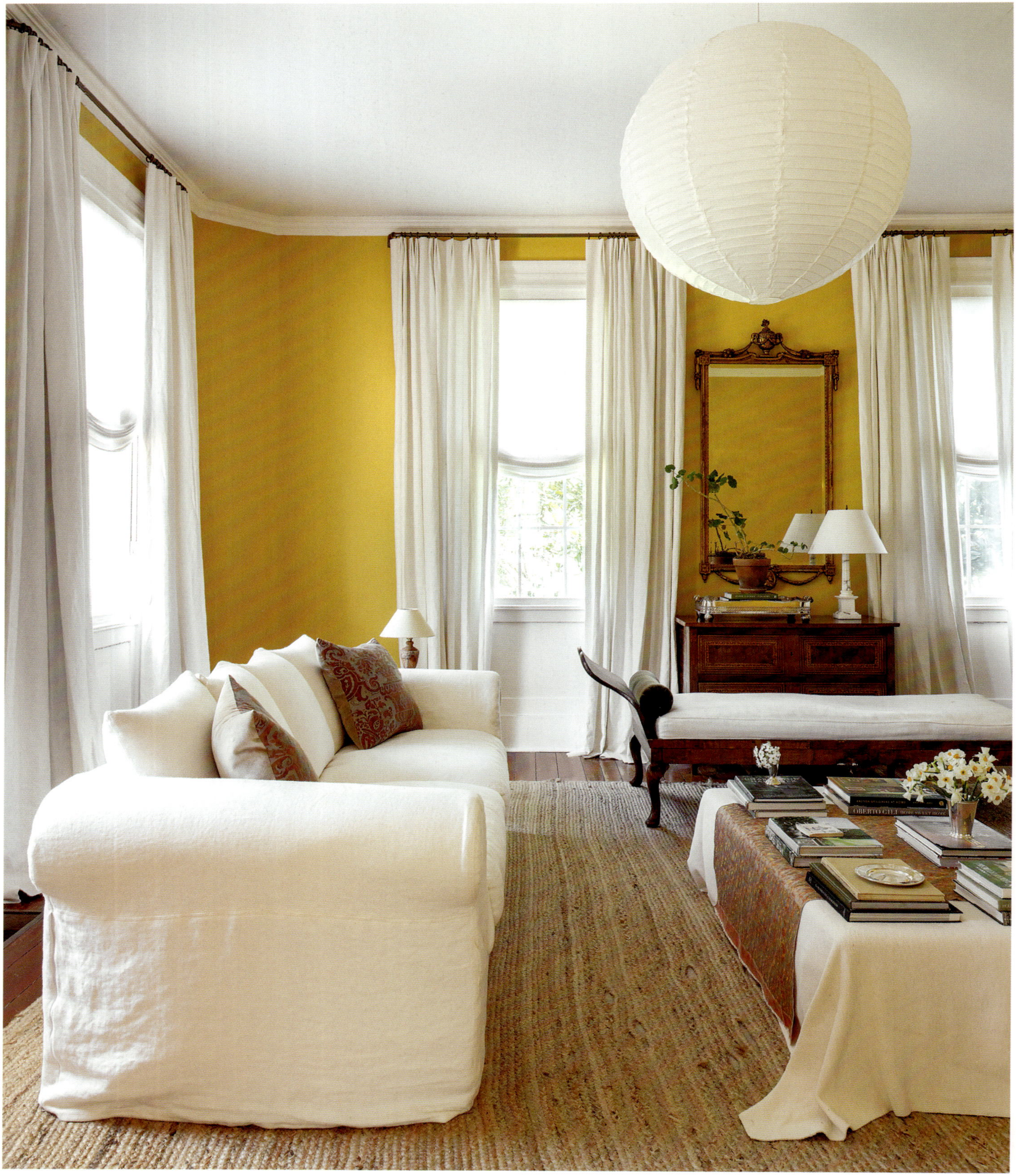

Opposite: While the furnishing tends toward more traditional pieces, Kristin wanted bright and happy colors on the walls in the living room. Above: In her workspace, Kristin, with her mother's help, covered her walls in brown-and-white ticking fabric, which provides a backdrop for her design inspirations.

Below and right: With walls of windows, light floods into the simply adorned sunroom, where the family spends most of their time.

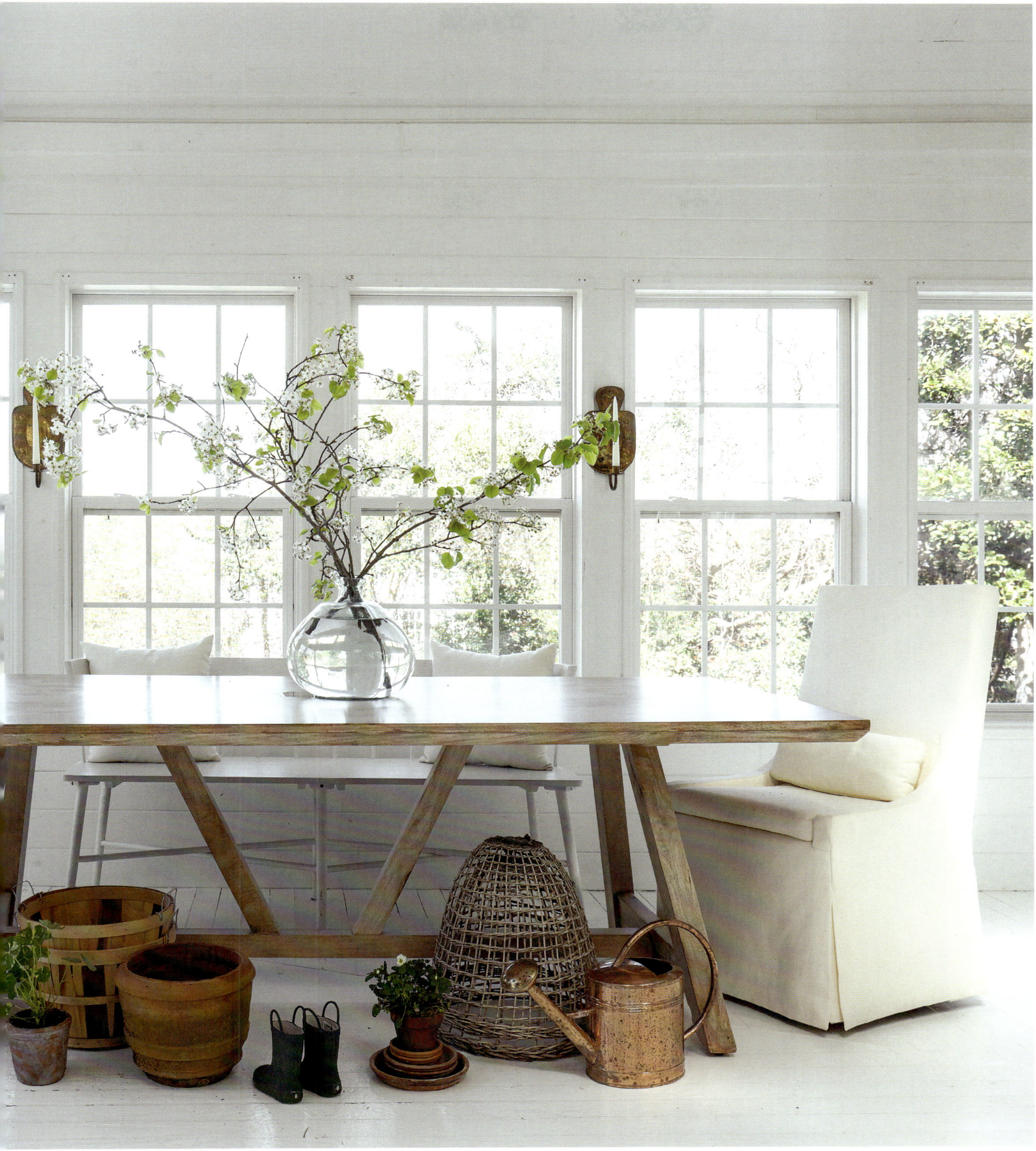

RACHEL ALLEN

LONDON, ENGLAND

Not long after moving to London from Wales, Rachel Allen decided to build a wide-beam barge for her home, not just for the romance of it all, but also as an alternative, affordable way to live in in the city. Fast forward to today: she has lived on the barge, located on the Regent's Canal in Islington, a northern district of the city, for more than ten years.

Rachel landed her first job in the city at Jamb London and quickly became enamored with design. Subsequently, she worked with Christie's Rita Konig and finally with Robert Kime, where she was the showroom manager. All of this prepared her to ultimately establish her own design firm, with projects in the United Kingdom as well as in the United States. Her well-developed eye for design can be seen in the choices she has made for her home.

Rachel had the barge built in the north of England. By designing her own barge instead of purchasing an existing one, she was able to create exactly the style she wanted. Even though it was brand-new when she moved in, Rachel was able to add depth and patina to the space by selecting items with history, like the antique floors

Above: The barge Rachel built as her home—which she shares with her dog, Abe—resides on the Regent's Canal in Islington. Opposite: In a space so compact, every inch has a purpose. This AGA stove found a home in her compact kitchen.

THE ESSENTIALS

NINE HOMES FOR INSPIRATION

The barge is small, but Rachel has kept the furnishings to a minimum, and the result is a comfortable home that feels anything but cramped.

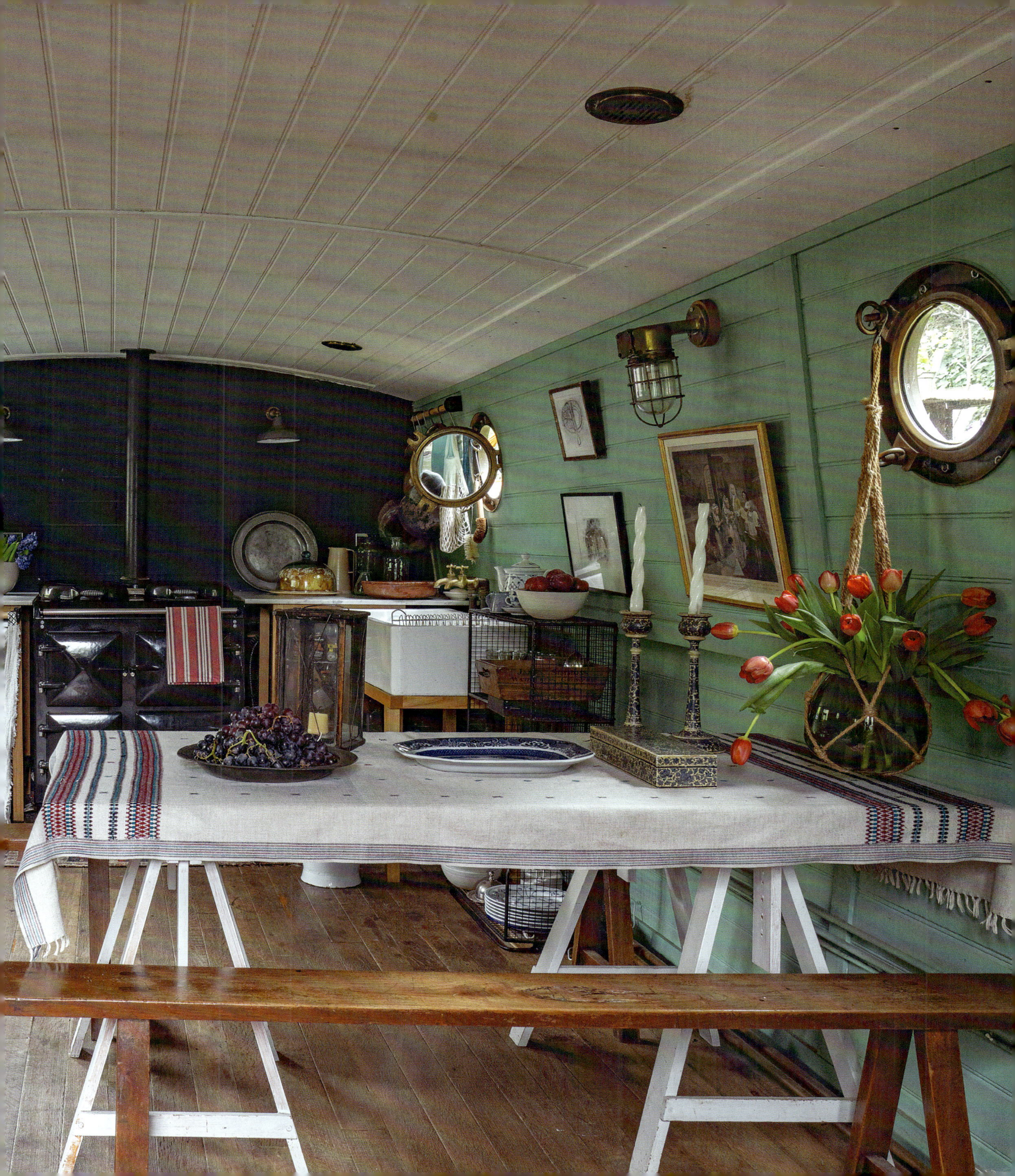

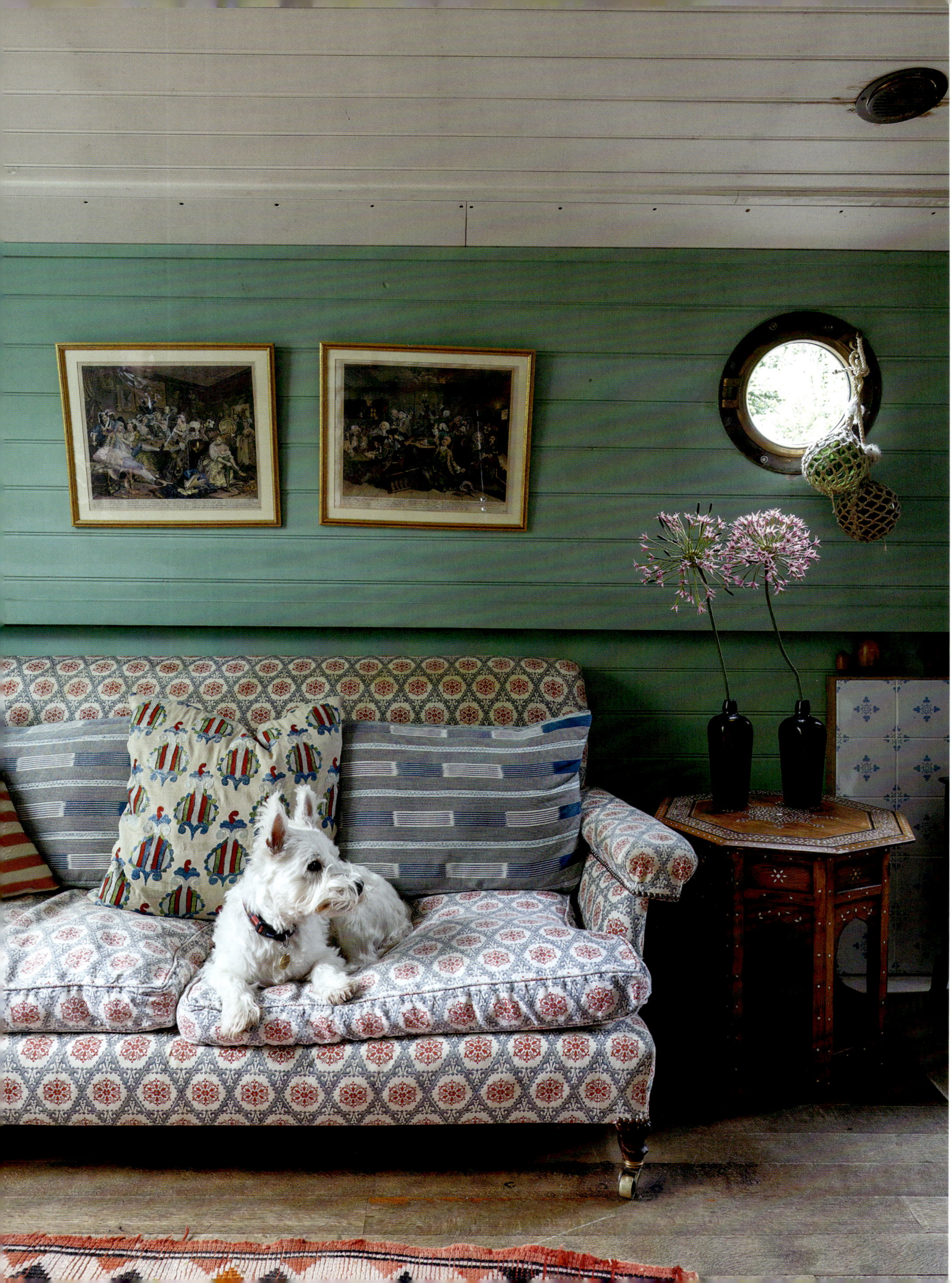

Opposite: Abe sitting on the sofa upholstered in Cordoba by Bennison Fabrics. Right: A smaller-size tin tub intended for pets is used in this small space.

THE ESSENTIALS

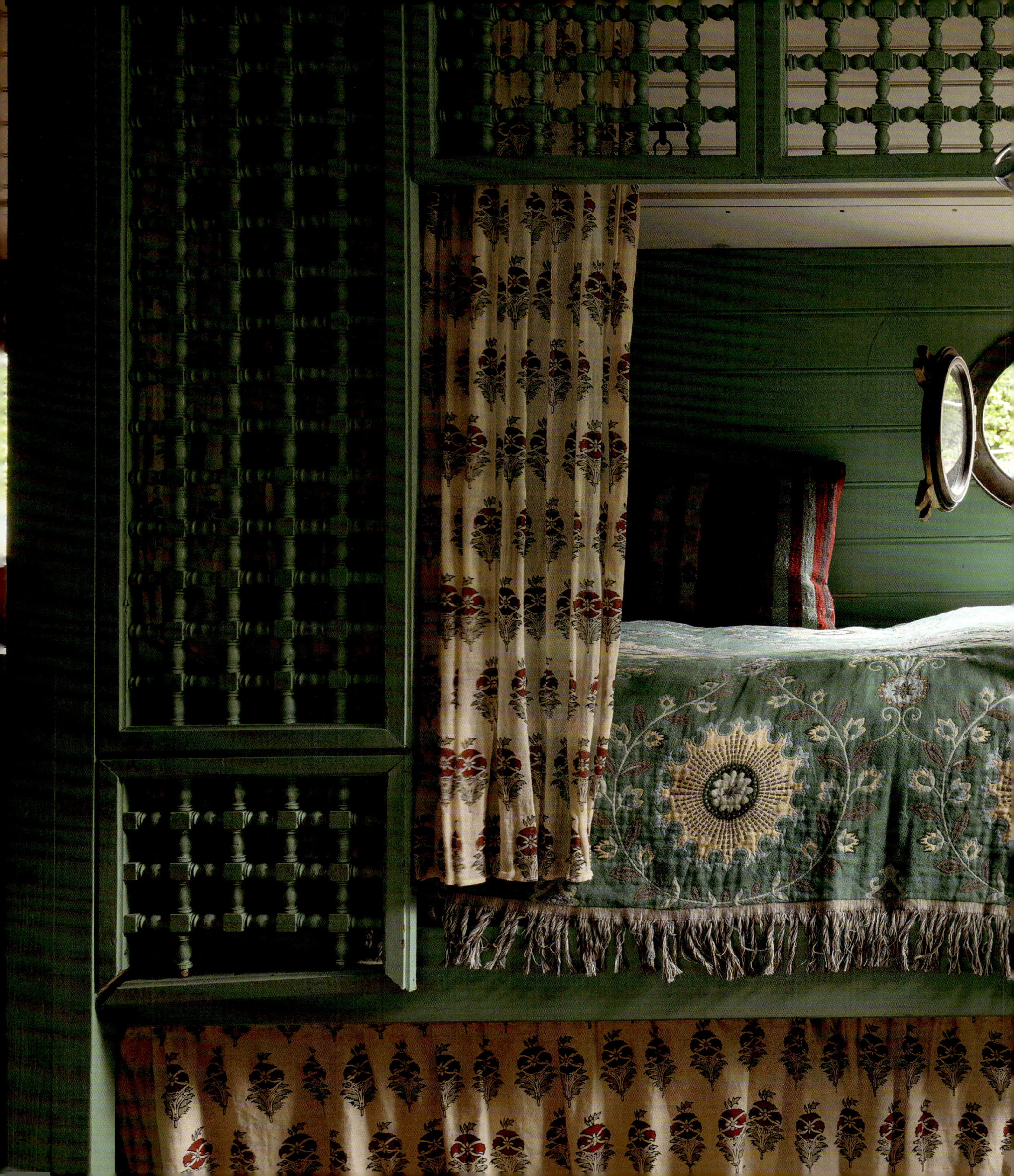

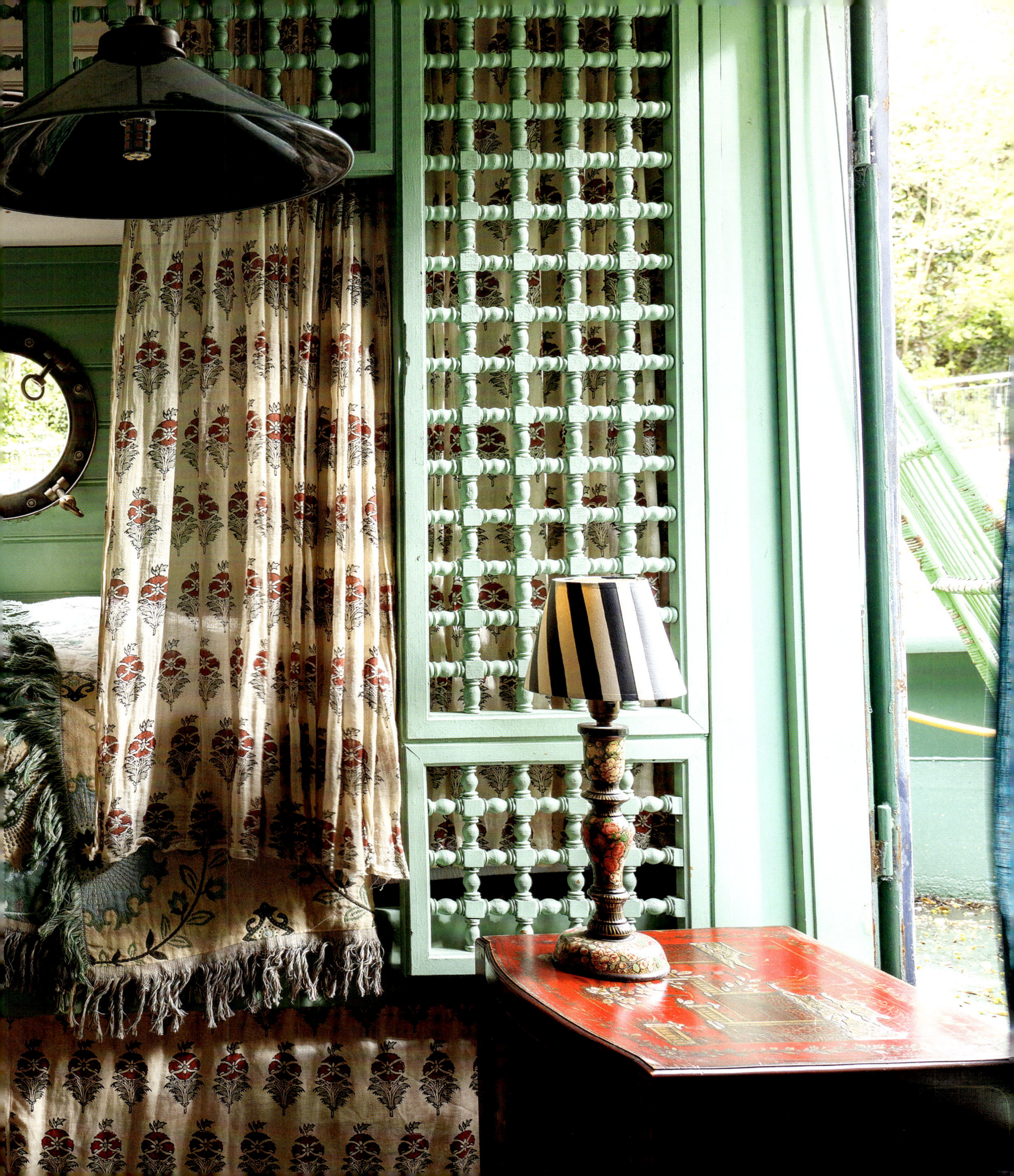

that came out of a former museum. She also selected a tin bathtub of a smaller-than-usual size (originally designed for bathing pets) to fit the footprint of the barge. But the addition that grounds the barge the most is probably the AGA stove. It not only feels cozy, but also makes the space look more like a traditional home.

As you walk down the path to the canal, you can see that Rachel's barge is one of four homes moored right before the Islington Tunnel. Transporting goods using barges like these has a long history in the UK, before engines or motors were common. "The boats used to be pulled by horses walking alongside the canals, but in the tunnel, people would use their feet against the walls to push their way through," says Rachel. There is a certain stillness on the canal that makes you feel worlds away from the bustling city.

As you step into the home, you feel an immediate warmth and comfort from the collected design of the space. The reclaimed floors, the paneled walls painted Arsenic by Farrow & Ball, and the eclectic mix of antique furnishings and colorful textiles make the space seem like it has always been there. The roof of the barge is home to a garden of potted plants and on the warmer days serves as an outdoor dining space. The intimacy and permanence within the barge tempt visitors to linger.

"I thought I'd only live on here a few years, but now I can't imagine living anywhere else," says Rachel. Living in such a small space, she needs to be mindful of not bringing too many belongings into the mix. Rachel has mastered this. Her home is not cluttered; instead it feels effortlessly layered, making for a peaceful, comfortable retreat from her busy life in London.

Previous spread: Rachel's bed is tucked into the corner and enclosed, so the sleeping area almost feels like it is in a separate room. Above, from left: With a spacious table, there is plenty of room for guests to visit. With optimal organization, everything has its place in the kitchen. Opposite: A Coalbrookdale wood stove heats the barge.

THE ESSENTIALS
196

NINE HOMES FOR INSPIRATION

CHARLOTTE BOUNDY

LONDON, ENGLAND

When Charlotte Boundy found her home in London, she knew she was moving into a white-walled blank canvas. What she didn't realize was she was also becoming a member of the vibrant, tight-knit community of Shepherd's Bush, where neighbors know one another and often find a reason to get together—like the street party they had for the coronation of King Charles III. Her home is on a quiet road with more of a village vibe, and she wouldn't have it any other way.

After Charlotte purchased the home, she made the conscious decision to live there and wait six months before making any changes. She wanted to have a chance for the house to speak to her. She loved the bones of the home—how the light streamed into the south-facing kitchen through a wall of windows looking out to the garden, the double living room, and the three bedrooms, which meant she could convert one into an office. It was the perfect space for her. "I looked forward to the opportunity to work out of my home," she explains.

Her love for design started while in boarding school. She was smitten with decorating her own dorm cubicle. "I'm a magpie. I love beautiful things," says Charlotte.

Above: Charlotte likes to think of herself as a magpie, collecting things that catch her eye. Opposite: The living room serves as a space for her library, its oversize couch an invitation to curl up with a good book.

THE ESSENTIALS

NINE HOMES FOR INSPIRATION   199

In this enticing space, where patterns play together for a harmonious moment, Charlotte not only uses patterns in her choices of textiles, but also in plates on the wall, paintings, and other vessels. The fireplace is made by Jamb.

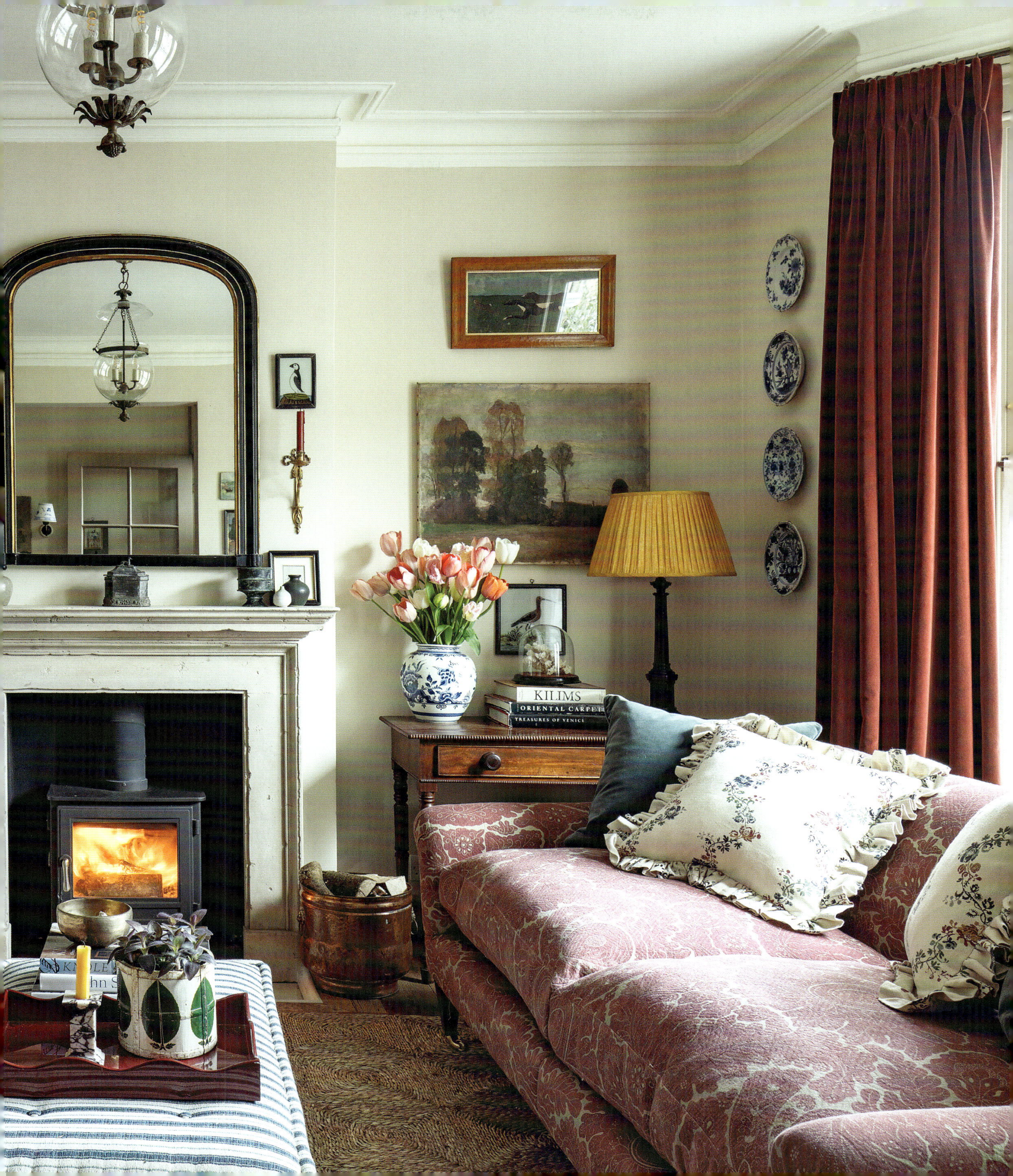
KILIMS
ORIENTAL CARPETS
TREASURES OF VENICE

River Cottage
COLEFAX & FOWLER
JOHN FOWLER
Giorgio Locatelli
Made in Italy
JERUSALEM

Opposite: A small secretary desk with a pull-man lamp defines the small space. Pig, her dog, rests comfortably next to the radiator. Right: Sometimes the simplest detail can be the most impactful—like this chair at the base of the stairway.

Although she was trained as a graphic designer in school, her work experience has focused on interiors. She launched her design studio in 2018, with expert training from her previous work, including jobs at Christie's, at *The World of Interiors* magazine, and with designers Max Rollitt and Rose Uniacke.

Charlotte, known for her traditional approach to decorating, works hard to retain the integrity of a home, as you can see in her approach to designing her own. After living six months in the house, Charlotte made changes that would help with the way she planned to use the different spaces. She realized that she would like to have a bathroom on the main floor, so one of the first changes she made was to add a powder room under the staircase there. The result is a small jewelry box of a room.

Charlotte began to add color to every wall, room by room. She also converted one of the bedrooms into her studio, adding a window with a view to the garden to help inspire her work. She added a cupboard for storing fabric samples in a corner and painted it the same color as the trim—Reddish Brown by Farrow & Ball. Although the bathroom upstairs is small, Charlotte thought that this size was integral to the home and chose to renovate it with the same footprint, adding texture and her own personality in the form of Zellige tiles, a Pierre Frey shower curtain, and a La Chapelle sink from Lefroy Brooks. Charlotte's bedroom, which runs the entire width of the home, has a four-poster bed and a headboard from Ensemblier, upholstered in a floral textile from Nicholas Herbert, along with ticking from Cloth Shop. The whole room, including the fireplace, is painted in Setting Plaster by Farrow & Ball. Her bedroom and the entire second floor have floors covered in sisal.

Above, from left: Charlotte's kitchen, painted in Lilac Pink and Brunswick Green natural paints by Edward Bulmer, is the heart of her home and where people often gather around her farmhouse table. Opposite: The antique hutch adds character to the room.

NINE HOMES FOR INSPIRATION

205

Charlotte brings a style that is both collected and approachable. Her home is a mix of all her treasured pieces. The living room houses her sizable library along the main wall. The ebonized antique mirror hanging above the Portland stone fireplace is from Jamb and was purchased at an antique store on London's Lillie Road. Also in the living room, a Lorfords Elmstead sofa upholstered in GP & J Baker's Thornham Spice, which was a win at a National Health Service (NHS) charity auction during the COVID-19 lockdown, brings pattern to the space, along with lampshades made of vintage silk saris from India from Nushka, a local store in Notting Hill.

While Charlotte has always dreamed of a big country house, her home in Shepherd's Bush has everything she needs—a much-needed home studio in a comfortable home and a community she doesn't want to leave anytime soon. Her home is where she likes to be.

THE ESSENTIALS

Opposite: The canopy, done in Nicholas Herbert fabric with a ticking interior fabric above the primary bed, adds warmth and an additional layer to the bed. Above: A simple fireplace gives the room another focal point. Charlotte's ability to mix an array of patterns is displayed here in full glory.

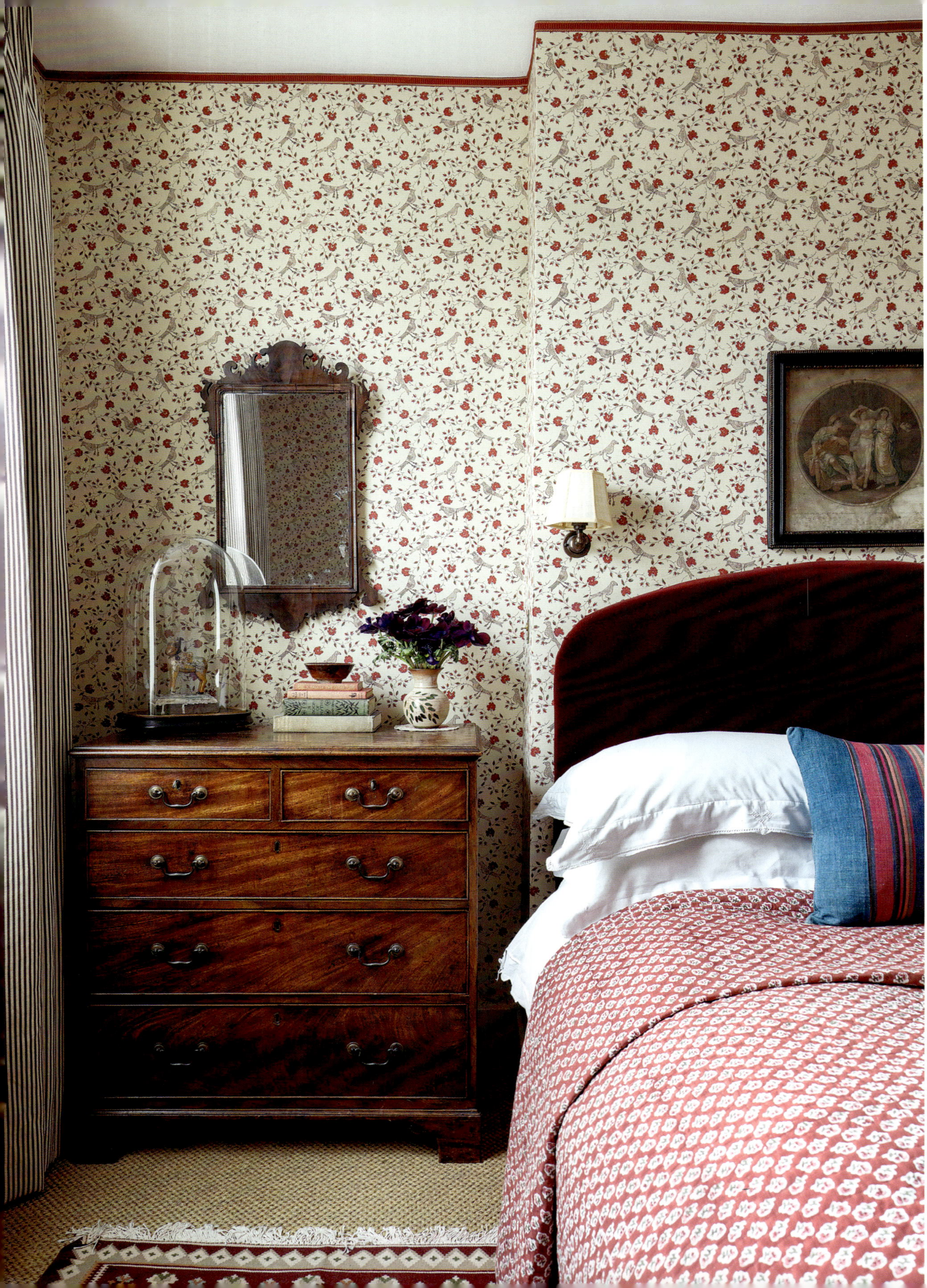

Opposite and above: A cheerful guest bedroom is enveloped in Pierre Frey wallpaper.

Above: The colorful mood board, gathered striped desk skirt, and pretty boxes containing fabric samples all contribute to the inviting warmth of Charlotte's design office. Opposite: The small space at the landing of her staircase is accentuated by a beautiful table and hats that become art.

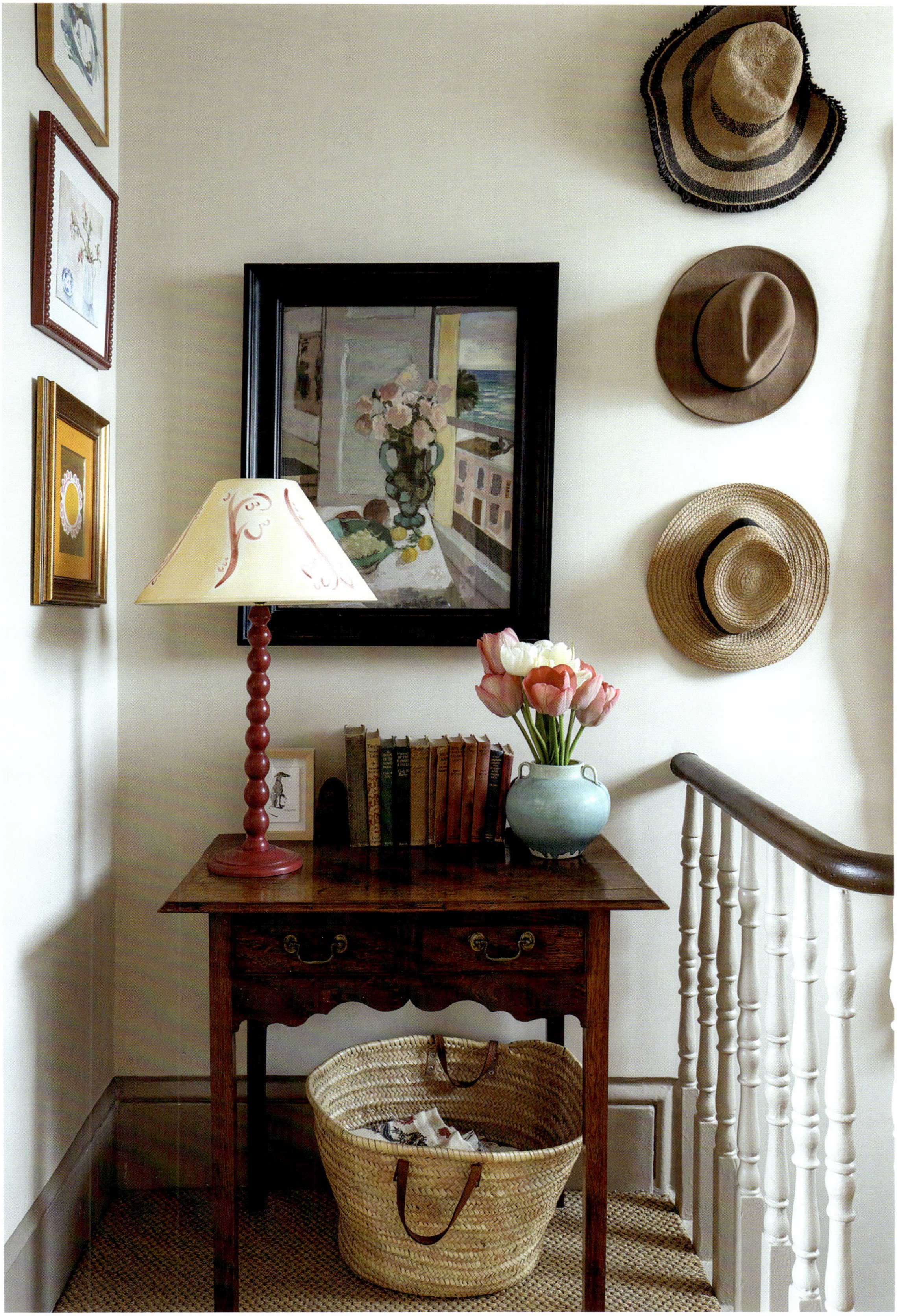

GLENN BAN

EAST HAMPTON, NEW YORK

glenn Ban, who has his own interior design firm based in East Hampton, New York, specializes in both residential and commercial projects. He is known for combining clean architecture with modern and vintage furniture, as well as contemporary art. For more than twenty years, Glenn Ban has enjoyed living on Long Island, New York, and raising his son, Charlie, there. He was drawn to the small-town feeling of East Hampton. Although it has an influx of summer vacationers, there is also a strong year-round community. "You learn to live around it," explains Glenn. He loves the proximity to the beaches, less than two miles away. "We usually ride our bikes there, although I also love to walk," he says.

Glenn found the home through a friend of a friend. The house, built in 1820, offered everything he wanted, including three bedrooms upstairs and a downstairs with three main rooms—a kitchen, dining room, and living room. When they moved in, Glenn painted all the walls white and moved the shutters from the top half of the windows to the bottom half, leaving the top without curtains, an arrangement that provides light but also allows for privacy. Glenn prefers using something

Above, from left: White walls create the perfect backdrop for the simple shutters and wood furniture. Glenn relaxes in his kitchen. Opposite: His light-filled multi-purpose dining room is an effective mix of modern and vintage and wood and metal.

The Private House
Rose Tarlow
ARCHITECTURE TO LANDSCAPE
LE CORBUSIER MY WORK

Above: The inviting living room, with a coffee table by Adrian Pearsall, is a space that the family enjoys. Opposite: An antique chest in the corner next to the sofa provides space for a reclaimed-wood lamp and peonies.

already there to buying new items. "I'm always teetering between wanting to improve the home or just embracing the imperfection," he says. For Glenn, imperfection does a better job in telling the story and history of the space.

He also loves living with a mix of things from different styles and periods, a quality that dances flawlessly with Glenn's love of imperfection. The coffee table in his living room is by mid-century modern designer Adrian Pearsall. It was from his former partner's uncle, a priest, who also had a formidable collection of mid-century furniture in his residence. "I've found and used this table in many of the homes I've designed," states Glenn. In his home, a mix of periods—traditional, Arts and Crafts, mid-century modern, and rustic pieces live comfortably together. A perfect example of this can be found in his dining room, where he pairs an Arts and Crafts table with mid-century chairs, a metal

THE ESSENTIALS

Sometimes less is more. In the case of Glenn's kitchen, he chose not to build new cabinetry and embraced the original cabinet and fireplace. The result is a kitchen that feels like a room you want to spend time in.

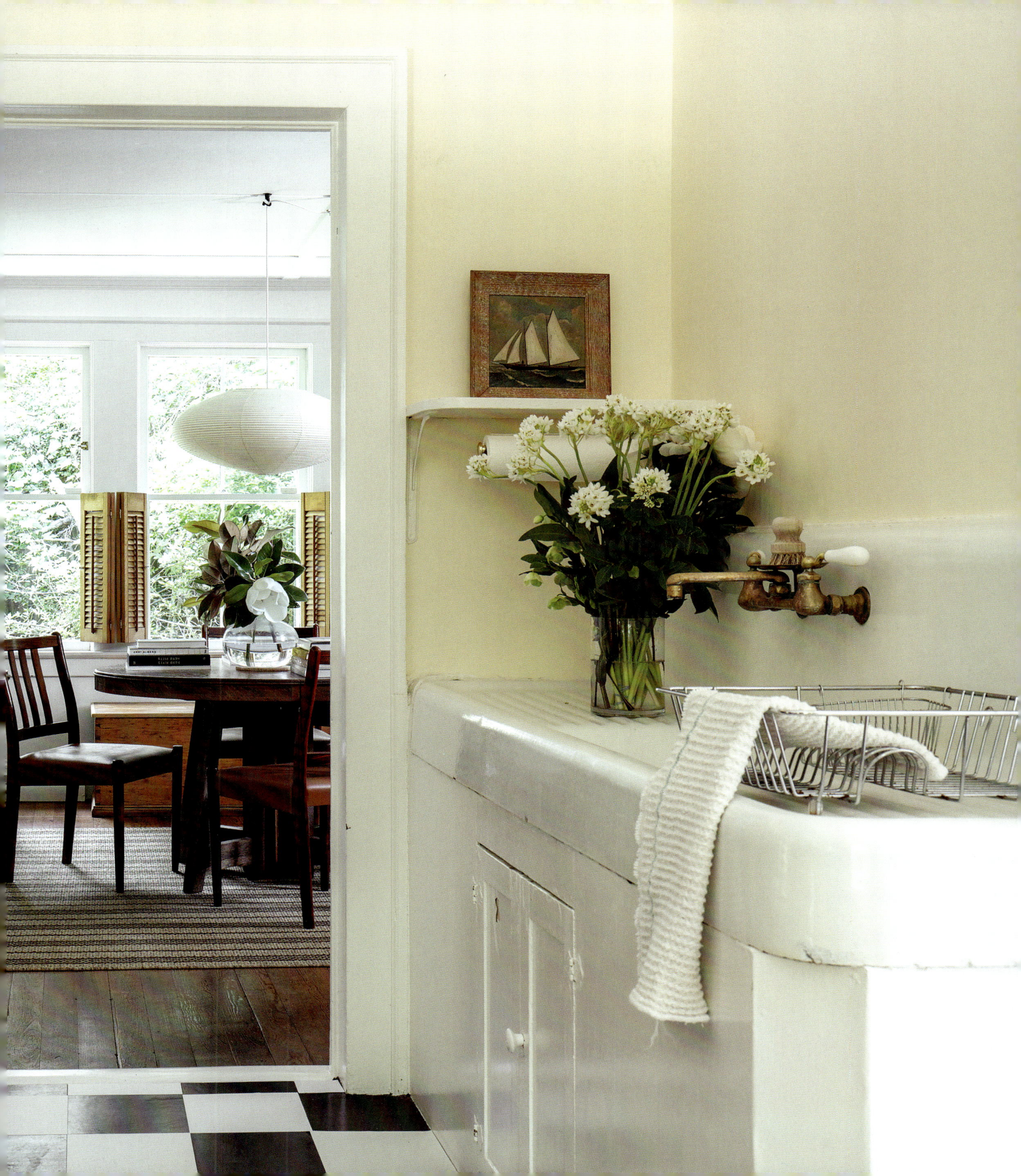

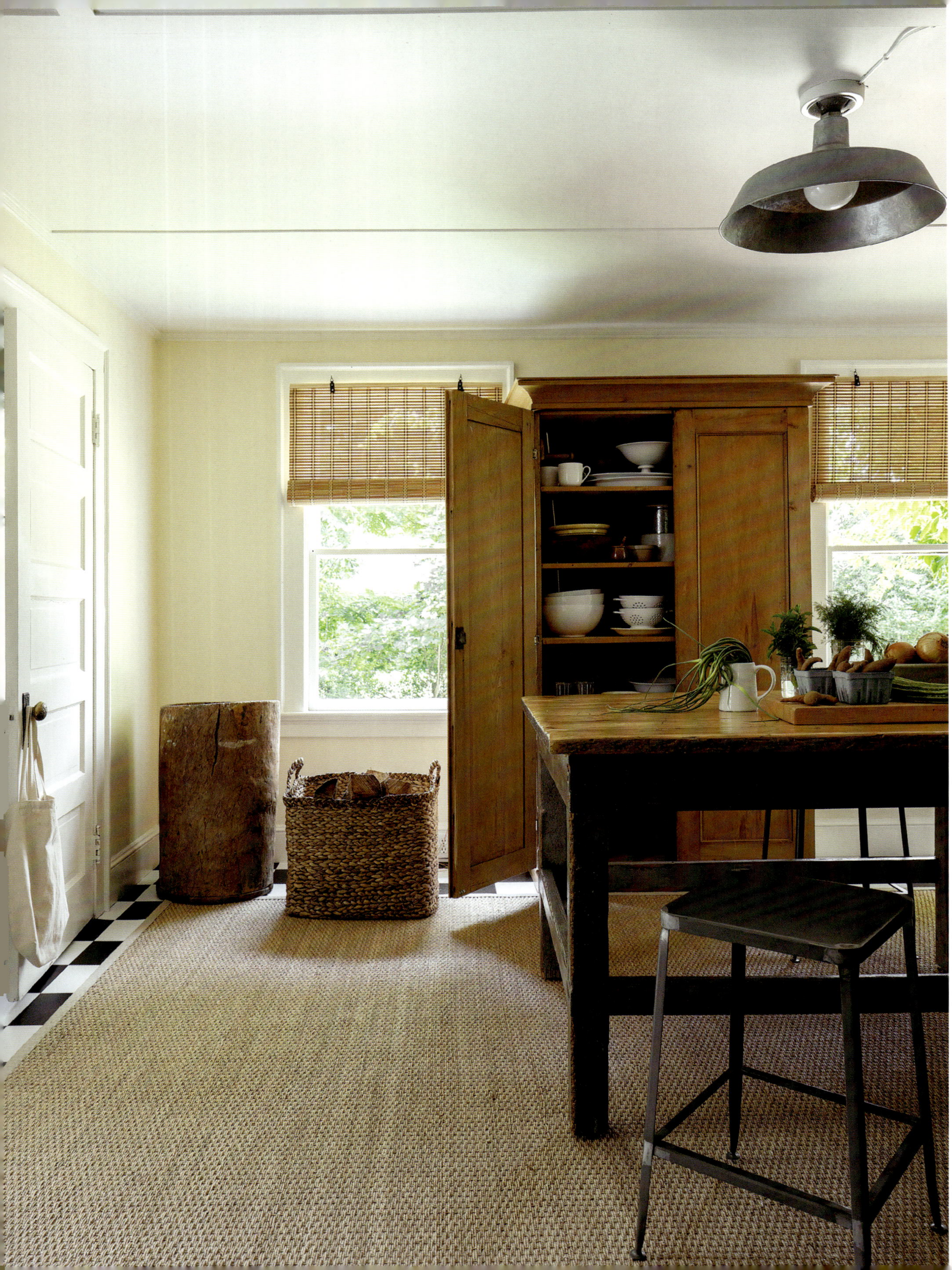

Opposite: Simple woven shades, a basket of wood, and a sisal rug add texture to the kitchen. A large armoire provides much-needed storage. Above: The island was an old Abercrombie & Fitch fixture. A wood burning stove provides heat in the winter.

daybed, and a more ornate chest with a marble top. "I believe Arts and Crafts is such an underrated period of furniture," Glenn says. The pillows on the daybed are all made from textiles he has collected.

The living room and the other ground floor rooms are used all of the time by Glenn, his partner, and his son. The spaces are connected but also are separate from each other. In the winter months, Glenn hangs curtains on the windows to add weight to the rooms. The kitchen has minimal built-in cabinets, so instead, he uses furniture to fulfill the needs of the room—including a large armoire he stores things in and a large floating island he purchased at auction, which in a previous life was a fixture in an Abercrombie & Fitch store. He sanded the top but kept the remainder as he found it.

Everything in Glenn's home has meaning to him, and he doesn't feel the need to spend a lot of money on things. "I'm very resourceful and thoughtful about what I buy—I also move my things around all of the time," says Glenn. The daybed that resides in his dining room has lived in many spaces as the needs of his home have evolved. His home is a testament to "Less is more"—a lesson in design we can all learn.

THE ESSENTIALS

Above: Glenn is not only an expert at showing restraint in his decorating, but also blending aesthetics to create a warm and comfortable home. Opposite: This small room upstairs functions beautifully as a guest bedroom.

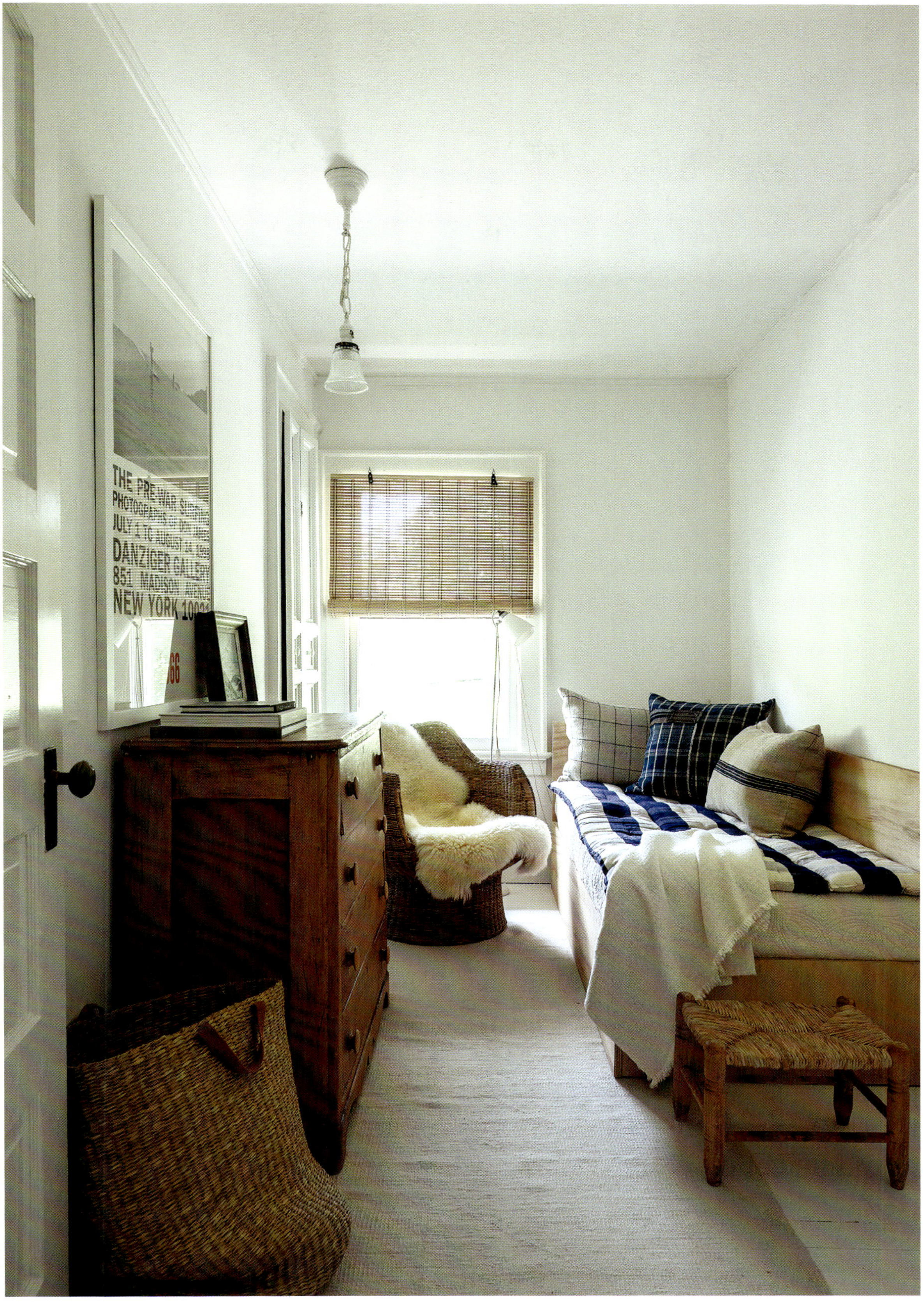
DANZIGER
851 MADISON
NEW YORK

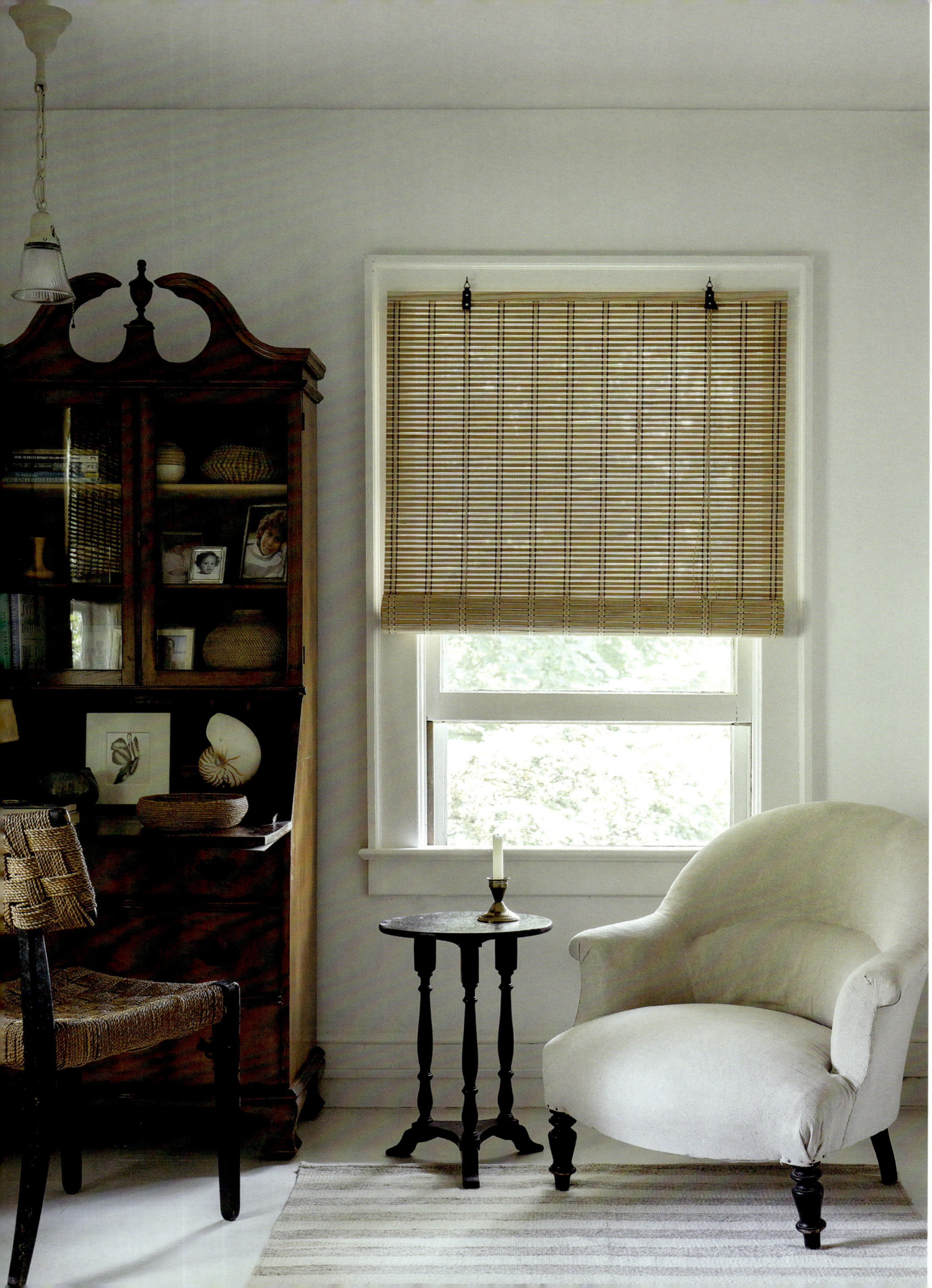

Opposite: A secretary desk and upholstered chair reside in the corner of the primary bedroom. Above: Simplicity rules in the bedroom, where a linen cover and a woolen blanket draped over the end of the bed add dimension.

NINE HOMES FOR INSPIRATION

224

"I'm always teetering between wanting to improve the home or just embracing the imperfection."

—GLENN BAN

Opposite and above: The covered porch has a vintage wicker sofa and table at one end and a refurbished wooden swing at the other, each adorned in striped cushions.

THE ESSENTIALS

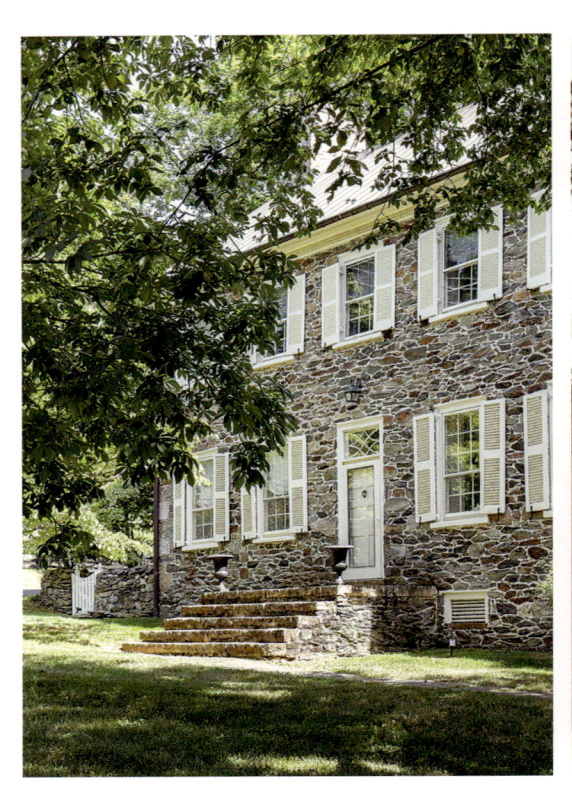

JOSH YOUNG

MIDDLEBURG, VIRGINIA

a deep reverence for the past can be seen in Josh Young's art and his homes. But don't be fooled: his feet are firmly planted in the modern world. For Josh, the past and present can live comfortably together.

Josh has been painting since the age of five and built his first art studio in his family home's basement when he was a teenager. After high school, he moved to Milan, Italy, where he studied media, communications, and production design at the Universitá Cattolica del Sacro Cuore. "Milan had a huge impact on me. The depth of history is everywhere but there is also a strong current of modernity," says Josh. He continues to gravitate to a mixed-media technique on canvas, using textiles, loose paper, antique documents, and mesh.

When Josh returned to the United States, he moved to New York City and worked at Swavelle Mill Creek Fabrics in textile design. He then moved to Chicago, where he worked in public relations and marketing. When he was laid off from his corporate job, his partner encouraged Josh to dive deep into what he really loved—art and design. In 2019, Josh Young Design House was born. His business has

Above: Josh and his partner were looking for a country retreat. They found the perfect home in a stone house in Middleburg, Virginia, which they named Sycamore House. Right: A beautiful moment in the entryway: the stairway accentuated with art, a pair of riding boots, and an elegant settee.

THE ESSENTIALS

NINE HOMES FOR INSPIRATION
227

Josh finds the perfect balance of antique furniture, wicker baskets, well-positioned art, and a touch of modern, with the floor lamps that flank the sofa. Soft linen roman shades can be found on many windows.

CLASSIC ART
Treasures of the HERMITAGE
ARCHITECTURAL DIGEST
HOUSE & GARDEN

focused on his portrait-style paintings, geometric collages, and his interior design services. Josh has also had several successful collaborations, including with Williams Sonoma Home and Framebridge. He is also the author of *Artful Home* (2024).

In 2020, Josh and his partner made the decision to move back to the East Coast and chose Washington, DC, where they purchased an 1885 town house on Capitol Hill. The bottom level contains Josh's art and design studio (see pages 118–121). After a few years, they felt the pull to buy a house in the countryside and found the perfect stone house in Middleburg, Virginia: Sycamore House. Middleburg, a town of about 650 people, has been the rural playground of many well-known individuals, including Jacqueline Kennedy Onassis, who loved to fox hunt there. "Having a second home in the country has been an extension of defining who I am," Josh says.

Sycamore House was built in 1780. For many years, it was owned by Quakers who remained neutral in both the American Revolution and the Civil War. They had soldiers from both sides board at their home. When the previous owners were working in the

Above, from left: Books are an important part of this home, many of them about art or regional lore from the Middleburg area. Opposite: A Ralph Lauren sofa, which had a former home in a local fraternity, is now recovered and taking center stage in one of the main sitting rooms.

THE ESSENTIALS

230

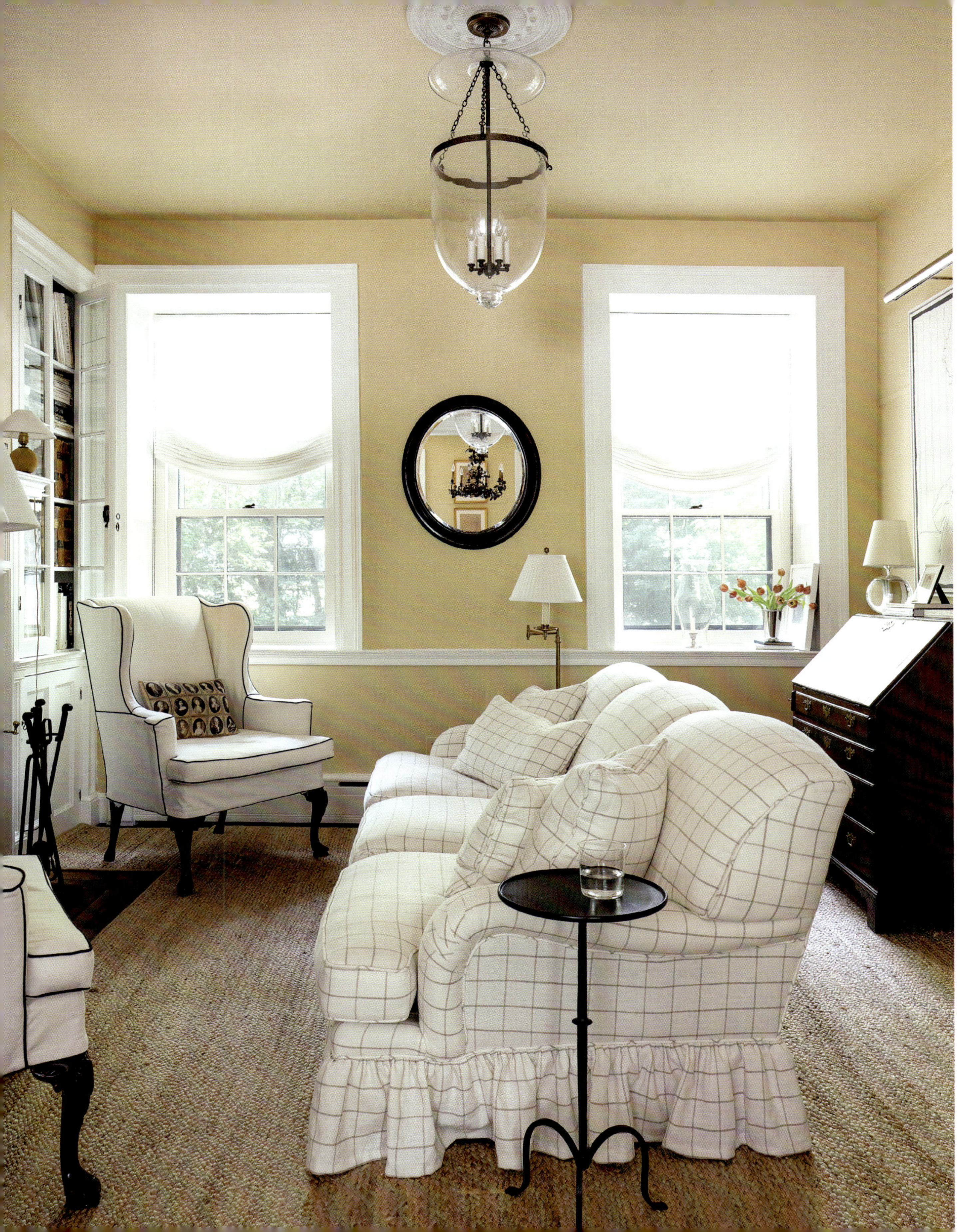

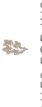

Above: Portraits can be found throughout the home. The painting above the fireplace is one of Josh's works of art. Right: The formal dining room is transformed by antique chairs with white linen–gathered skirts.

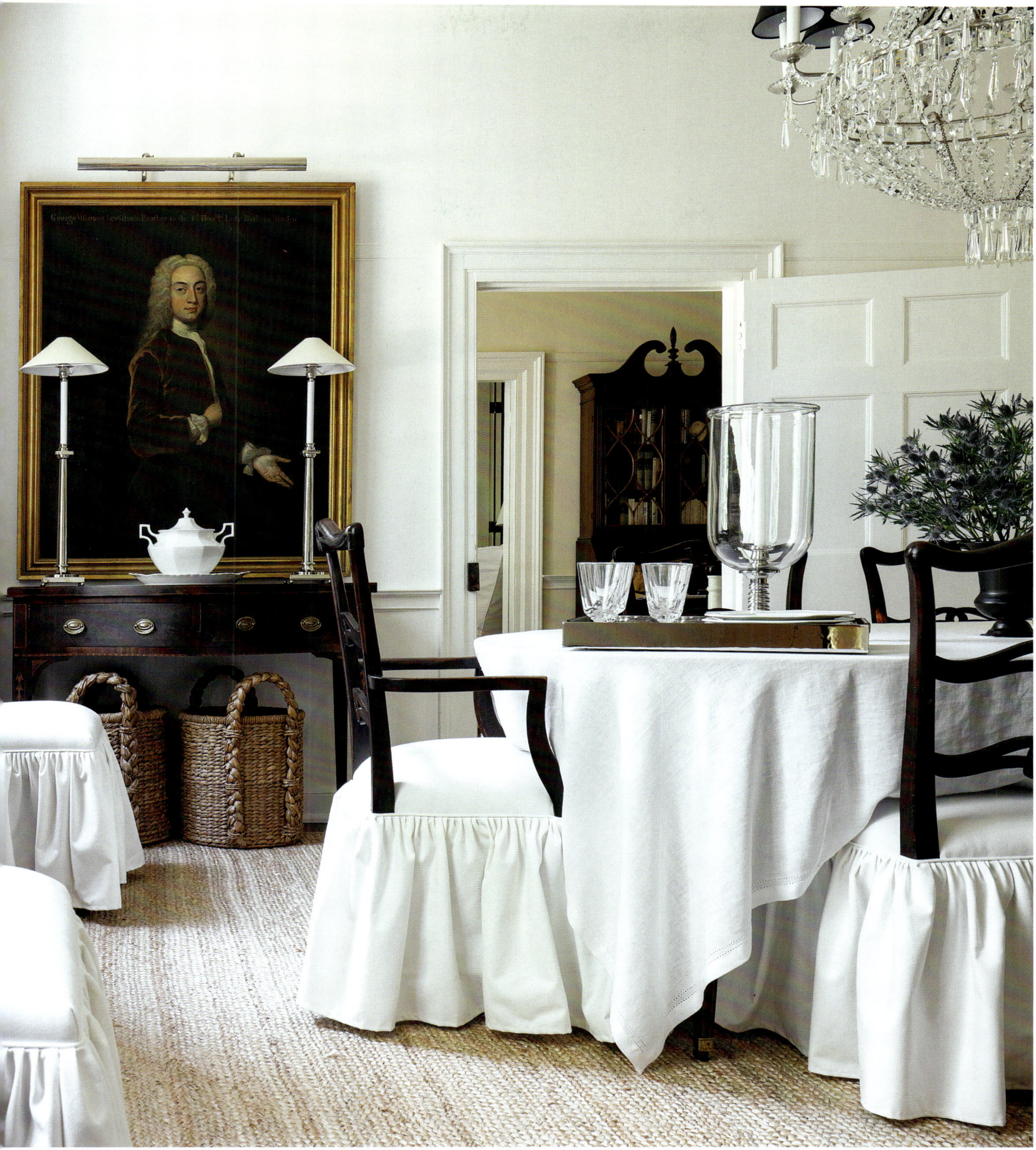

garden, they uncovered possessions of these soldiers from both wars. Josh was drawn to the sense of character and patina of the home. "I find there is a beautiful tension between the historical elements of the home and modern parts of life today," he says.

The house is filled to the brim with antiques sourced primarily from nearby shops. Old silver, furniture sourced locally, vintage books—many about Middleburg—make the home feel as if it's all been here for generations. The Ralph Lauren sofa came out of a fraternity house and was recovered in a windowpane brown-and-cream linen. "I wrote my book *Artful Home* sitting on that sofa," Josh recalls. In addition to antiques, the home also houses equestrian accessories in different spots around its rooms. Riding boots, black riding helmets, and polo sticks reference the horse culture of Middleburg.

Although their home in Washington, DC, is more neutral, here Josh plays with color. Bright yellow walls in one of the living rooms add a sense of modernity. The primary bedroom has Persian rugs in tones of reds and blues, and the curtains of the four-poster bed are in red ticking. Blue-and-white transferware covers the wall of a small cove. Sycamore House is another beautiful design accomplishment for Josh, with many of his own creations within the walls.

Above: A stunning stone wall and wide-plank floors make the kitchen look as if it were original to the house. Opposite: In the corner of the kitchen, a marble-topped bistro table is paired with four wicker chairs, both from Williams Sonoma Home.

THE ESSENTIALS

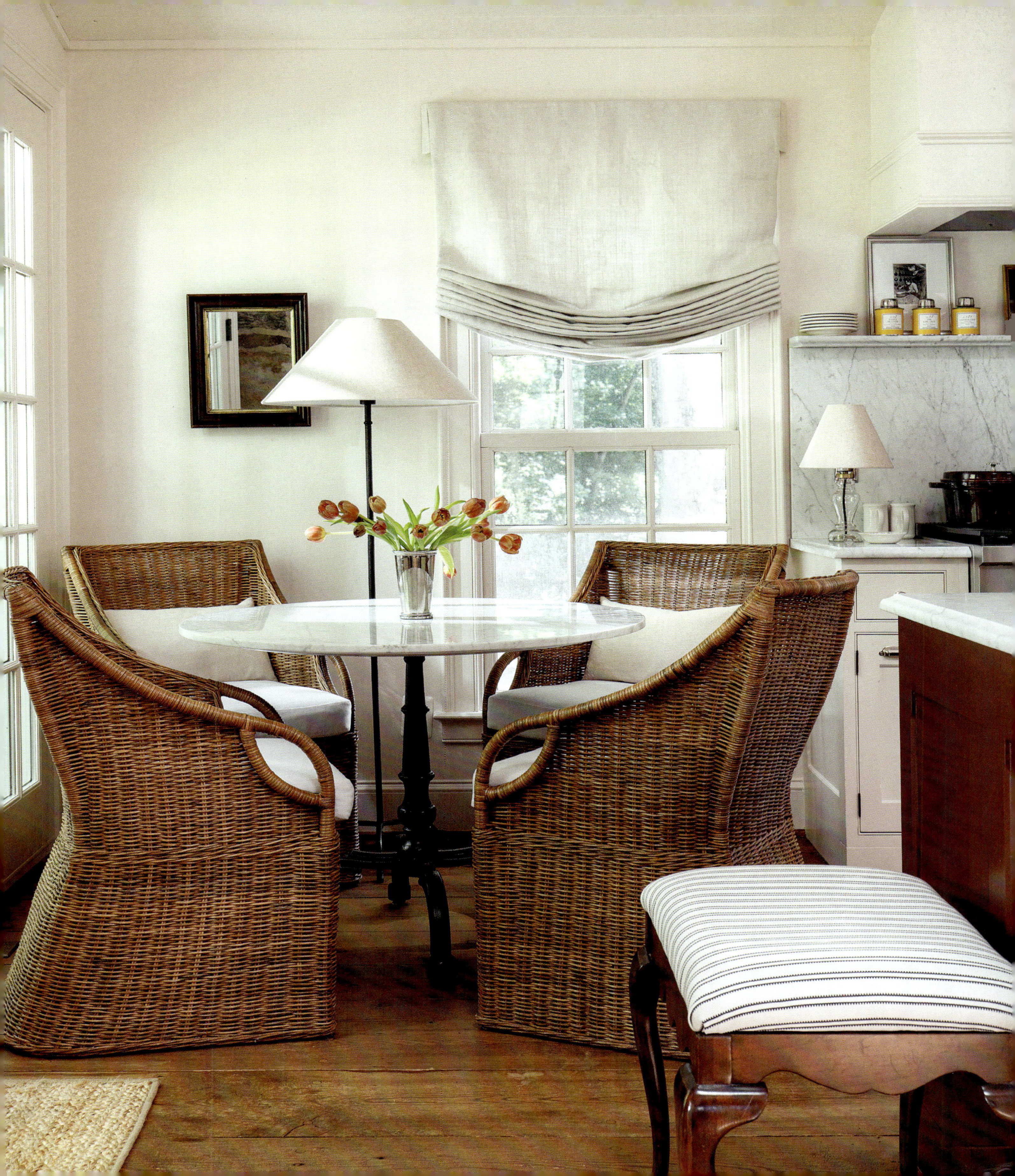

THE ESSENTIALS

Opposite, insets from top: More of Josh's book collection, riding hats, and, of course, portraits occupy the fireplace surrounds. In another nook, the television is surrounded by blue-and-white transferware. Above: In this sitting room, two sofas face each other to create an intimate spot in the home.

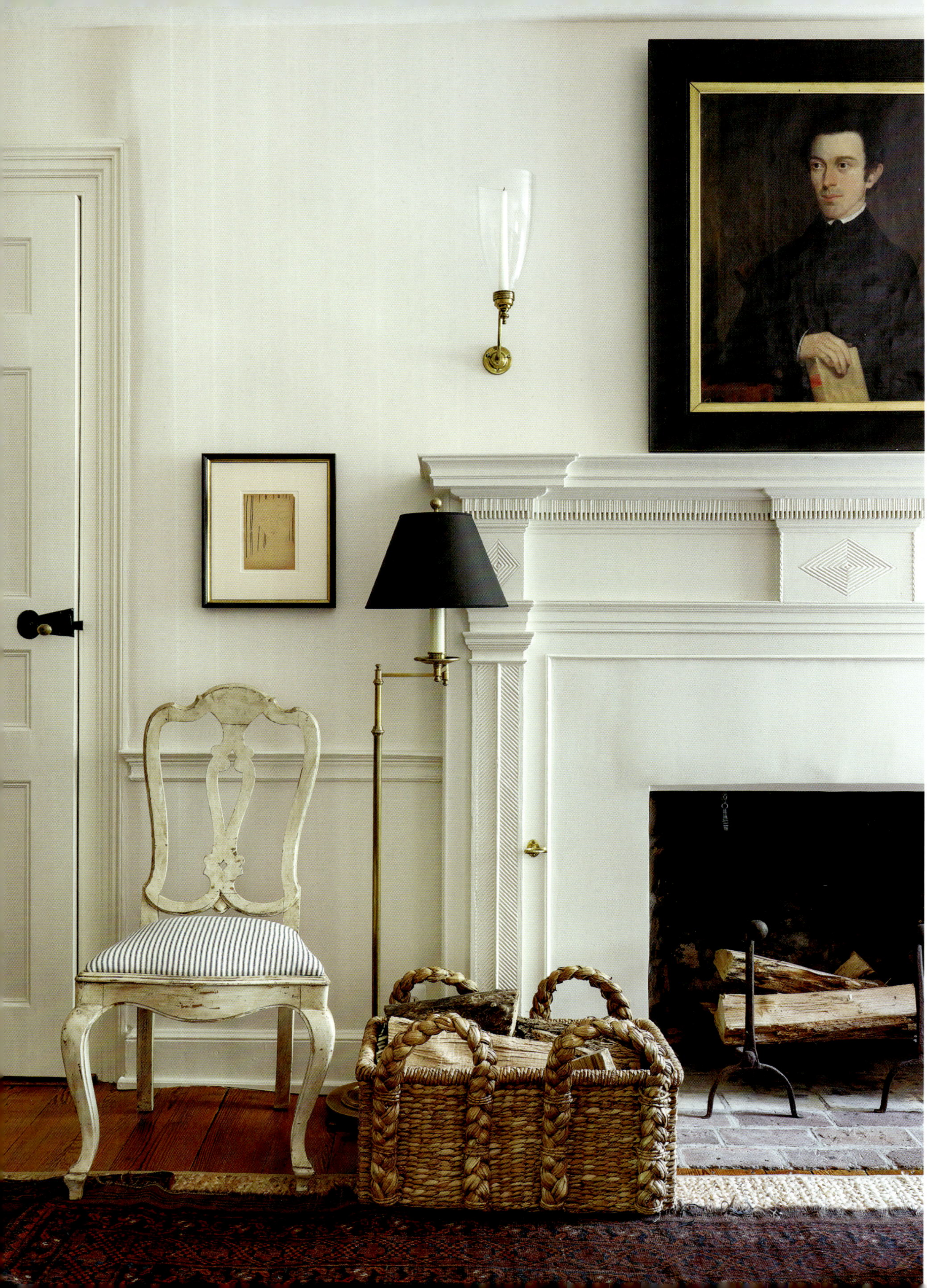

Opposite: A Swedish chair sits next to the fireplace in the primary bedroom. Right: The four-poster bed has curtains that soften the room. Artwork is playfully hung on the door.

THE ESSENTIALS

Above: The two upstairs guest rooms carry on the theme of portraits, books, and neutral tones, with the added nuance of wallpaper in one of the rooms (bottom row). Opposite: Josh takes every opportunity to showcase his vast art collection.

NINE HOMES FOR INSPIRATION

COURTNAY DANIELS

NEW YORK, NEW YORK

Courtnay Daniels has loved every minute of living in New York City, where she moved after marrying her husband, Gil Schaefer, an architect, in 2018. With an apartment a block away from Central Park, Courtnay has taken full advantage, walking six to nine miles in a loop in the park each day. "You start to see the same people. I like to walk counterclockwise so I can see people's faces," she says. "Walking in the park is such a nice way not to feel alone, because there is always someone there," she adds.

Courtnay began her design firm in San Francisco, where she and her family owned and lived in the house used for the television show *Full House*. It was an adventure, with a constant stream of tourists walking by to see the house—and even a few peering into the windows. For her New York home, she had envisioned a classic city apartment, but with enough space to be able to provide the same comforts of home that she grew up with for her two children. And this is precisely what she has achieved.

Designing their home was primarily Courtnay's project. Her husband helped with the structural puzzles, including how to put in central air conditioning, which

Above: In Courtnay's living room, a vignette of family photos finds a home on the corner table. Opposite: The dark green walls create a sense of drama in the entry of the home. The vintage stool is covered in ikat silk.

THE ESSENTIALS

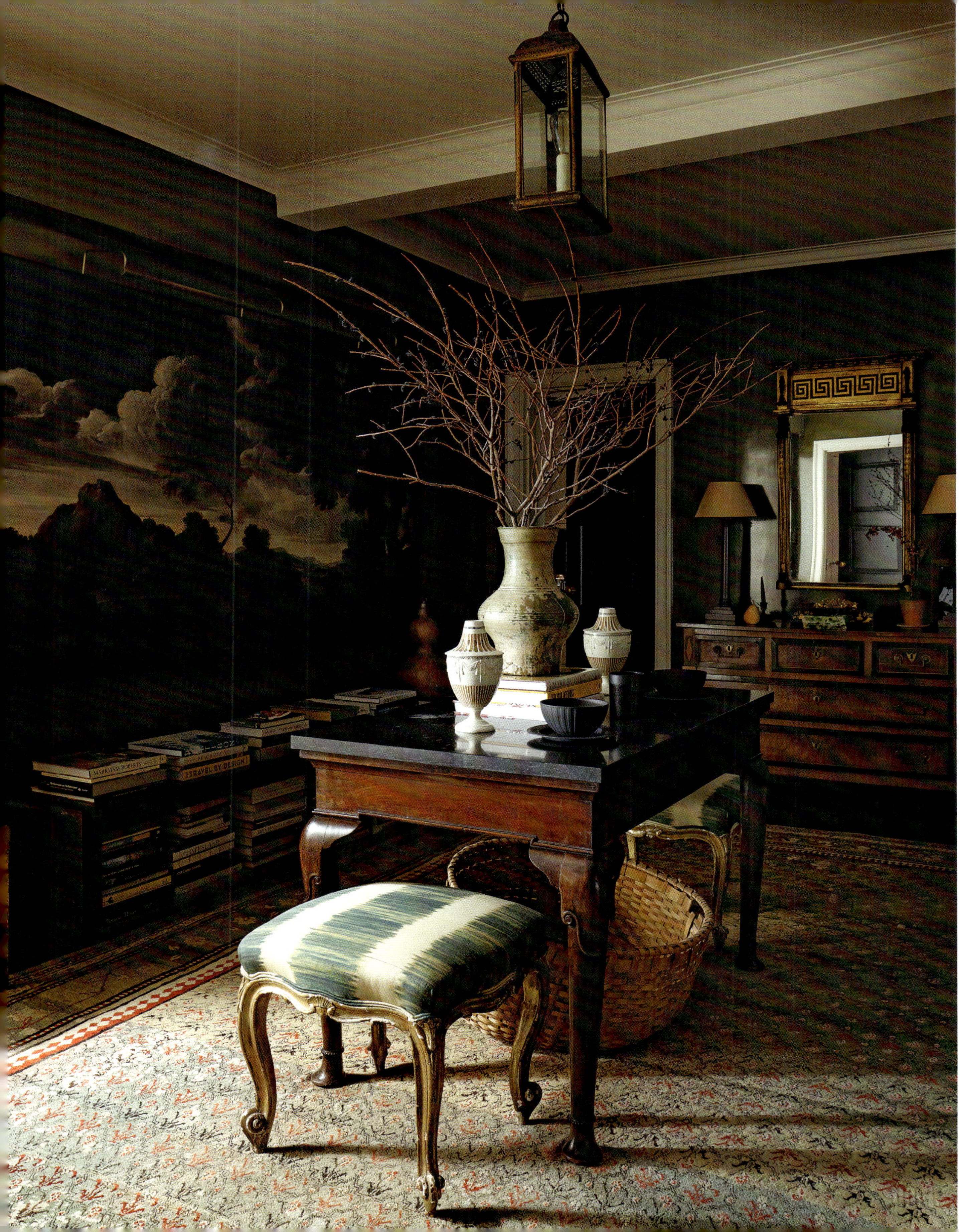
MARKHAM ROBERTS
TRAVEL BY DESIGN

The entryway features a seventeenth-century Italian landscape that fits in with the mood of the home. With a variety of sitting areas in the living room, there are multiple places for an intimate conversation.

THE ESSENTIALS

HENRY ADAMS
THE FAÇADES OF PARIS
Ellsworth Kelly
Plant Drawings

was a huge challenge. Courtnay conferred with Gil about the choices she was considering. She showed him the colors and fabrics she had pulled, and he gave input, offering a second set of trained eyes. "The only room Gil had no say in was the kitchen," Courtnay says.

Talking about how she planned the living space for the home, Courtnay says, "I always start in the living room." Unlike many designers, who start with a rug, Courtnay begins with a fabric and then branches out from there. "I knew I wanted a Lee Jofa chintz fabric that had been discontinued. I got them to bring it out of their archives to reprint it for me. From there, the rest of the house fell into place," she recalls. The living room has a series of sitting areas that all flow together. "I often gravitate to the living room to read," she says.

Above: The mantel is set off with a large oval mirror and a variety of topiaries on either side.
Right: The living room curtains are made with a fabric from Lee Jofa that had been discontinued, which Courtnay convinced them to bring back for her drapery.

"I knew I wanted a Lee Jofa chintz fabric that had been discontinued. I got them to bring it out of their archives to reprint it for me. From there, the rest of the house fell into place."

—COURTNAY DANIELS

Above: Throughout the home, Courtnay's art and photography collections line the walls. The dining room is distinguished by its darker paint color.

THE ESSENTIALS

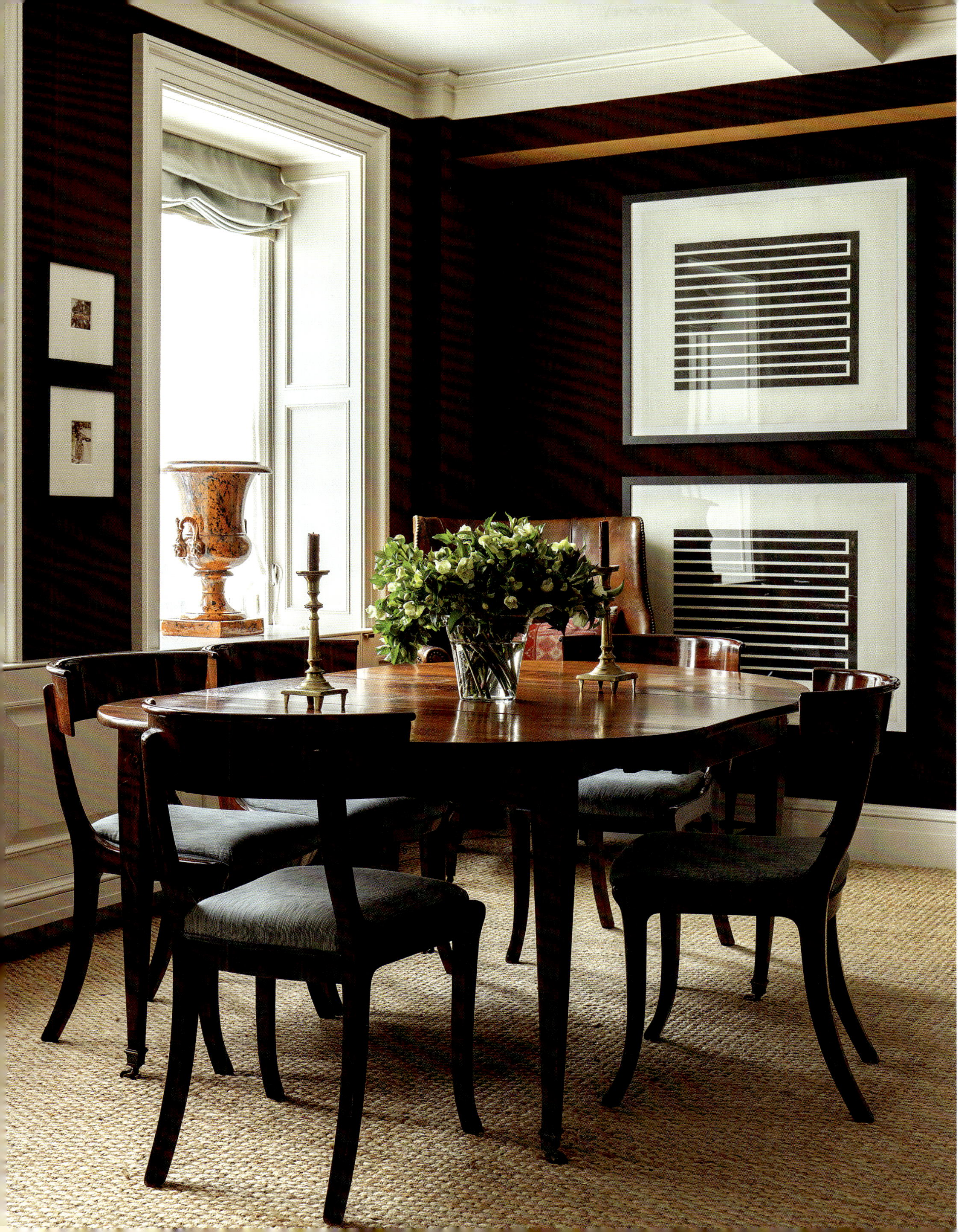

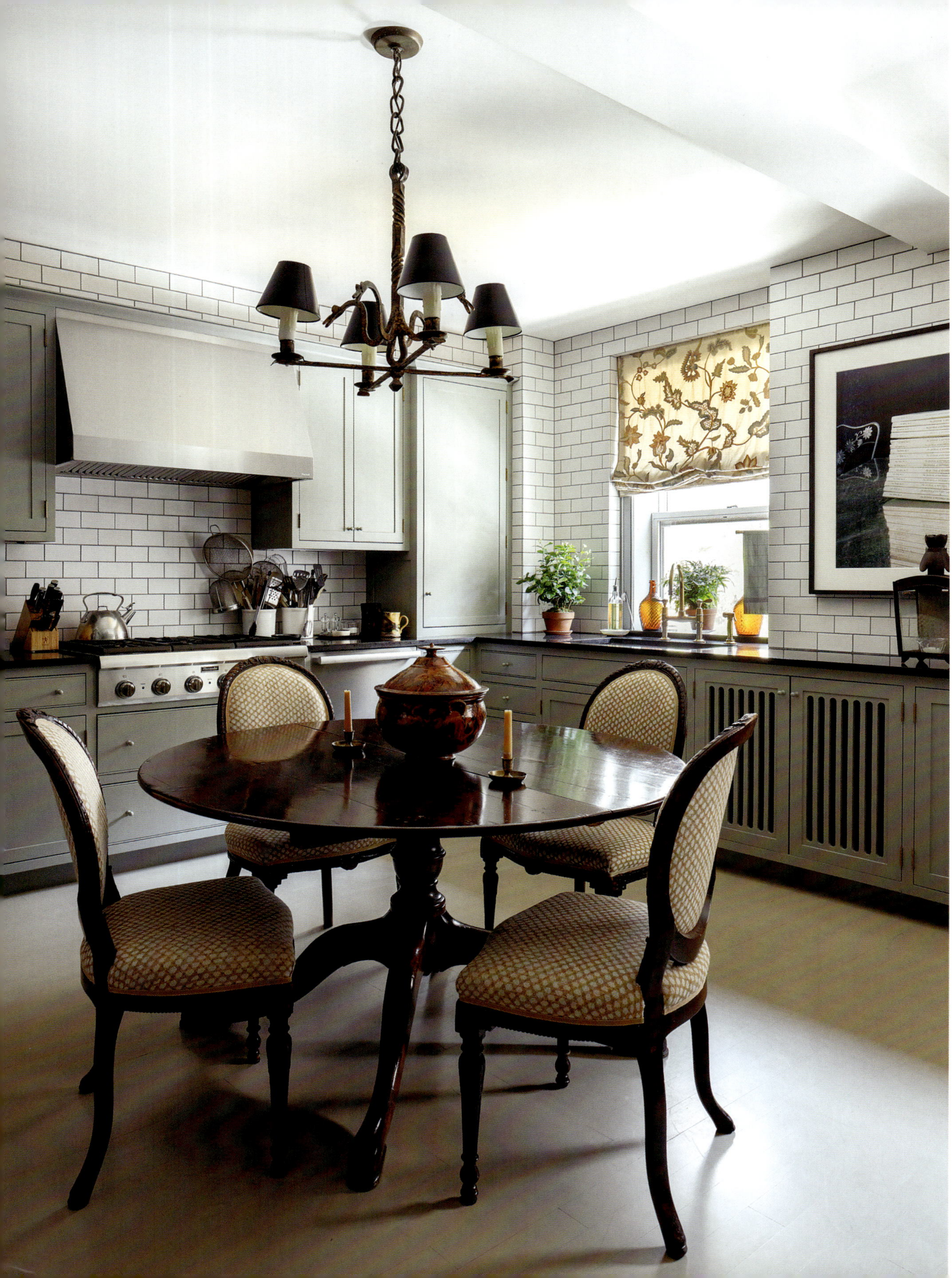

The kitchen is the gathering hub for the family. Courtnay loves to cook, and her kids and husband, Gil Schaefer, love to sit around the table while she is preparing meals.

Her photography collection is scattered throughout the home, but her way of displaying the photos alongside vignettes of accessories is personal and tells a story of the family. "My kids' art is mixed into the rooms. It makes me so happy," Courtnay says. For example, her daughter made a Day of the Dead whistle in school, and it sits next to a small Roman sculpture. "When you insert those personal items, it feels more used and authentic," she adds.

If there is a room that Courtnay is drawn to the most, it's her kitchen. "I love to cook. It's my stress reliever," she says. The whole family often gathers here. "We all love the kitchen, but we really use the entire home." Even within the confines of a Manhattan apartment, the considered design of the home allows for all of the family members to have privacy and also spend time together. Their home supports and reflects a strong family bond.

THE ESSENTIALS

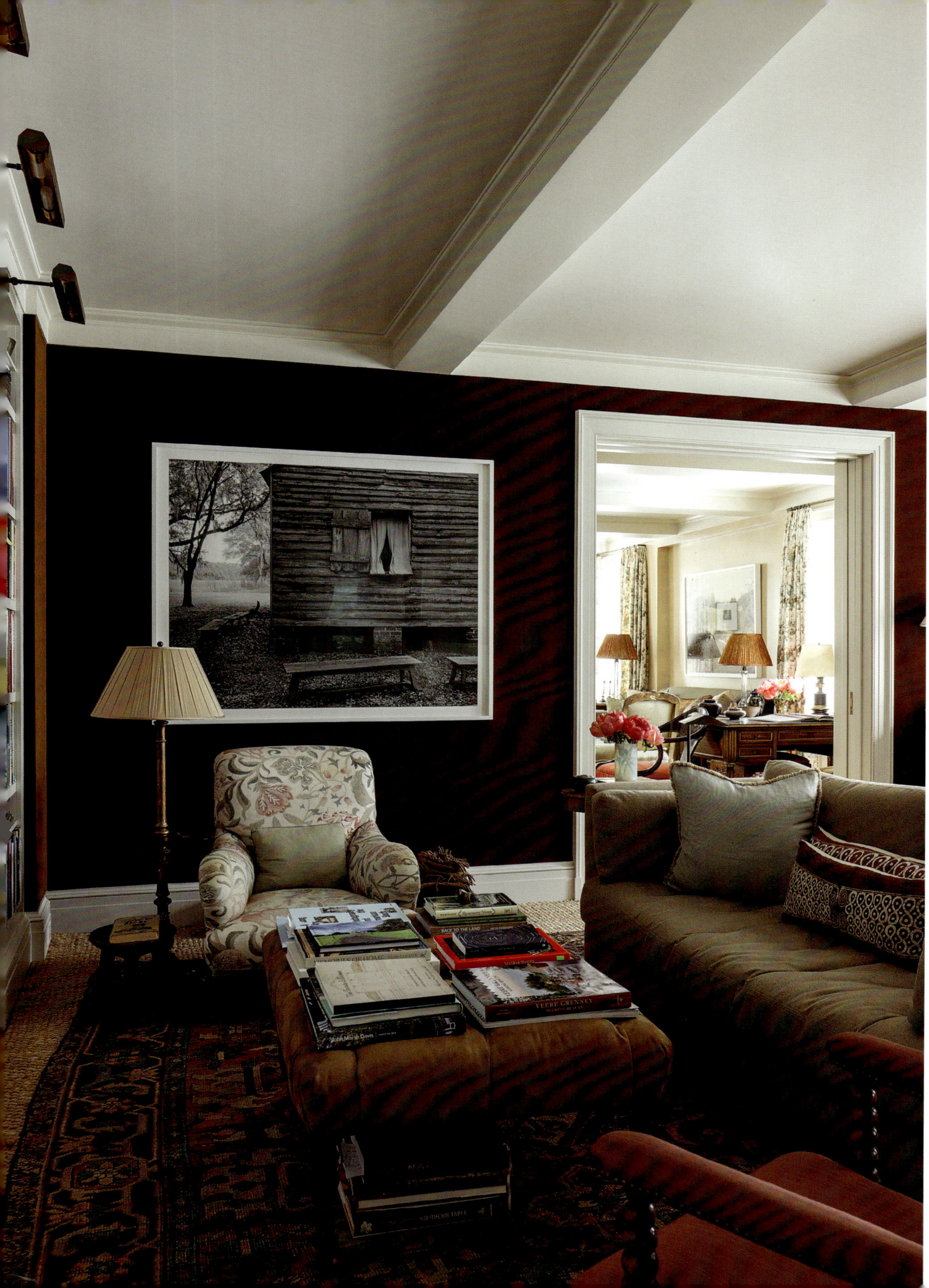

Opposite: The library is where you will often find Gil Schaefer working on his projects as an architect. Below: A small table is home to many of Courtnay's cherished objects.

NINE HOMES FOR INSPIRATION   253

LAN JAENICKE

SAN FRANCISCO, CALIFORNIA

during the pandemic, Lan Jaenicke, a fashion designer, made the decision to sell a condominium she had and find a different home in San Francisco. She and her partner, Anthony Perliss, loved their condo, which was featured in *Travel Home*, but they were ready for a home with more access to the outdoors. As luck would have it, Lan and her son, Alex, visited a house for sale in Pacific Heights that seemed perfect. And as a bonus, the house has a strong artistic, creative history that appealed to Lan.

In 1908, the outside of the home was featured in the *San Francisco Chronicle* when the owner—a fireman—painted a mural of Yosemite across the front of the house so he would feel closer to nature. In the 1920s, sculptor Erwin Winterhalter purchased the home and added an area for his art studio, which is now the dining and living room area. Under the area rug in the dining room is a large trap door that connects to the garage, which was useful for easy loading of Winterhalter's sculptures.

When Lan moved into the home, she felt it was important to keep the core integrity of the space intact, in particular preserving the features embodying the

Above: There are plaster reliefs embedded in the walls and fireplace surface. Opposite: Lan wears a dress she designed for her collection.

THE ESSENTIALS

NINE HOMES FOR INSPIRATION 255

Left: The small entry to the home is accentuated with a tile floor and wrought-iron chandelier. Opposite: The furnishings in the living room are kept to a minimum. Lan likes to change arrangements frequently to keep it fresh.

home's creative energy. A huge metal-paned window sweeps across a large portion of the wall and continues to arch onto the ceiling. There is a sculpture of a woman with a paint palette in her hand above the front door. But perhaps the most remarkable details of the space are the reliefs embedded in the walls.

Lan did make a few important changes, like removing the wrought iron that had been added to a balcony above the dining room. She painted the entire house white, ripped out the carpet on the steps and top floor, and plastered the fireplace.

How Lan uses the different spaces in the home is fluid and always changing. The first time we visited the home there was a defined dining room with a table and chairs around it. On our latest visit, she and Anthony had turned the room into a workspace

THE ESSENTIALS

NINE HOMES FOR INSPIRATION   257

The main living space has sweeping ceilings that have been painted to look like wood. There is a trap door in the floor so artwork by a former tenant could be lowered out.

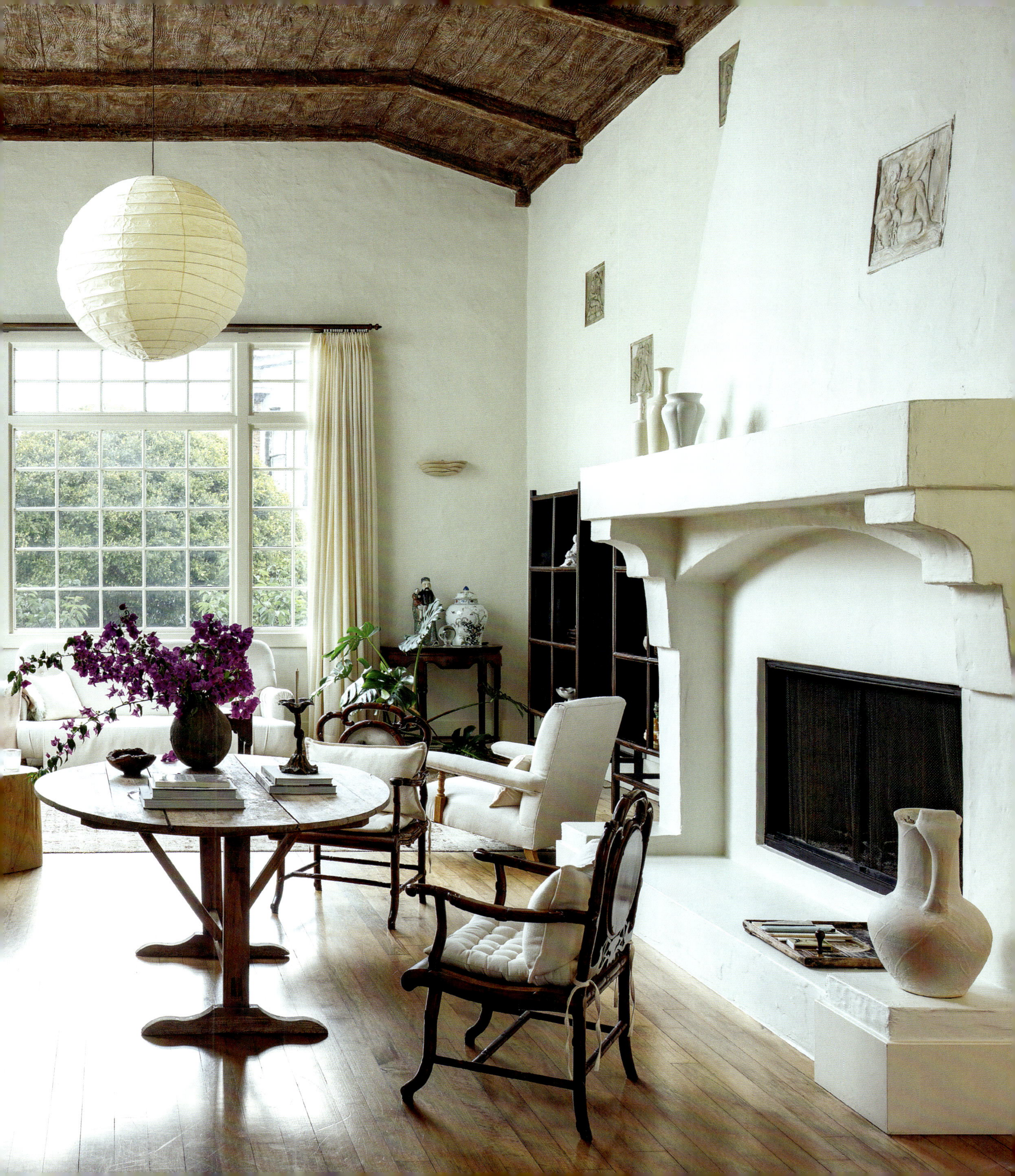

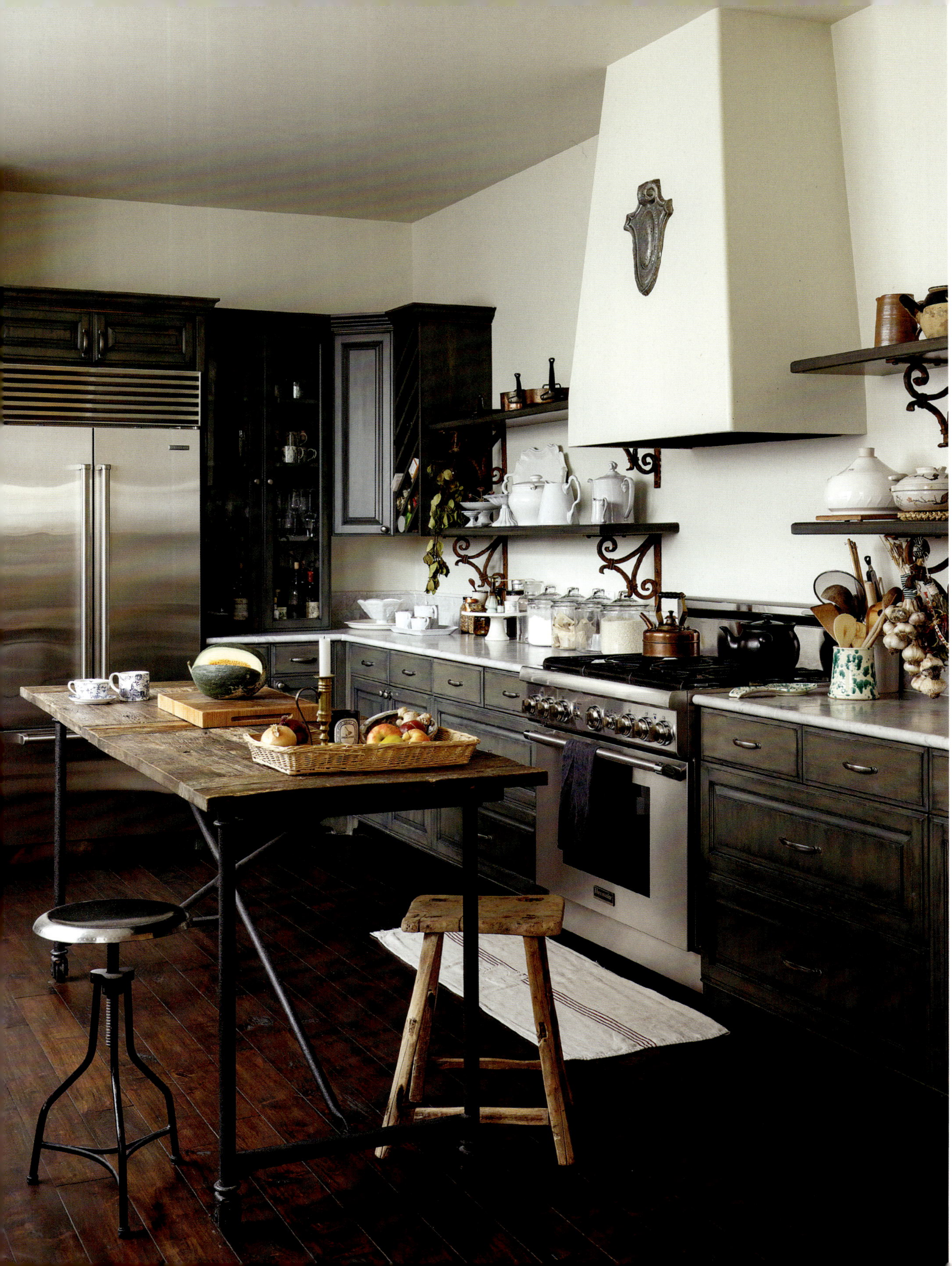

Opposite: Lan and her partner, Anthony, love to cook and entertain, and the expansive kitchen lends itself to gatherings. Above: A comfortable seating area is tucked away in the corner of the kitchen.

with a large table pushed against the wall. The room felt more open and airier. "The house should serve you in how you wish to live," Lan says. They have come to prefer smaller, more intimate gatherings instead of big parties.

As you move toward the back of the home, there is a spacious sofa and a table and chairs in the corner of the expansive kitchen. "We love gathering in this spot to unwind," says Lan. Continuing further back, you arrive at an antechamber to the principal bedroom. The mood is set with incense burning on a small table. As you open the door to the bedroom, there is a sense of calm. A double-ply cashmere bed covering is elegant and simple. Lan has a special ability to take fabric and drape it to enhance a room. Before you enter into the bedroom, there is white velvet fabric draped over a rod that falls perfectly and cocoons the room. "Since the bed is what you face walking into the room, I wanted a buffer and created it out of fabric. It's better feng shui," she explains.

THE ESSENTIALS

The upper level of the house is where Lan has her at-home studio. This is where many of her ideas for the clothing she designs are born. She practices her calligraphy here most days, and her work adorns one of the walls.

The layout of the home is perfect for her eighteen-year-old son. He has his own space, the entire bottom level, which includes a bedroom, bathroom, hangout area, and access through the garage. He enjoys having friends over.

The home that Lan and Anthony have aptly named "Atelier Lyon" after the street they live on is in very many ways a combination of all of her former homes, with elements collected over her lifetime, styled in a fresh way. "I don't really buy a lot. I prefer using what I have," says Lan. One thing to learn from Lan is to find a way to use all your spaces, moving furniture around frequently and adding new life to your home.

Above, from left: There is a small sitting area in the primary bedroom. The main bath provides a luxurious retreat from their busy lives. Opposite: In the bedroom, Lan used a thick cashmere from her clothing collection to create a warm bed cover.

THE ESSENTIALS

NINE HOMES FOR INSPIRATION 263

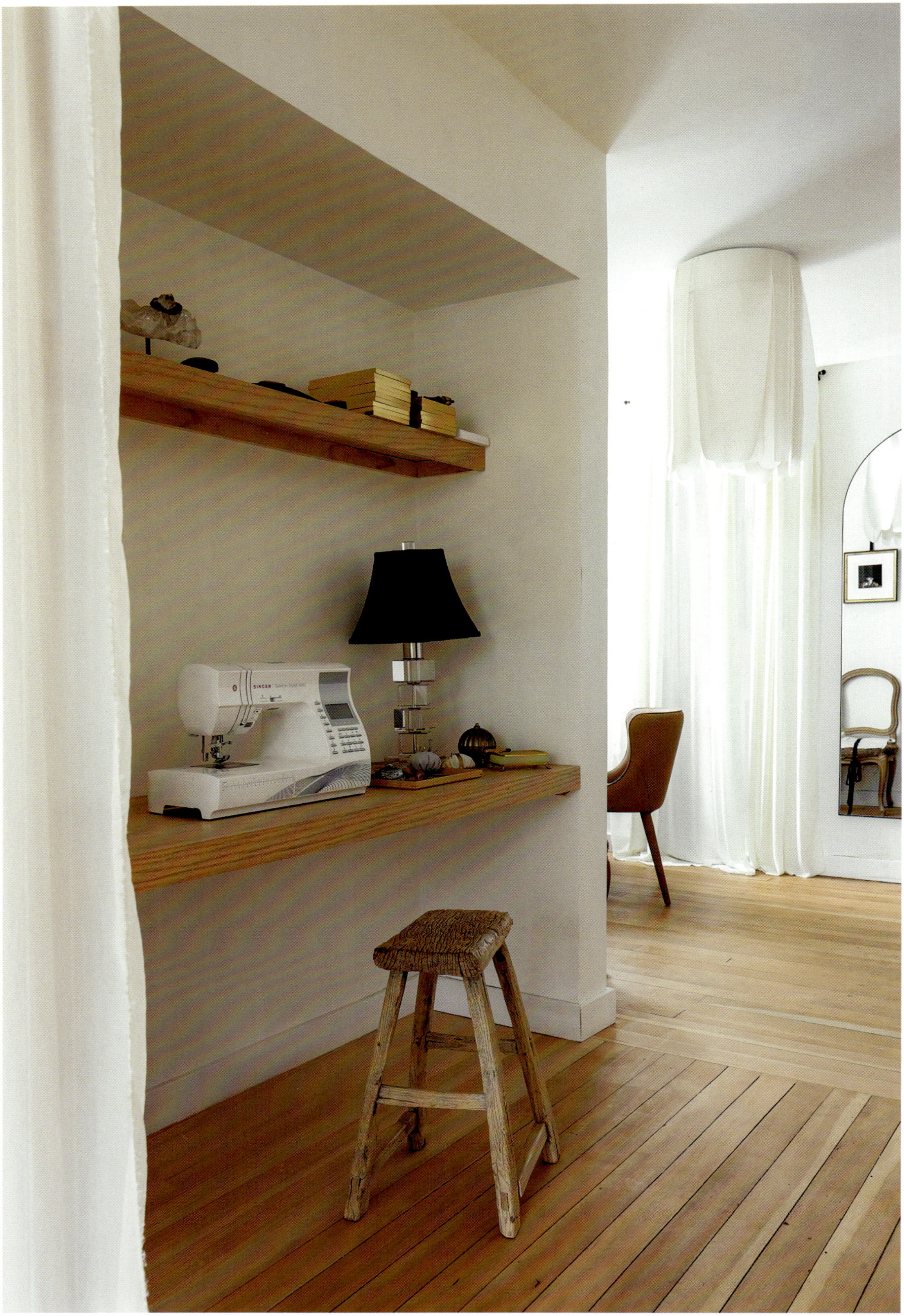
SINGER

"The house should serve you in how you wish to live."
—LAN JAENICKE

Opposite: Lan's workspace is on the top floor of the home, separated from the main level.
Above: The dining room is currently being used as a workspace for Anthony.

THE ESSENTIALS

AMY MEIER

RANCHO SANTA FE, CALIFORNIA

You could say Amy Meier was born into her career as an interior designer. Her father was in the furniture business for his entire career, and her mother was a seamstress who had a window treatment workroom. "I am sure that is where I got my love of fabric," says Amy. She has always found a way to be creative. She studied photography as an undergraduate and then moved on to Parsons School of Design. Ultimately, she turned to interior design because of the personal relationships she could build with clients and colleagues alike.

Amy and her husband, Kevin Meier, were drawn to Rancho Santa Fe, California, by its history and the equestrian charm of the village, located thirty minutes from San Diego. The house has its original Adirondack siding, also known as brainstorm siding. This is usually horizontal siding and has a live edge left on the revealed face. The house is a 1950s California Ranch, which they love and embrace. "We will continue to tweak and remodel, probably forever," Amy says.

Amy and her husband started their careers in New York and Boston, where they thought they would live forever. But fifteen years ago, fate had other plans for them.

Above: Amy tends to a horse in the front yard of her ranch-style home. Opposite: A vintage daybed sits below the beamed ceilings of her living room.

THE ESSENTIALS

NINE HOMES FOR INSPIRATION

267

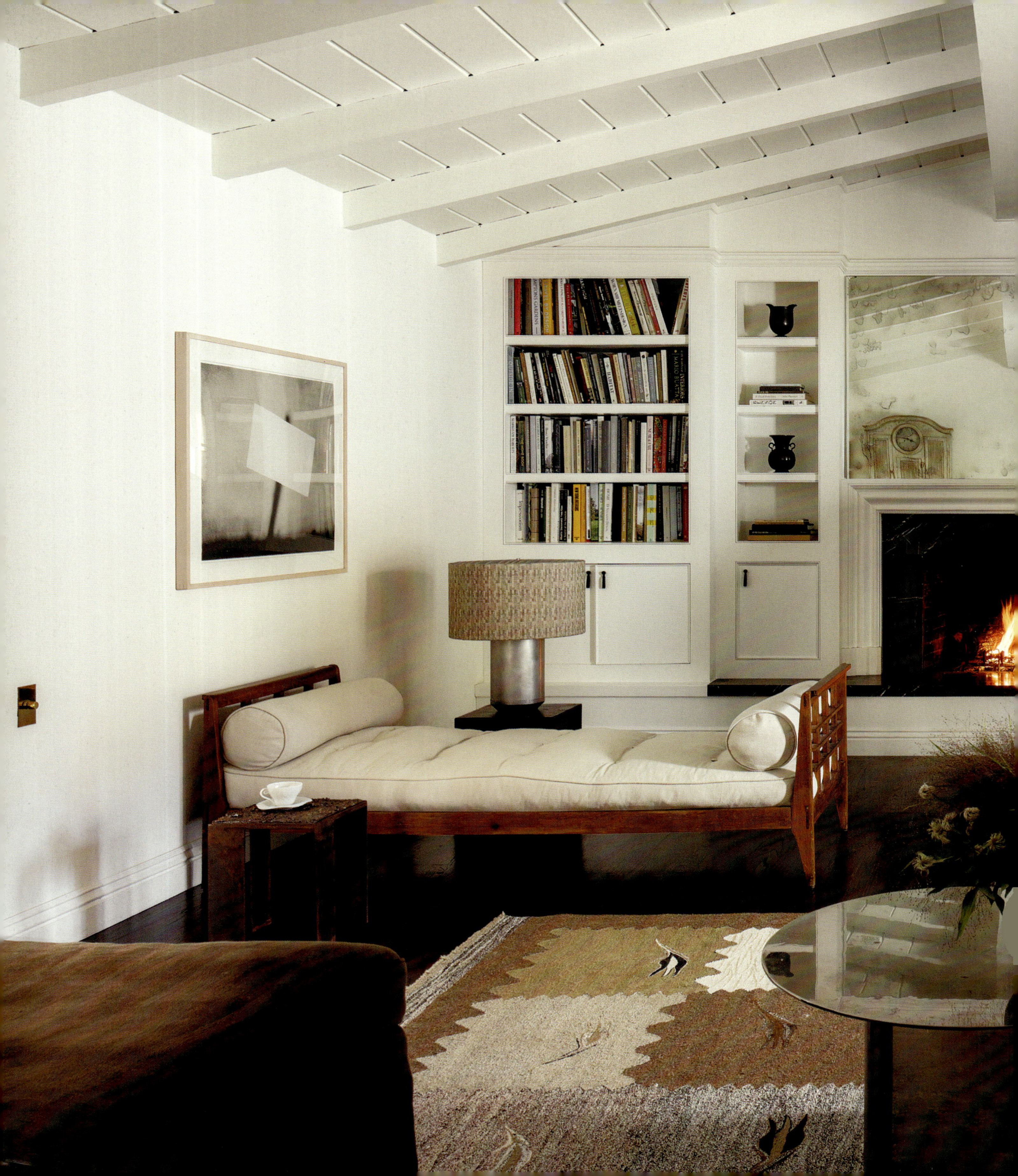

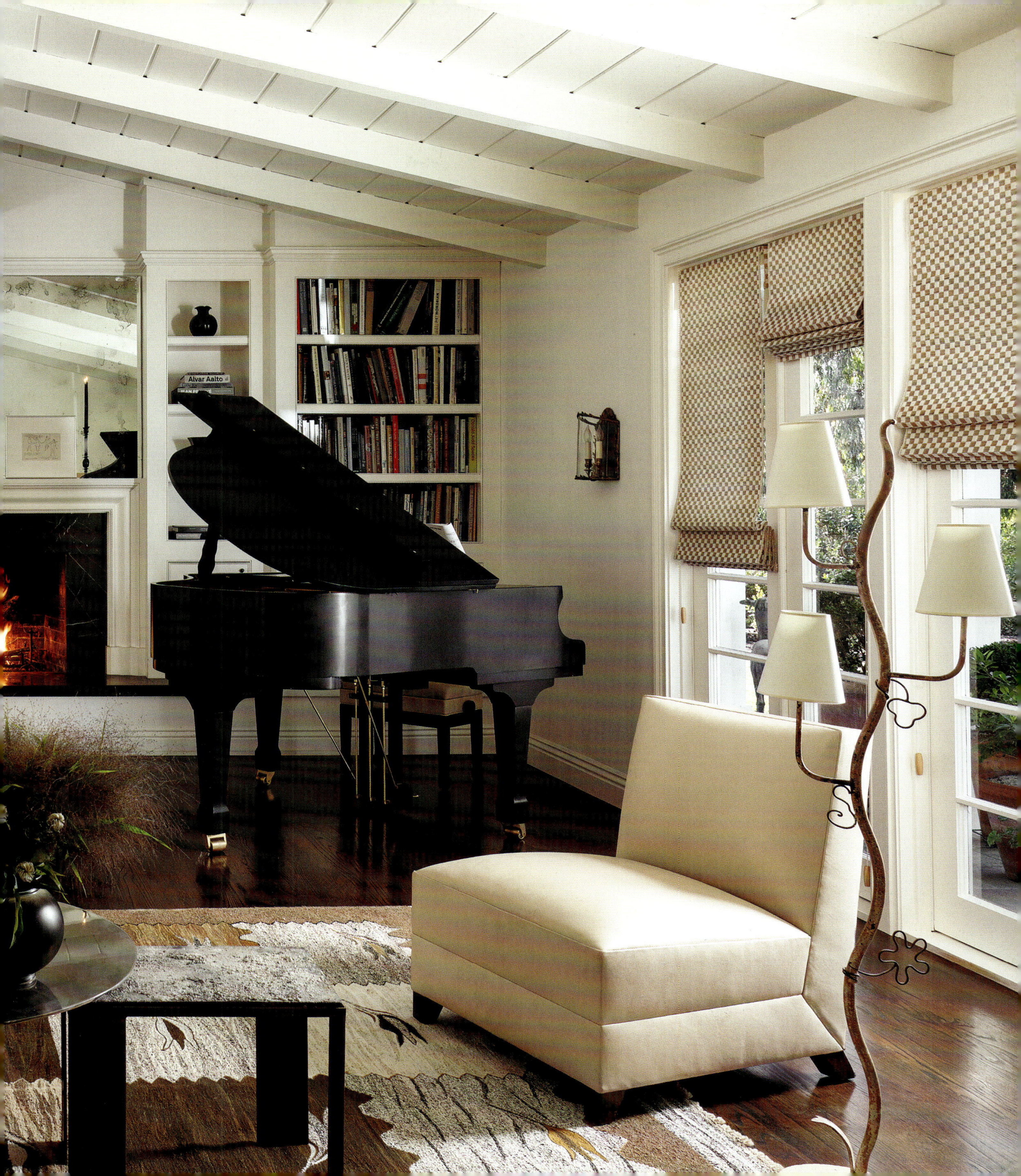
Alvar Aalto

Previous spread: In this full view of the living room, the fireplace takes center stage. Left: They kept the Dutch door and also have French doors that span the entire living room, creating an indoor-outdoor living space. Right: Tin portraits taken annually of Amy's children hang on the wall next to a vintage wood school crate that displays Emily Ridings's sculptural conch basket.

> "I believe that when you can cohesively fit together seemingly disparate or disjointed components like a puzzle, the vibrant and cohesive composition can create a home far more special than just the sum of its parts."
> —AMY MEIER

Kevin had a business opportunity in California, and so they decided to move to the West Coast for just a few years. The plan was always to go back to the Northeast, but they began to put down roots and now believe this is their forever home. The setting is the showstopper, so they wanted the house to be modest and inviting, to honor its simple charm and classic-leaning features, while also celebrating the natural environment.

As you enter the home, you see that Amy is inspired by the unique and authentic things that are handmade, well made, and rare or hard to find. "I am constantly learning and exploring different eras and genres, and I believe that when you can cohesively fit together seemingly disparate or disjointed components like a puzzle,

THE ESSENTIALS

NINE HOMES FOR INSPIRATION

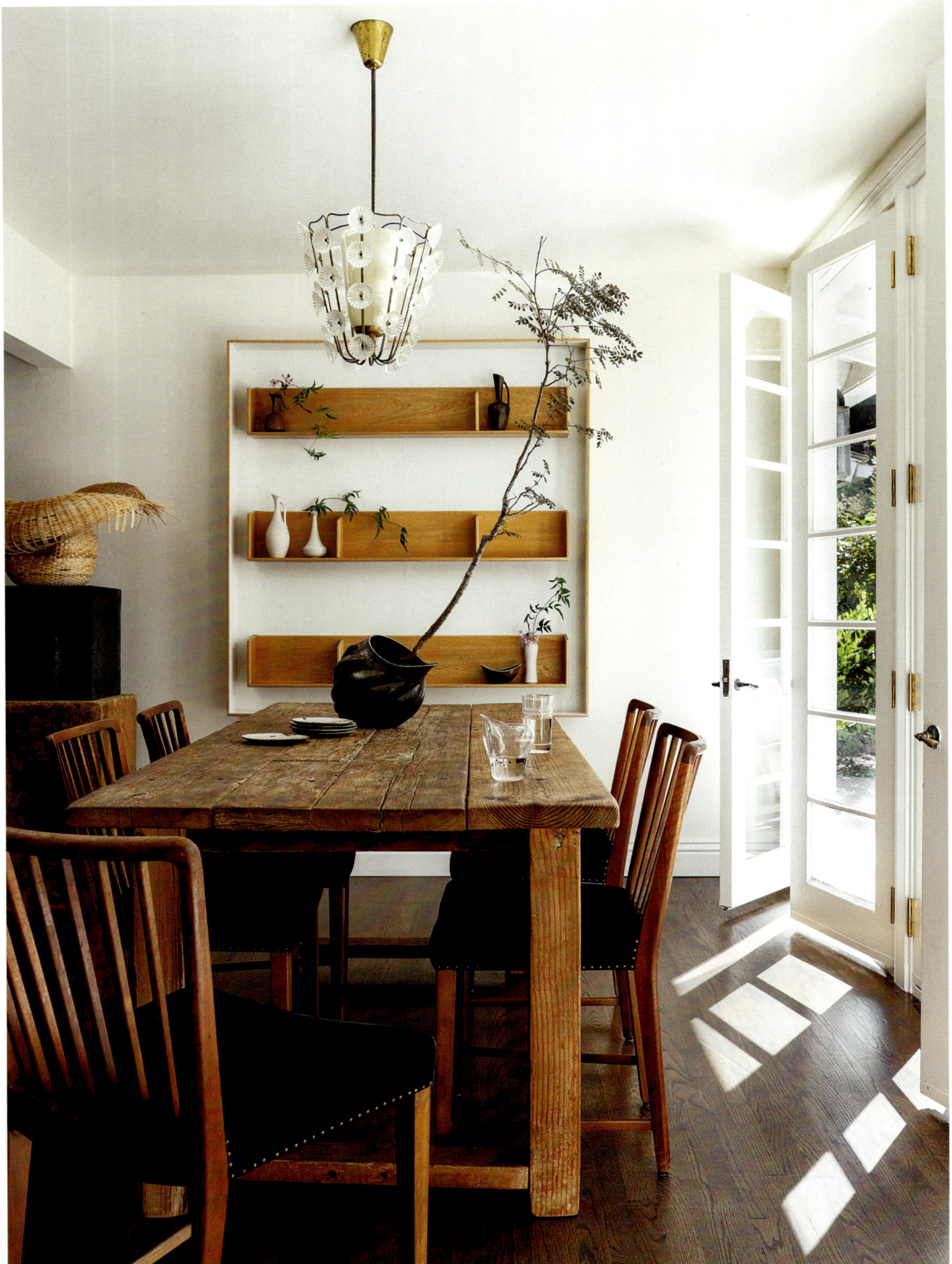

Opposite and above: The dining room is flooded with light from the three sets of French doors.

the vibrant and cohesive composition can create a home far more special than just the sum of its parts," she says.

There is a calm, restrained thread to Amy's home. With white walls and woven shades, the house feels connected to the beautiful light that streams through the windows. "The light, especially September through April, is so special," she notes.

Every piece Amy has chosen for the home seems to harmonize with the others. Tin photographs sit comfortably next to a pedestal with an exquisite handmade basket displayed on top. Although there is restraint, the house is anything but austere. There is simply care in everything brought into the home. Neutral tones in both furniture and window treatments add calm to the spaces.

Outdoors there are raised beds where plants grow that the family uses in their daily meals. The home is next to an equestrian center, and Amy loves to watch the horses from her home. The family is a busy one, with three spirited young girls. "Our home needs to be easy to live in, and therefore it needs to be well thought out," Amy says. She and her husband often say, "Keep everything that is needed and nothing that is not." A great mantra to live by!

THE ESSENTIALS

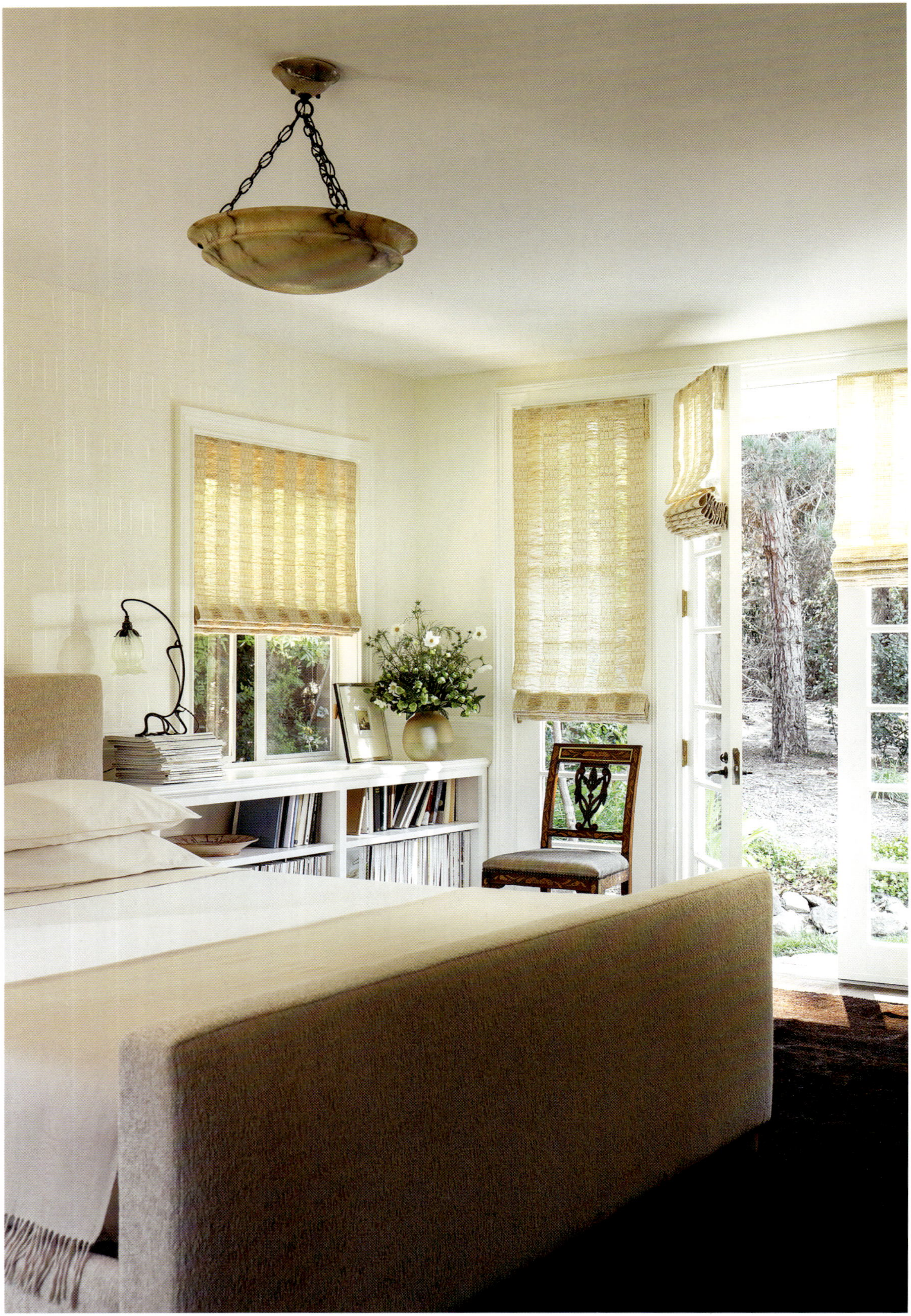

Opposite and right: Amy collaborated with Hartmann & Forbes to create woven shades that allow light to filter into the primary bedroom. Low bookshelves house her collection of books.

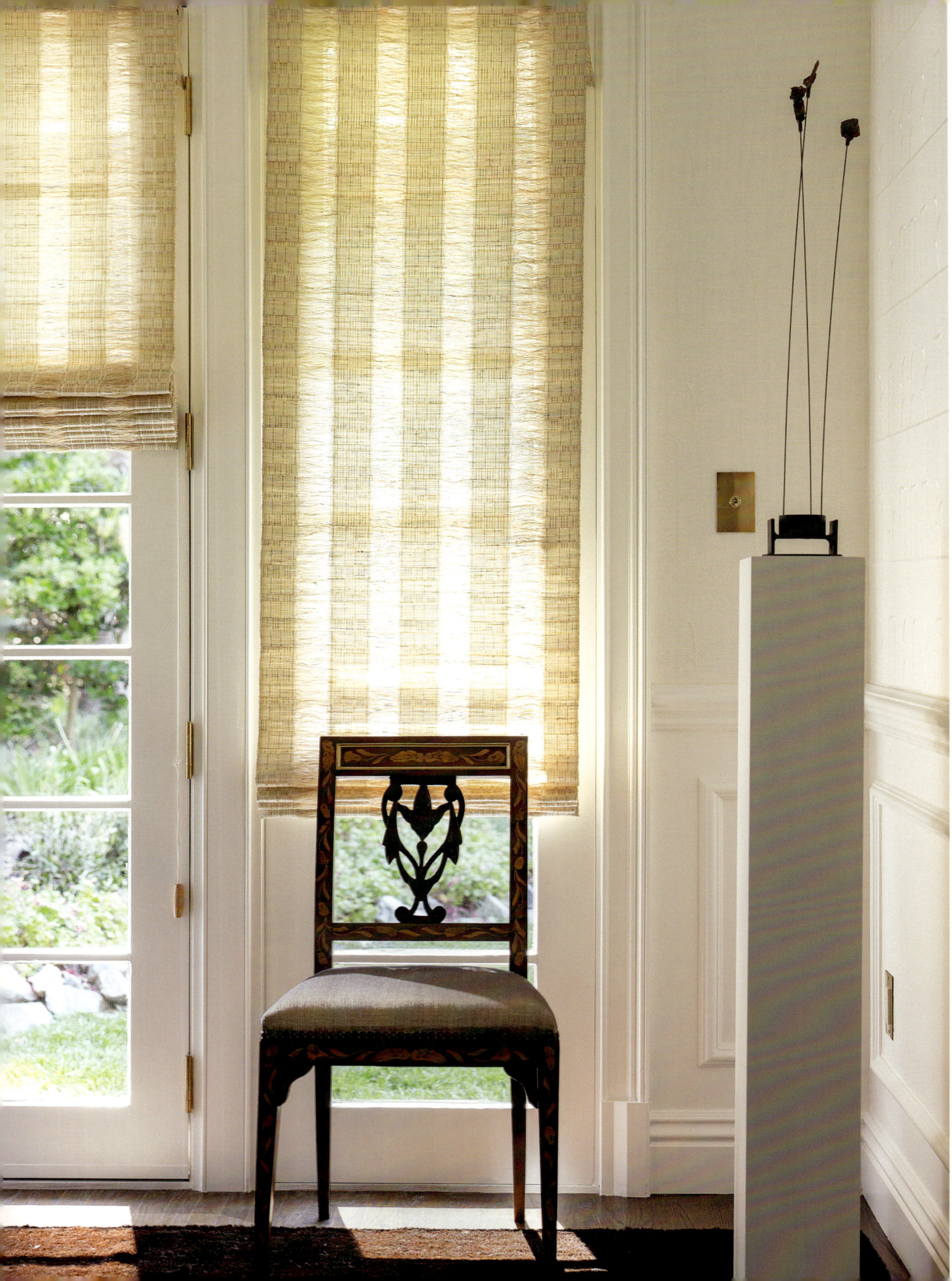

Opposite: Amy's primary bedroom delicately balances antiques and modern pieces.
Above: The primary bathroom showcases her custom-designed woven shade.

THE ESSENTIALS

Above: Gardens are cultivated in willow-branch raised beds made by Amy's husband, Kevin.
Opposite: The plentiful grounds provide ample area for outdoor living.

THE ESSENTIALS

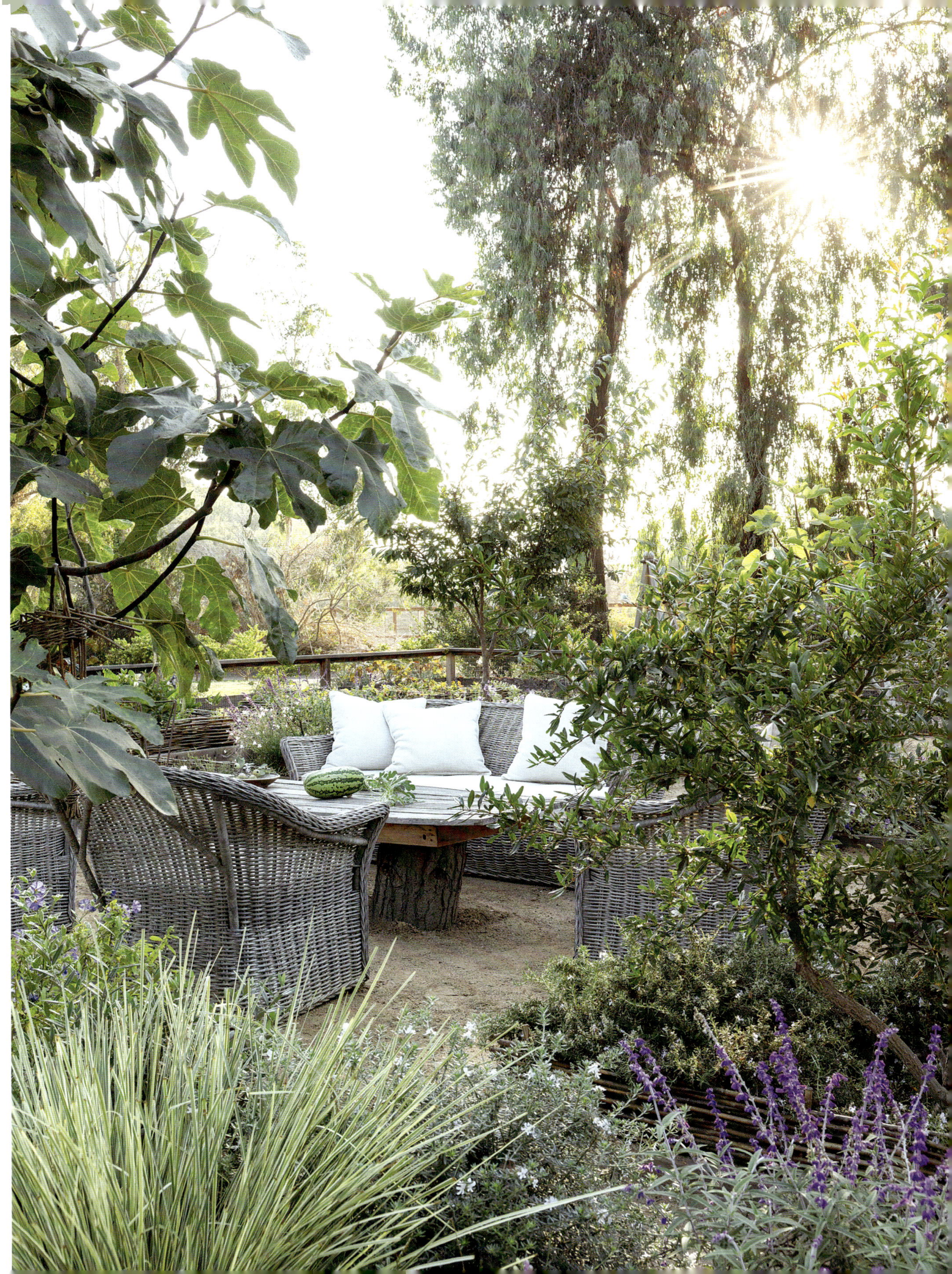

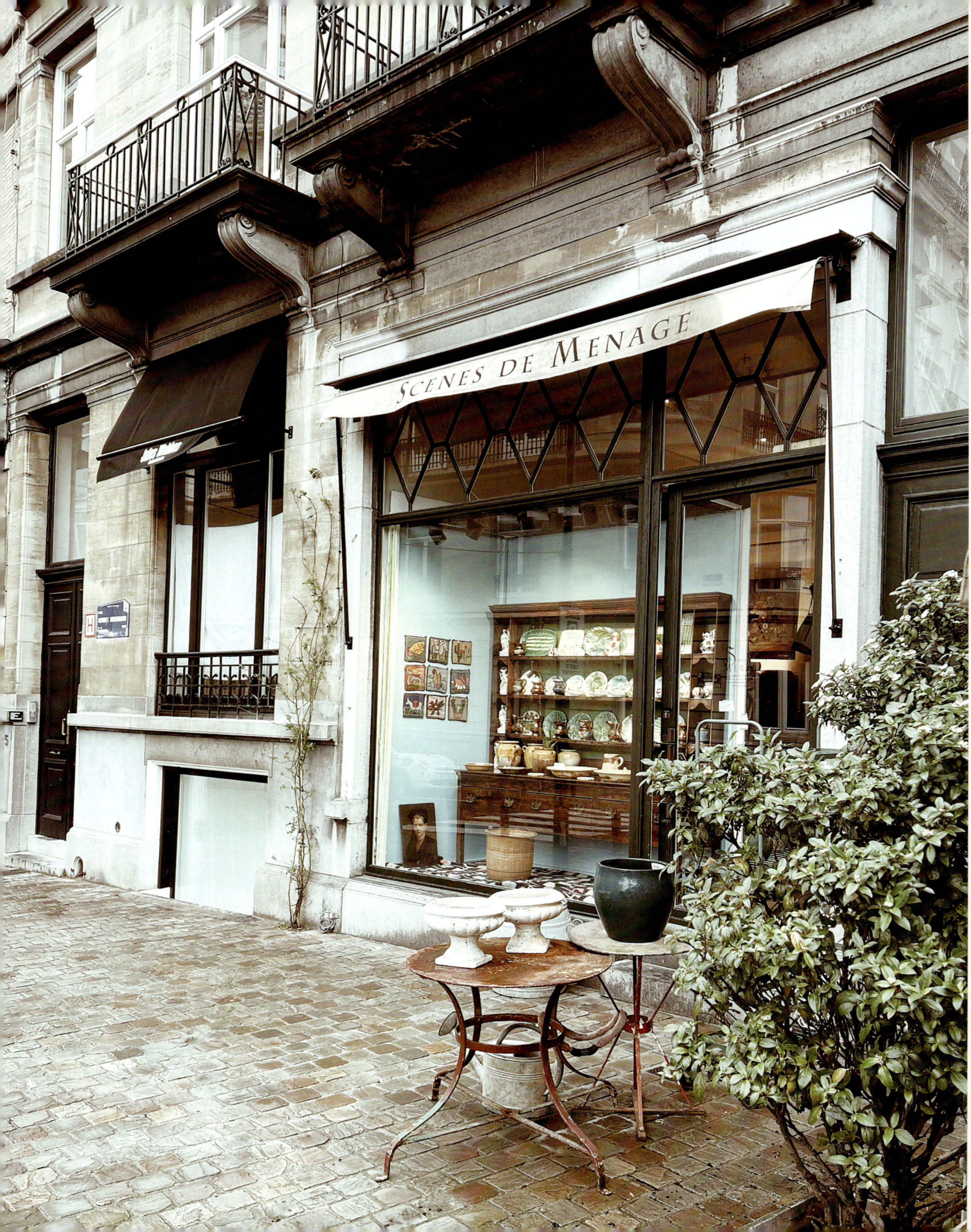
SCENES DE MENAGE

LITTLE BLACK BOOK

*We have been cultivating this list for years
and hope you find as much inspiration from these makers,
designers, brands, and shops as we have.*

Happy shopping!

Opposite: This inviting shop was one of our favorite finds on a trip to Brussels, Belgium.
Travel is when we often acquire our most prized pieces for our home.

HARDWARE

Brick and Mortar

DEVOL KITCHENS
devolkitchens.com
London, Bath, and Leicestershire, England; New York, New York
These three locations showcase the handcrafted items deVOL Kitchen manufactures—forged iron and brass pulls, ceramic light fixtures, and most importantly, their bespoke cabinetry.

HISTORISCHE BAUELEMENTE
historische-bauelemente.com
Marwitz, Germany
A great source for architectural pieces, old doors, and other items for building and replacing structures in your home.

LIZ'S ANTIQUE HARDWARE
lahardware.com
Los Angeles, California
Floor-to-ceiling mecca of vintage hardware and lighting for the home.

REJUVENATION HARDWARE
rejuvenation.com
Portland, Oregon
This was our go-to place for lighting and hardware in Portland when we lived there. It also has a great selection of vintage parts for the home. Everything can also be found online.

Online

ART AND FORGE
artandforge.com

CLASSIC BRASS
classic-brass.com

EMTEK
emtek.com

HOUSE OF ANTIQUE HARDWARE
houseofantiquehardware.com

ROCKY MOUNTAIN HARDWARE
rockymountainhardware.com

SIGNATURE HARDWARE
signaturehardware.com

OUTDOOR LIVING

Brick and Mortar

EMILY JOUBERT HOME & GARDEN
emilyjoubert.com
San Francisco, Woodside, and Montecito, California
Excellent source for home and garden items, including antiques, design books, and smalls.

MICHAEL TRAPP
shopmichaeltrapp.com
West Cornwall, Connecticut
Antiques and architectural fragments from Michael Trapp's travels (see pages 80–81).

TERRAIN
shopterrain.com
See website for various locations
Houseplant paradise with other unique items for the garden and home.

THE WELL
instagram.com/thewellsummerland
Summerland, California
Art and garden items from around the world.

Online

FRONTGATE
frontgate.com

JANUS ET CIE
janusetcie.com

TEXTILES, COLOR & PATTERN

Brick and Mortar

ANTOINETTE POISSON
antoinettepoisson.com
Paris, France
Wallpapers, fabrics, ceramics, interiors, and perfumes.

CLOTH HOUSE
clothhouse.com
London, England
A true treasure trove of exquisite fabrics. You'll find something unique to bring home to make into a pillow.

THE CLOTH SHOP
theclothshop.net
London, England
This mother-and-son team has a curated selection of fabric, wool blankets, items for the kitchen, trims, and more. Worth a stop when you are in the Portobello neighborhood.

THE GREAT ENGLISH OUTDOORS
greatenglish.co.uk
Hay-on-Wye, Wales
Located in a town famous for its bookstores and book festival, this store has an excellent collection of Welsh woven and woolen items for the home.

HEATHER TAYLOR HOME
heathertaylorhome.com
Los Angeles, California
Looking for gingham for your home? Heather Taylor Home has beautiful textiles handcrafted in Chiapas, Mexico. The color combinations are stunning.

HEIR LOOMS RUGS + INTERIORS
heirlooms.co
West Palm Beach, Florida
One-of-a-kind vintage and antique rugs from around the world.

IKSEL DECORATIVE ARTS
iksel.com
Paris, France
If you are in search of the perfect wallpaper print, this is where you'll find it.

LES INDIENNES
lesindiennes.com
Hudson, New York
Retail outlet of the revered Les Indiennes hand-block printed fabrics.

NUSHKA
nushka.co.uk
London, England
On the hunt for patterned lampshades? This shop is filled to the brim with every size, color, and pattern imaginable. Most of the stunning lampshades are made with Indian saris.

PENNY MORRISON
pennymorrison.com
London, England
Penny's shop not only houses her fabric collection but also showcases other designers' textiles. It's also filled with her collection of lampshades and pottery.

ROBERT KIME
robertkime.com
London, England
This must-visit shop off Pimlico Road that has timeless textiles, wallpaper, custom lampshades, and antiques.

SHIPROCK SANTA FE
shiprocksantafe.com
Santa Fe, New Mexico
The best collection of historic Navajo rugs, blankets, and Indigenous American jewelry. Owned by a fifth-generation dealer who was raised on the Navajo Nation and formerly ran four trading posts.

SOANE BRITAIN
soane.co.uk
London, England
Thoughtfully made Lighting, textiles and wallpaper. Every single piece is made in Britain, using a network of craftsman and workshops that excel in traditional crafts.
(see pages 110–111)

TULU TEXTILES
tulutextiles.com
Istanbul, Turkey
If you love textiles, both vintage and modern of the best quality, you must visit this shop.

Online

ALICE SERGEANT
alicesergeant.com
(see endpapers)

BENNISON FABRICS
bennisonfabrics.com

CAROLINA IRVING TEXTILES
carolinairvingtextiles.com

CW STOCKWELL
cwstockwell.com

DÉCORS BARBARES
decorsbarbares.com/fabrics

DE GOURNAY
degournay.com

ELIZABETH EAKINS
elizabetheakins.com

GUY GOODFELLOW COLLECTION
guygoodfellowcollection.com

HOLLAND AND SHERRY
hollandandsherry.com

HOWE AT 36 BOURNE STREET
36bournestreet.com/product-category/textiles

Above: Robert Kime

LITTLE BLACK BOOK
284

TEXTILES, COLOR & PATTERN (cont.)

Online

IKSEL DECORATIVE ARTS
iksel.com

JASPER TEXTILES
michaelsmithinc.com

JOHN ROBSHAW
johnrobshaw.com

KATHARINE POLE
FRENCH ANTIQUES & TEXTILES
katharinepole.com
(see pages 86–89)

KATHRYN M IRELAND
TEXTILES & DESIGN
kathrynireland.com

KETTLEWELL COLLECTION
kettlewellcollection.com

LAKE AUGUST
lakeaugust.com/collections/textiles

LAUREN LIESS
shop.laurenliess.com/collections/textiles

LEAH O'CONNELL DESIGN
TEXTILES & WALLCOVERINGS
leahoconnelltextiles.com
(see pages 28–31)

LES INDIENNES
lesindiennes.com

LISA FINE TEXTILES
lisafinetextiles.com

MCLAURIN & PIERCY
mclaurinandpiercy.com

MICHAEL S SMITH INC
michaelsmithinc.com

MOLLY MAHON
mollymahon.com/collections/fabric

MORRIS & CO.
wmorrisandco.com/uk/

NAMAY SAMAY
namaysamay.com

NICOLE FABRE DESIGNS
nicolefabredesigns.com

PENNY MORRISON
pennymorrison.com

PETER DUNHAM
TEXTILES & WALLPAPER
peterdunhamtextiles.com

RAOUL TEXTILES
raoultextiles.com

ROBERT KIME
robertkime.com/collection/fabrics

ROSE CUMMING
wellstextiles.com/collections/rose-cumming

ROSE TARLOW
rosetarlow.com

SARAH VANRENEN
sarahvanrenen.com/products/category/fabrics

SCHUYLER SAMPERTON TEXTILES
schuylersampertontextiles.com

SERENA DUGAN STUDIO
serenadugan.com

SISTER PARISH DESIGN
sisterparishdesign.com

SUSAN CONNOR NEW YORK
susanconnorny.com/collections/fabric

TULU TEXTILES
tulutextiles.com

WALTER G
walter-g.com

LIGHTING

Online

ALLIED MAKER
alliedmaker.com

APPARATUS
apparatusstudio.com

CHRISTOPHER BUTTERWORTH
christopherbutterworth.com

FERM LIVING
fermliving.com

HECTOR FINCH
hectorfinch.com

HOME & FOUND
homeandfound.com/finds
(see pages 100–103)

LAWSON FENNING
lawsonfenning.com

MADE BY JIM LAWRENCE
jim-lawrence.co.uk

NOTARY
notaryceramics.com

PERROTINE
perrotine.co

POOKY
pooky.com

URBAN ELECTRIC & CO
urbanelectric.com

VISUAL COMFORT
visualcomfort.com

Opposite: Christopher Butterworth

FURNITURE & ACCESSORIES

Brick and Mortar

Opposite: Brownrigg

A LA TURCA
alaturcahouse.com
Istanbul, Turkey
This town house is filled with treasures you won't find anywhere else—kilims, old globes, art, furniture. Plan at least a few hours to explore.

ALDER & CO.
alderandcoshop.com
Hudson, New York
This gem is beautifully tucked into a town house in Hudson, New York. It's filled to the brim with clothes, accessories, and smalls for your home.

ANECDOTE
shopanecdote.com
La Grange, Illinois
This shop offers curated design elements for your home, including furniture, home decor, art, and more.

ANTIQUES OF SOUTH WINDERMERE
instagram.com/antiquessouthwindermere
Charleston, South Carolina
Timeless antiques drawn from regional sources.

AXS DESIGN
axsdesign.fr
Paris, France
Curated antiques shop for the home.

BOX ROAD
boxroad.net
Albuquerque, New Mexico
A perfect mix of antique furniture, transferware and vintage smalls for the home.

BROWNRIGG
brownrigg-interiors.co.uk
Tetbury, England
For timeless antiques for the home, this is worth a visit. This shop is one of our favorites for unique antiques. Tetbury is a wonderful town to visit.

CHELSEA ANTIQUES
sonomacounty.com/profiles/chelsea-antiques
Petaluma, California
A regular spot we visit a few times a month for light fixtures, oil paintings, and other bits and bobs for the home.

CHOOSING KEEPING STATIONERY
choosingkeeping.com
London, England
A bespoke stationery that makes our favorite handmade books with cloth bindings.

THE COLLECTIVE SANTA FE
thecollectivesantafe.com
Santa Fe, New Mexico
The ultimate destination for antiques in Santa Fe.

COMER & CO.
comerandco.com
Charlottesville, Virginia
This shop is filled with antique furniture, gold-leaf mirrors, and an abundance of decorative items.

COURTYARD ANTIQUES
antiquesintents.co.uk
Presteigne, Wales
This shop has a one-of-a-kind selection of china, paintings, and other small accessories. Check their website as they also go to tent shows around the UK.

DEAN ANTIQUES
deanantiques.co.uk
Tetbury, England
This shop specializes in pieces by Howard & Sons, as well as working with local craftsmen to craft one-of-a-kind pieces.

DEWILDE HAUS ANTIQUITIES
dewildehaus.com
Roseville, California
A curated collection of antique and vintage furnishings for your home.

DIANI LIVING
dianiboutique.com/
Santa Barbara, California
This Santa Barbara shop custom pillows, linens, clothing, accessories, and uniquely sourced pieces from around the world.

DURHAM HOUSE ANTIQUES
durhamhouseantiques.co.uk
Stow-on-the-Wold, England
In the heart of the Cotswolds, this antique shop has something for everyone.

ELSIE GREEN
elsiegreen.com
Concord, California
One of the best sources in the United States for French vintage home items. (see pages 50–53)

EMILY JOUBERT HOME & GARDEN
emilyjoubert.com
San Francisco, Woodside, and Montecito, California
Excellent source for home and garden items, including antiques, design books, and smalls.

ERICA TANOV
ericatanov.com
Berkeley, California
Beautifully curated clothing and home items designed by Erica Tanov along with wares from other carefully chosen designers and artists.

FOUND BY MAJA
foundbymaja.com
San Francisco, California
Emerald green and turquoise tones dominate this shop, where you can find vintage items from around the world.

GALERIE DES MINIMES
galeriedesminimes.com
Brussel, Belgium
Antique store with unique items that range from the fifteenth century to mid-century modern.

LITTLE BLACK BOOK
287

LITTLE BLACK BOOK
288

FURNITURE & ACCESSORIES (cont.)

Brick and Mortar

LA GALLERIE, BY LAURA GONZALEZ
lauragonzalez.fr
Paris, France
Furniture and accessories with unique combinations of motifs and materials.

GARDE
gardeshop.com
Los Angeles, California; Dallas, Texas; New York, New York
The owners are always finding the next wave of beautiful new objects.

GLENN BAN DESIGN
glennban.com
East Hampton, New York
We fell completely in love with his studio where Glenn sells beautiful vintage furniture and accessories. (see pages 212–225)

HELEN STOREY ANTIQUES
helenstoreyantiques.com
Charlottesville, Virginia
It's impossible to leave this shop without a treasure. Each item is carefully sourced.

HOLLYWOOD AT HOME
hollywoodathome.com
Los Angeles, California; New York, New York
A showroom that houses all of our favorite textile designers as well as one-of-a-kind pieces.

HOMESONG MARKET
homesongmarket.com
Kansas City, Missouri
A mindful home goods shop that honors the earth and elevates the everyday through simplicity.

HOWE LONDON
howelondon.com
London, England
Antiques and bespoke furniture items with a timeless design and functionality.

HUDSON GRACE
hudsongracesf.com
Check website for various locations
Timeless décor for those who love to entertain. A great source for design books and antique silver.

JAMB
jamb.co.uk
London, England
Exquisitely restored antiques, fireplace mantels, and lighting. Don't forget to go to the basement.

JAMES ILES ANTIQUES
jamesilesantiques.com
London, England
Beautiful antiques at reasonable prices and the kindest owner.

JAYSON HOME
jaysonhome.com
Chicago, Illinois
A beloved vintage and modern store in Chicago. They purchase items from the far corners of the globe.

JEFFERSON WEST
jeffersonwest.com
A must stop in Los Angeles. This shop is filled to the brim with wonderfully curated antique furnishings and accessories.

JOHN DERIAN
johnderian.com
New York, New York; Provincetown, Massachusetts
A rich trove of furniture and houseware, famous for decoupage, filled to the brim.

JUXTAPOSITION HOME
juxtaposition.com
Newport Beach, California
A collection of industrial pieces, furniture, textiles, rugs, and natural elements for your home.

KRB NEW YORK
krbnyc.com
New York, New York
Located on the Upper East Side, the boutique from Kate Rheinstein Brodsky offers a curated collection of antiques, unique finds, and anything you need for your home. It's a must!

LARGER CROSS
largercross.com
Oldwick, New Jersey
The perfect shop for when you're doing the finishing touches for your home.

LEFTOVERS ANTIQUES
leftoversantiques.com
Brenham, Texas
Awe around every corner of this shop.

LORFORDS ANTIQUES
lorfordsantiques.com
Tetbury, England
This is packed to the brim with antiques. You are guaranteed to find something for your home here.

M. CHARPENTIER ANTIQUES
mcharpentier.com
London, England
Specializing in decorative furniture, mercury mirrors, garden ornaments, and unique objects of charm from the eighteenth to the twentieth century.

MAISON
maisonshoppe.com
Mountain Brook, Alabama
Carefully curated shop with furniture, antiques, and found objects.

MARCH
marchsf.com
San Francisco, California
Furniture, art, and objects for the home with a handmade, artisan vibe.

MARCHÉ
marche-ct.com
Falls Village, Connecticut
Nestled in the heart of Falls Village, Marché resides in the old bank building and houses vintage treasures.

Opposite: Plain Goods

FURNITURE & ACCESSORIES (cont.)

Brick and Mortar

Opposite: Jefferson West

MARSTON HOUSE VINALHAVEN
marstonhouse.com
Vinalhaven, Maine
Half the year, the owners are in France where they buy textiles and furnishings for their shop. The other half, you can find them in Maine and buy the carefully selected finds. You can find their schedule on Instagram.

THE MART COLLECTIVE
themartcollective.com
Venice, California
Antique collective filled with vintage items for your home.

MATE GALLERY
mategallery.com
Montecito, California
Nautical items for your home; it's New England in Montecito.

MCINTOSH COTTAGE ANTIQUES
mcintoshcottageantiques.com
Columbia, South Carolina
This curated antique shop has a beautiful mix of vintage items—oil paintings, china, transferware, antique furniture, and more. We filled our suitcases with treasures!

MERCI
merci-merci.com
Paris, France
Located in the Marais, this three-story building is filled with curated items for your home as well as clothing. You'll leave the shop feeling inspired by their displays.

MICHAEL DEL PIERO GOOD DESIGN
michaeldelpiero.com
Chicago, Illinois; Wainscott, New York
Beautifully sourced items for the home and garden from around the world.

MICHELE ARAGON
Paris, France
Vintage textiles and antiques for your home. Not to be missed.

MIDDLEBURG ANTIQUE GALLERY
middleburgantiquegallery.com
Middleburg, Virginia
If you are on the hunt for classic Americana antiques this is the spot for you.

NELLIE'S OF AMAGANSETT
nelliesofamagansett.com
Amagansett, New York
Nellie's is a gem where you'll walk in and immediately not want to leave. You'll be leaving this antique shop after discovering at least one, if not a handful of treasures. From quirky sculptures to timeless furnishings, there's something for everyone here.

NEST
nestsf.com
San Francisco, California
Playful shop with both new and vintage items from around the world.

NICKEY KEHOE
nickeykehoe.com
New York, New York; Los Angeles, California
Home decor shop with furniture and accessories. One-of-a-kind vintage and new items are mixed seamlessly.

NIMMO & SPOONER
nimmoandspooner.co.uk
London, England
A distinctive mix of Continental and English items from the eighteenth to the twentieth century.

OLIVE ATELIERS
oliveateliers.com
Culver City, California
They source objects with old souls. You will find curious, unique pieces here.

PANOPLIE
panoplie.com
Los Angeles, California
Vintage finds and curated items for the home. There is always something here we can't resist.

PATINE
euro-linens.com
Santa Cruz, California
Store specializing in European rustic antiques and linens—bread boards, old linen sheets, and much more.

PINCH
pinchdesign.com
London, England
Design shop with furniture and lighting you won't want to miss.

PLAIN GOODS
plain-goods.com
New Preston, Connecticut
Let us just tell you that this shop is not to be missed. It's a true gem! You'll need to walk through a few times to take it all in. With various textiles, vintage lighting, and tableware, there is truly something for everyone.

PRESERVATION COMPANY
preservationco.com
Huntsville, Alabama; Round Top, Texas
Architectural salvage store that also carries antiques and reclaimed pieces for your home.

PRIZE HOME + GARDEN
prizeantiques.com
Kansas City, Missouri
The owners are keen antique hunters who offer one-of-a-kind pieces found worldwide.

QUINDRY
quindry.net
London, England
Twentieth-century furniture, lighting, and decorative arts, with an emphasis on timeless lines and fine materials.

QUITTNER
quittnerhome.com
Germantown, New York
Workshop and retail store with artifacts from the past.

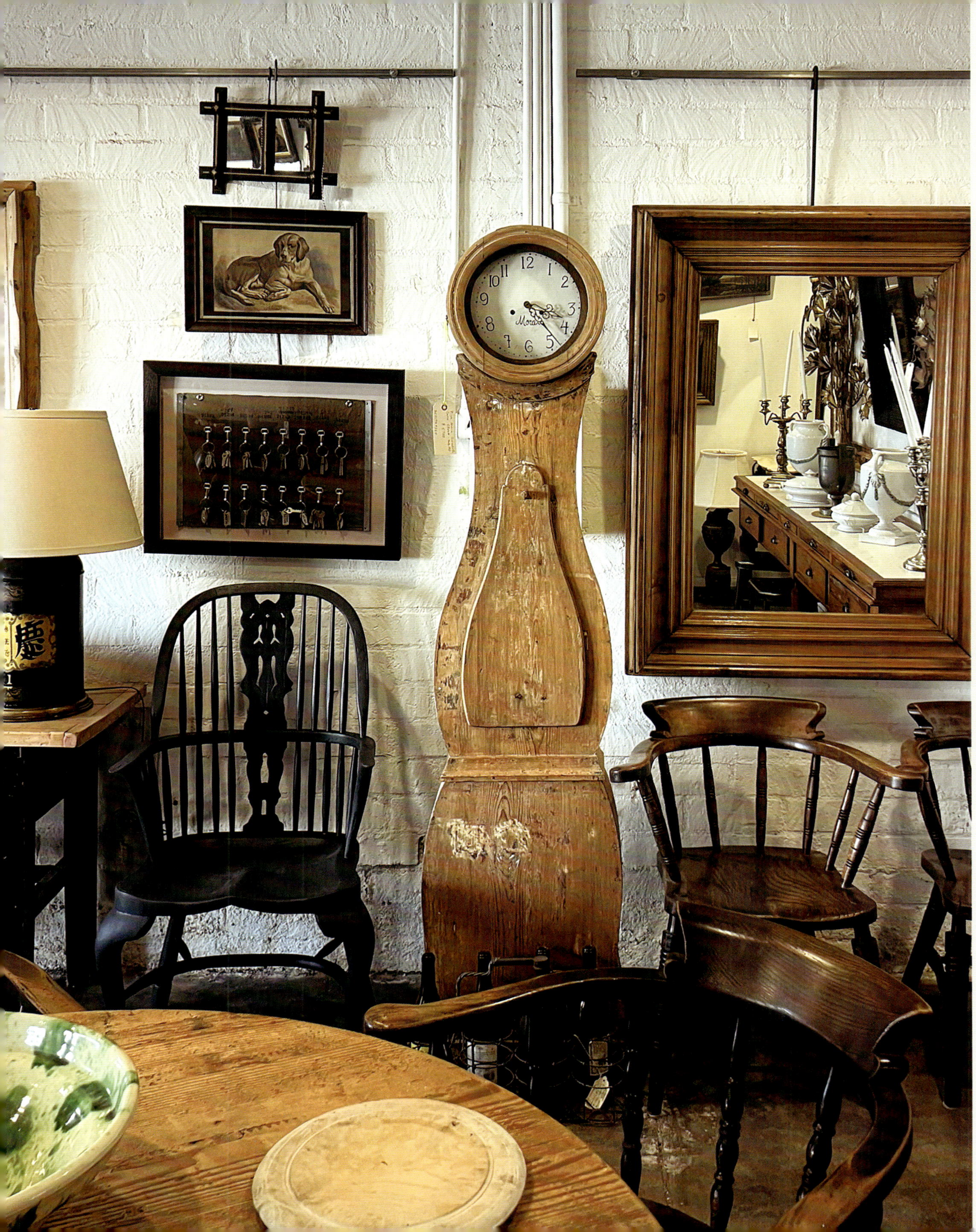

LITTLE BLACK BOOK
292

FURNITURE & ACCESSORIES (cont.)

Brick and Mortar

RED CHAIR ON WARREN
redchair-antiques.com
Hudson, New York
When visiting the Hudson Valley, you can't miss this shop filled to the brim with European and American treasures for the home.

RED TICKING
redticking.com
Seattle, Washington
This is a treasure trove of items from both Europe and the East Coast. Pam has a talent for finding the best items for the home.

RICHARD SCOTT ANTIQUES
richardscottantiques.co.uk
Holt, Norfolk, England
This shop has a wide array of antiques, furniture, and bespoke items for the home.

ROBERTSON ANTIQUES
robertsonsantiques.com
Carmel by the Sea, California
We've been popping into this antique store for more than fifteen years.

ROMAN AND WILLIAMS GUILD
rwguild.com
New York, New York
Beautifully curated home design, furniture, lighting, and textiles that are of the highest quality and style. Not to be missed!

ROOMS & GARDENS
roomsandgardens.com
Montecito, California
Perfect mix of furniture, textiles, and other items for your home.

SCÈNES DE MÉNAGE
instagram.com/scenesdemenage_bruxelles
Brussels, Belgium
A treasure chest filled with one-of-a-kind vintage textiles, silver, china, and much more.

SERENA & LILY
serenaandlily.com
Check website for various locations
Furniture and accessories for the home, with a wide selection of upholstered items that will last you generations. They also have a beautiful selection of lighting, bedding, and wallpaper.

SEVENTEEN SOUTH ANTIQUES
Charleston, South Carolina
Eclectic collection of furniture and décor for all types of homes.

SHOPPE AMBER INTERIORS
shoppeamberinteriors.com
Calabasas, Larkspur, Newport Beach, and Montecito, California
California-inspired home decor shops stocked to the brim with pillows, bed linens, furniture, rugs, art, books, and everything else for creating a layered home. (see pages 134–135)

SIENNA ANTIQUES
Petaluma, California
A local favorite of ours; we make regular stops here. Filled with a well-curated mix of antique furniture, paintings, and small items for the home.

SONOMA COUNTRY ANTIQUES
sonomaantiques.com
Sonoma, California
A great source for vintage and antique furniture in the wine country of Northern California.

SPARTAN
spartan-shop.com
Portland, Oregon
Minimalist contemporary furniture and housewares.

STARS ANTIQUES
starsantique.com
Portland, Oregon
A junk lover's paradise. One of our favorite places in Portland to source.

STREET MARBURG
streettmarburg.co.uk
London, England
Stylish antiques to fill your home.

STUDIO FAEGER
faegershop.com
London, England
A gem in the heart of London filled with curated interiors and homeware for the slow living.

SUD
sudneworleans.com
New Orleans, Louisiana
After traveling to Sicily, William and Richard opened a beautiful boutique that offers Sicilian antiques, art, and contemporary crafts.

SUE FISHER KING
suefisherking.com
San Francisco, California
Offering an impressive collection of Astier de Villatte ceramics, bed and table linens, and design books.

SUMMER HOUSE
summerhousemillvalley.com
Mill Valley, California
Carefully chosen gems, including furniture, smalls, bedding, rugs, and lighting.

TANCREDI & MORGEN
tancrediandmorgen.com
Carmel, California
French mercantile that is filled with treasures that are handpicked by the sweetest family.

TAPISSERIE
tapisserie.co.uk
London, England
Tapisserie is a beautiful shop on the second floor right next to the Victoria and Albert Museum. You can sift through the hundreds of needlework canvases and embroidery patterns, as well as customize the colors to work perfectly with your home.

Opposite: Robert Kime

FURNITURE & ACCESSORIES (cont.)

Brick and Mortar

TARA ANTIQUES CENTRE
tara-antiques.co.uk
Stow-on-the-Wold, England
Located in a manor house, this antique store boasts four floors of gems.

TERRACE OAKS ANTIQUES
terraceoaksantiques.com
Charleston, South Carolina
An antique mall with more than sixty vendors. Beautiful stock of antiques with new items added daily.

VIA ANTICA
viaantica.be
Brussels, Belgium
Vintage furniture and art objects for the home.

THE VINTAGE RUG SHOP
thevintagerugshop.com
Berkeley, California
A large collection of vintage rugs and an excellent source of design and art books. You can also find furniture and other unique items for the home.

VW HOME
vicentewolfhome.com
New York, New York
Personally curated shop of items from design connoisseur Vicente Wolf's far-flung travels. (see pages 36–37)

WATSON KENNEDY
watsonkennedy.com
Seattle, Washington
A long-time favorite that is packed to the ceiling with irresistible items for the home.

WELL MADE HOME
wellmadehome.com
Larkspur, California; Palm Beach, Florida
Beautiful selection of textiles, pillows, fabric lampshades, pottery, and more.

WHEARLEY & CO.
shop.whearleyandco.com
Redwood City, California
Perfect selection of home items, including wool throws, candles, as well as tabletop and decorative items.

WILLA GRAY HOME
willagrayhome.com
Indianapolis, Indiana
Sophisticated home decor shop with a wide and deep array of textiles, furniture, books, and smalls for the home.

WOODNUTT ANTIQUES
woodnuttantiques.com/shop
London, England
Unique antique glassware, furniture, and trinkets that will add beautiful depth to your home.

WYNSUM ANTIQUES & INTERIORS
wynsum.shop
Charleston and Mount Pleasant, South Carolina
Beautiful antiques and art showcased by different vendors.

100 MAIN
100mainst.com
Falls Village, Connecticut
This shop, owned by Bunny Williams, is a treasure trove for your home, with local artisans featured and one of the best book collections we have seen for design. (see pages 62–64)

Online

ALICE PALMER & CO
alicepalmer.co

AMY MEIER SHOP
amymeier.com/shop
(see pages 266–279)

ANTHROPOLOGIE
anthropologie.com/anthroliving

BLOOMIST
bloomist.com

BUNNY WILLIAMS HOME
bunnywilliamshome.com
(see pages 62–64)

CAROLINA IRVING & DAUGHTERS
ci-daughters.com

CASAMIDY
casamidy.com

CB2
cb2.com

CHAIRISH
chairish.com

CLAIBORNE & OLIVE
claiborneandolive.com

COYUCHI
coyuchi.com

CRATE & BARREL
crateandbarrel.com

ERIN LANE ESTATE
erinlaneestate.com

ETSY
etsy.com

FRAGMENTS IDENTITY
fragmentsidentity.com

GALERIE PROVENANCE
galerieprovenance.com

JUNE HOME SUPPLY
junehomesupply.com

LAUREN LIESS
shop.laurenliess.com

LES TABLES D'EVA
lestablesdeva.fr

MARIGOLD LIVING
marigoldliving.com

MCGEE AND CO.
mcgeeandco.com

ART

NATE BERKUS
nateberkus.com
(see pages 106–107)

PALECEK
palecek.com

THE PARSON'S NOSE ANTIQUES
theparsonsnoseantiques.com

PARTERRE
shopparterre.com

REVITALISTE
revitaliste.com

SHARLAND ENGLAND
sharland-england.com

STUDIO HAM
studioham.co.uk

TOTEM HOME
totemhome.com

VINTAGE FRENCH
vintagefrench.com

1ST DIBS
1stdibs.com

GALERIE ETNA
instagram.com/galerieetna
Paris, France
Old-world charm, filled with oil paintings and furniture.

JEN AMENT
jenniferament.com

JOSH YOUNG
joshyoungdesignhouse.com
(see pages 118–121 and 226–241)

LOST ART SALON
lostartsalon.com
San Francisco, California
Carefully curated collection of art. You won't leave without a new piece.

PABLO GOEBEL FINE ARTS
pgfinearts.com
Mexico City, Mexico
A beautifully curated art gallery of the best Mexico has to offer.

Below: Helen Storey Antiques

HANDCRAFTED ITEMS
Brick and Mortar

ALIX D. REYNIS
alixdreynis.com
Paris, France
A beautiful shop curated by Alix Depondt-Reynis. The pottery is stunning.

ASTIER DE VILLATTE
astierdevillatte.com
Paris, France; Milan, Italy
Features incredible handmade pottery with a glaze you won't believe, as well as a publishing house and perfume workshop that creates candles, incense, and more.

CAN GARANYA
cangaranya.com
Manacor, Mallorca
Basket shop with beautiful handmade items, including handwoven stools.

CERAMICHE NICOLA FASANO
fasanocnf.it
Grottaglie, Italy
Handmade ceramics in a wide range of colors and shapes.

FARMHOUSE POTTERY
farmhousepottery.com
Woodstock, Vermont
Artisanal potters who make unique pottery, decor, and candles. They also host pottery workshops throughout the year.

GORDIOLA
gordiola.com
Algaida, Mallorca
The fourth-oldest company in Spain and a seventh-generation business creating amazing hand-blown glass and chandeliers.

LA TUILE À LOUP
latuilealoup.com
Paris, France
Playful rustic handmade tableware.

LUBAROL
lubarol.com
Copenhagen, Denmark
Multibrand design and fashion boutique.

HANDCRAFTED ITEMS (cont.)

Brick and Mortar

MIMBRERIA VIDAL
mimbreriavidal.com
Palma, Mallorca
A beautiful basket shop with handwoven stools.

MIRI MARA CERAMICS
mirimara.com
Carpinteria, California
Handmade ceramics with stunning details and form.

NOTARY CERAMICS
notaryceramics.com
Portland, Oregon
One of our personal favorites. Their lamp bases are made with quality and care. Everything in the shop is swoon-worthy.

ONORA
onoracasa.com
Mexico City, Mexico
A modern take on Mexican crafts.

POTTEMAGER ERIK B. BENDTSEN
Copenhagen, Denmark
Handmade pottery.

RIVESTO ITALIA
rivestoitalia.com
Lecce, Italy
Unique antique and vintage antiques. Some of the most beautiful pieces of antique ceramics.

SAWKILLE CO.
sawkille.com
Rhinebeck, New York
Handcrafted furniture that has raw beauty.

Online

AMANDA MOFFAT POTTERY
amandamoffatpottery.com

DEBORAH NEEDLEMAN
deborahneedleman.com
(see pages 122–129)

HEATH CERAMICS
heathceramics.com

MICHAEL FINIZIO WOODWORKING
mfwoodworking.com/

REBEKAH MILES
rebekahmiles.com

SHELDON CERAMICS
sheldonceramics.com

STEPHANIE DARN MATTHIAS
stephaniedawnmatthias.com

FLOORING

Online

ARMADILLO & CO
armadillo-co.com

ELIZABETH EAKINS
elizabetheakins.com

ERNESTA
ernestarugs.com

FIRECLAY TILE
fireclaytile.com

HEIR LOOM CO
heirloomartco.com

SISAL RUGS DIRECT
sisalrugs.com

WINDOW TREATMENTS

Online

EVERHEM
everhem.com

HUNTER DOUGLAS
hunterdouglas.com

THE SHADE STORE
theshadestore.com

WOVN HOME
wovnhome.com
(see pages 142–145)

FLEA AND CRAFT MARKETS

ALAMEDA POINT ANTIQUES FAIRE
alamedapointantiquesfaire.com
Alameda, California
Many items in our homes come from this monthly flea market.

ALFIES ANTIQUE MARKET
alfiesantiques.com
London, England
Antique market with an eclectic ran of antiques and vintage items.

BRIMFIELD FLEA MARKETS
brimfieldantiquefleamarket.com
Brimfield, California
Miles of fields, as well as online auctions, with gems waiting to be discovered.

BROOKLYN FLEA
brooklynflea.com
Brooklyn, New York
Urban flea market at its best.

CHELSEA FLEA MARKET
chelseaflea.com
New York, New York
Chelsea Flea is an outdoor antique and collectible market that has been around for over forty years.

KAPALI ÇARSI (GRAND BAZAAR)
kapalicarsi.com.tr
Istanbul, Turkey
One of the most comprehensive bazaars, selling items from around the world, including ikat fabrics, textiles, and lanterns.

MARCHÉ AUX PUCES DE LA PORTE DE VANVES
pucesdevanves.com
Paris, France
This quaint flea market on the edge of Paris is our favorite! Be sure to arrive early.

MARCHÉ AUX PUCES DE SAINT-OUEN
pucesdeparissaintouen.com
Paris, France
This market is unlike any other. While it has outside vendors it also houses permanent vendors that have shops. It's one of a kind.

MERCADO DE ARTESANÍAS LA CUIDADELA
laciudadela.com.mx
Mexico City, Mexico
A perfect-size market with handicrafts from every region of Mexico.

THE ORIGINAL ROUND TOP ANTIQUES FAIR
roundtoptexasantiques.com
Round Top, Texas
You'll be blown away by the merchandising at this antique fair.

PORTOBELLO ROAD
portobelloroad.co.uk
London, England
Festive market of both shops and outside vendors, held on Saturdays.

SABLON ANTIQUES MARKET
sablonantiquesmarket.be
Brussels, Belgium
A wonderful antique market in the heart of Brussels, held every Saturday and Sunday since 1960 on Place du Grand Sablon.

Top: SUD, a New Orleans antique shop, is a must for pieces found in Sicily. Bottom: Robert Kime

A moment in Glenn Ban's home. Let what you love surround you in your spaces.

"I don't know how you describe romance actually… but some objects have it, they just have something that is more than themselves. If you're interested in them you can communicate it and they can communicate it too, and it's just magic, it's just how life is."

—ROBERT KIME

MIDDLEBURG,
VIRGINIA

ACKNOWLEDGMENTS

Writing a book is a huge task, and this is our third time going through the process. It has become increasingly clear to us that we need to remember why we do this: to meet and learn from the talented, interesting, and generous people we feature here. We feel as if we have deepened our love of design even more than we thought possible, and we are grateful.

We would like to thank everyone at Abrams for giving us another opportunity to write a book we care deeply about. We are grateful to those who played a role in the making of this book, but especially to our editor, Laura Dozier, who always helps us be better versions of ourselves.

To our agent, Kate Woodrow, who has been with us from the very beginning. You have always been able to gently nudge us to clarify our ideas and improve our thoughts. Your support and advice is so important to our success.

To our graphic designer, Emily Wardwell. We still can't believe you have designed all three of our books. You have taken our work and transformed it into a work of art!

To Stephanie Russo, our primary photographer. Thank you for long trips away from your family, long days of driving from one shoot to the other, and of course, many many laughs along the way. We will always appreciate what you have done for this book!

To Jenna Carli, thank you for stepping in to photograph the beautiful home of Calhoun Sumrall in New Orleans, Louisiana. Your images take our breath away. And to all of the other photographers who have contributed their images to the book, we are grateful.

To Alice Sergeant, thank you for letting us include your exquisite Zahra textile design for our endpapers. It embodies *The Essentials* perfectly.

To my (Caitlin) client Lily Riesenfeld and her family, thank you for allowing us to share your beautiful home on the cover and throughout the book.

To my (Caitlin) clients who graciously opened up their homes and let us share them within the pages of this book.

To Julie Forrest and her designer, Patricia Giffen, for letting us into your home and photographing these beautiful examples of good design. We are so inspired by your work.

And lastly to Eric, for all of the solo-parenting while I (Caitlin) am off in the far corners of the globe creating this book. I love you and Amelia and Jackson!

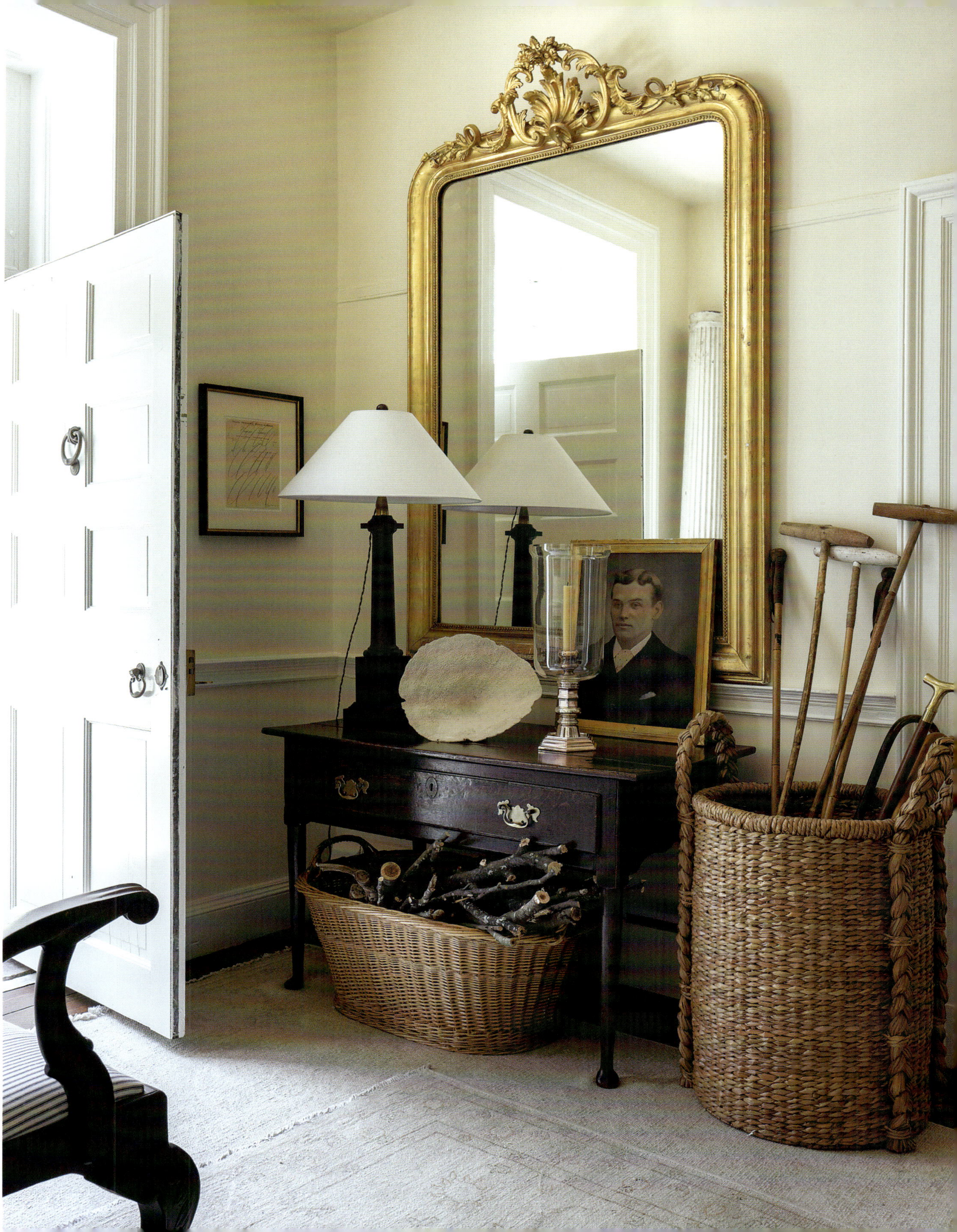

THE ESSENTIALS
302

LONDON,
ENGLAND

ABOUT THE AUTHORS

JULIE GOEBEL, and her daughter, Caitlin Flemming, are the coauthors of *Travel Home*, *Sense of Place*, and *The Essentials*. Julie is a humanities teacher and loves infecting her students with her passion for writing. In her free time, she enjoys traveling, and spending time with her grandchildren, Jackson and Amelia. Julie resides in a one-room cottage in Marin County, California, where she loves the redwood trees, sunshine, and small-town life. On the weekends, you will find her at the beach or curled up with a stack of design books and a cup of tea.

CAITLIN FLEMMING is coauthor of of *Travel Home*, *Sense of Place*, and *The Essentials*. She wrote both books with her mother, Julie Goebel. Caitlin has had her own design firm since 2012 and has projects throughout the Bay Area as well scattered throughout the United States. She continues to train her eye through travel and finding inspiration through travel. She especially enjoys antiquing and loves to find out the stories behind the pieces she finds. Caitlin lives in Marin County, California, with her husband, Eric, their two children, Jackson and Amelia, and their dog, Penny.

Editor: LAURA DOZIER
Designer: EMILY WARDWELL
Design Manager: DANIELLE YOUNGSMITH
Managing Editor: JAN HUGHES and KRISTA KEPLINGER
Production Manager: DENISE LACONGO

Library of Congress Control Number: 2025931147

ISBN: 978-1-4197-7878-0
eISBN: 979-8-88707-516-7

Text copyright © 2025 CAITLIN FLEMMING and JULIE GOEBEL
Photography copyright © 2025 STEPHANIE RUSSO except:
Pages 15, 57, 98 (left), 99, 140, 156–171 by JENNA CARLI | pages 16, 19, 28 (left), 29, 30 (center), 32, 34, 35, 48, 50 (left), 51, 52, 53, 280, 282, 284, 287, 288, 291, 292, 295, 297 by CAITLIN FLEMMING | pages 20–23 by GRANT GIBSON | pages 24, 26, 27, 28 (right), 30 (right) by LEAH O'CONNELL | page 37 by JULIEN CAPMEIL | pages 38, 40–41 (center photos) by JILL SHARP WEEKS | pages 42–47 by BESS FRIDAY | page 50 (right) by ELSIE GREEN | page 62 by LESLEY UNRUH for Williams Lawrence | page 74 by WILL BRINSON | page 94 by HARIS KENJAR | page 107 by HEATHER TALBERT | page 110 by DAMIAN RUSSELL | pages 122, 124, 125 by BRETT WOOD | pages 126–129 by CHRIS MOTTALINO | page 134 by SHADE DEGGES | page 142 by BRITTANY AMBRIDGE
Illustration credit: JUSTYNE DEWILDE
Endpaper credit: Zahra print by ALICE SERGEANT

Cover © 2025 Abrams

Published in 2025 by Abrams, an imprint of ABRAMS. All rights reserved. No portion of this book may be reproduced, stored in a retrieval system, or transmitted in any form or by any means, mechanical, electronic, photocopying, recording, or otherwise, without written permission from the publisher.

Printed and bound in China
10 9 8 7 6 5 4 3 2 1

Abrams books are available at special discounts when purchased in quantity for premiums and promotions as well as fundraising or educational use. Special editions can also be created to specification. For details, contact specialsales@abramsbooks.com or the address below.

Abrams® is a registered trademark of Harry N. Abrams, Inc.

ABRAMS The Art of Books
195 Broadway, New York, NY 10007
abramsbooks.com

CAPTIONS
Front cover: Home of Lily Riesenfeld, designed by Caitlin Flemming; front endpaper: Living room in Lan Jaenicke's home in San Francisco, California; pages 2–3: The entry of Josh Young's Middleburg, Virginia, home; pages 4 and 7: The studio of Kristin Ellen Hockman in Berkeley County, South Carolina; back endpaper: Garden entry to a project designed by Caitlin Flemming in Petaluma, California; back cover: Home of Glenn Ban in East Hampton, New York.

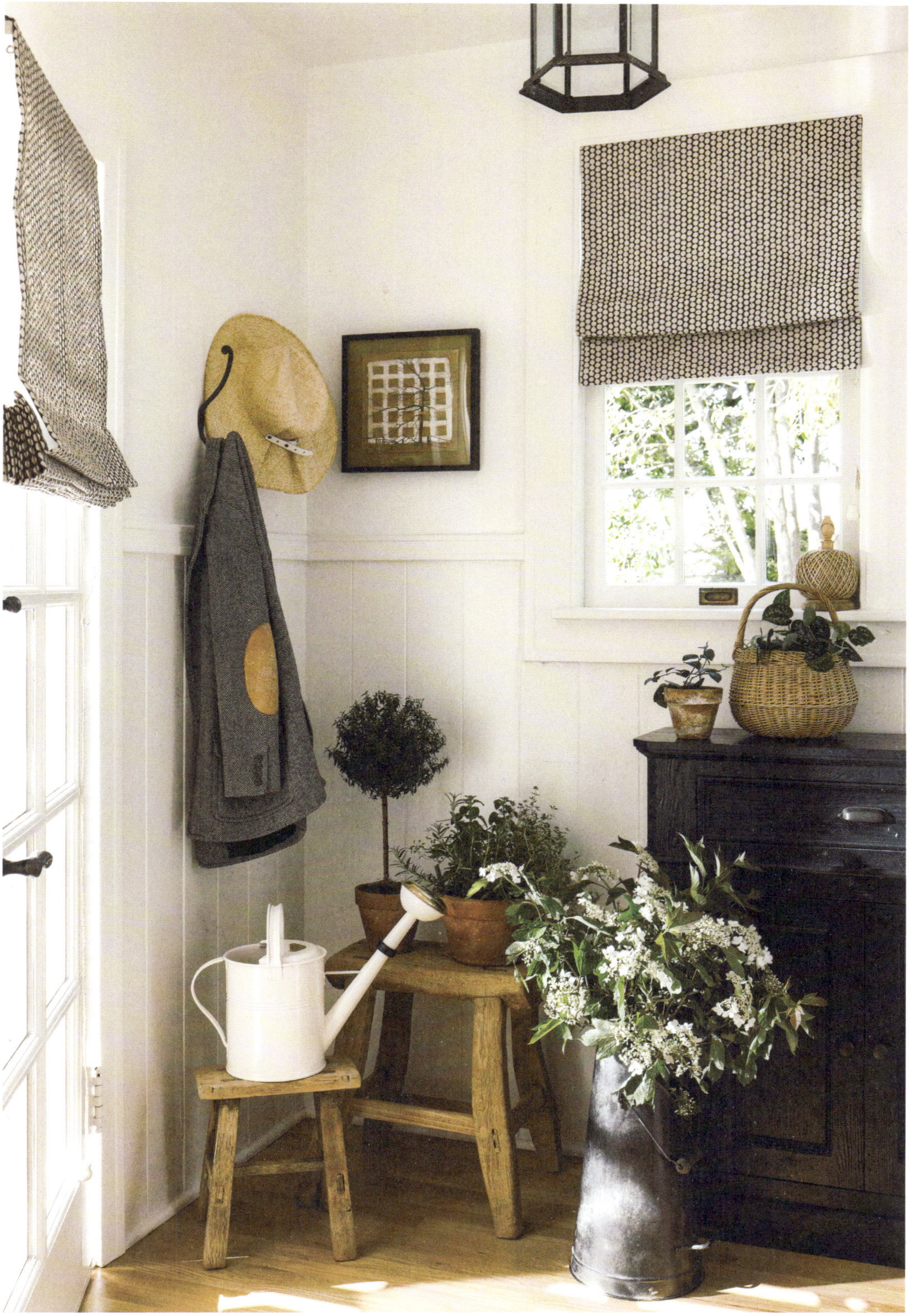